"To me, *Lights, Camera...Faith!* is the most imaginative and engaging contemporary contribution to the art of preaching: 72 well-known films integrated with the liturgical year, in dialogue with the Gospel. It makes Hollywood a splendid resource for the pulpit instead of simply a threat to morality. Informative and stimulating, provocative and practical, appreciative and critical, it should send preachers to the movies with fresh eyes, and bring revived enthusiasm into discussion groups. The homilies are still to be written by us, and many of the films are still to be seen, but the method is now ours for the taking."

WALTER J. BURGHARDT, SJ, SENIOR FELLOW
Woodstock Theological Center
Georgetown University

"It is clear from reading this book that Peter Malone and Rose Pacatte love movies, love Jesus, and love the Church. The movies they have chosen to bring into conversation with the Lectionary are broad-ranging and engaging. Use this book as a guide for your teaching and preaching, or use it for selecting (and later reflecting on) your next video from Blockbuster. It is excellent."

ROBERT K. JOHNSTON, PH.D.
Fuller Seminary, CA
Author, Reel Spirituality

"What a delightful idea! *Lights, Camera...Faith!* invites us into a conversation with the movies and the Sunday readings. More than an exercise book (in the line of St. Ignatius' Spiritual Exercises), more than a book about the cinema, it suggests ways of letting the Scriptures address contemporary culture.

"The real beauty of the book lies in the way it opens the door connecting the two realms we all too often keep separated. Once open, it is impossible not to see other connections, to hear the Scriptures in a new way, and to just watch the movies again.

"Because the book demands action on our part, it will serve as a great guide for parish or family discussions, for youth groups and religious education, and even for retreat groups."

PAUL A. SOUKUP, SJ, PH.D.
Professor of Communications
Santa Clara University

"Where do most of the stories in our culture today come from? Film! More and more people spend time at the cinema, in front of their cable TV, or renting movies from video stores. There is no doubt that the amount of time people, young and old, spend viewing films is increasing. Is there a way to refocus the audience's attention on those film stories and connect them with the Gospel?

"Malone and Pacatte do just that in *Lights, Camera...Faith!* This is a clever approach, long overdue. Connecting faith and culture is the challenge all ministers face today. Film, which is now woven into the fabric of our storytelling and conversations in everyday life, can be applied to the Gospel in unique and creative ways. This is one approach that is worth our consideration and investment of time and energy.

"How can faith and culture meet in the liturgical year celebrations? How can we influence Christians to approach film with a critical, reflective mind and to discern how Gospel values can challenge or affirm what we see and hear in a film? How can someone be challenged, the next time he or she sees a movie, to apply Gospel sensitivity and values to the experience? Malone and Pacatte's book guides us in this direction."

ANGELA ANN ZUKOWSKI, MHSH, D.MIN.
Unda World President
Member of the Pontifical Council for Social Communications

"Authors Malone and Pacatte have hit on a novel idea—a movie lectionary! They discuss the liturgical readings from the Old and New Testament and relate them to the films they have chosen for that week. This parallel is extremely well done and pushes the reader to discover links between the Bible passages and the film themes in ways that one would not readily discover on one's own.

"There are many ways this lectionary could be used. Teachers and youth leaders might want to use the films and Gospel readings to bring their young people closer to seeing connections between life as represented on screen, their own lives, and the messages of the Bible. Adult groups wishing to study the Bible in a less rigorous way than is traditionally offered might find its relationship with film thought-provoking. People of all Christian faiths will want to use the book!"

JOAN D. LYNCH, ED.D.
Communications professor
Villanova University

"The authors manage to throw open fresh new windows on ancient stories. The result is two-fold: we find Scripture coming alive in our hands and we gain a whole new perspective on the way God continues to show up in our culture."

BRYAN STONE
Professor of Evangelism
Boston University School of Theology
Author, Faith and Film

"Lights, Camera…Faith! offers an original and thought-provoking entry into the world of the Gospels through an invaluable resource for preachers, educators, discussion leaders, and anyone else who simply appreciates a fresh take on Scripture."

RICHARD A. BLAKE, SJ
Film Reviewer/ America Magazine
Co-director of Film Studies
Boston College

"What a treasure trove! I can just imagine many church communities launching programs using this material to enhance their congregation's grasp and application of the Gospel. This is a great service to the Church!"

SANDRA BOWDEN
President, Christians in the Visual Arts

LIGHTS CAMERA... FAITH!

By Peter Malone, MSC with Rose Pacatte, FSP

Pauline
BOOKS & MEDIA
Boston

Library of Congress Cataloging-in-Publication Data

Malone, Peter.
  Lights, camera...faith! : a movie lectionary. Cycle A / by Peter
Malone, MSC with Rose Pacatte, FSP.
      p. cm.
Includes bibliographical references and index.
  ISBN 0-8198-4490-X (pbk.)
  1. Bible. N.T. Gospels — Criticism, interpretation, etc. 2. Motion
pictures — Religious aspects — Christianity. I. Title.
  BS2565 .M27 2001
  261.5'7— dc21
                        2001001422
                        Rev.

ISBN 0-8198-4490-X

Cover design by Helen Rita Lane, FSP

Printed and published in the U.S.A. by Pauline Books & Media, 50 Saint Pauls Avenue, Boston, MA 02130-3491.

www.pauline.org

Pauline Books & Media is the publishing house of the Daughters of St. Paul, an international congregation of women religious serving the Church with the communications media.

2 3 4 5 6 7 8 9 10   08 07 06 05 04 03 02

WE ARE LIVING IN A MOVIE CULTURE. Whether we go to the movie theater, see a movie on television, videocassette, DVD, or download a film from the internet, movies and their themes are part of our daily lives.

In the words of one playwright and movie-watcher, several of whose plays have been turned into movies:

> "People created in the image and likeness of God are naturally called to peace and harmony with God, with others, with ourselves, and with all creation. The cinema can become an interpreter of this natural propensity and strive to be a place of reflection, a call to values, an invitation to dialogue and communion....

> "The cinema enjoys a wealth of languages, a multiplicity of styles, and a truly great variety of narrative forms: from realism to fairy tales, from history to science fiction, from adventure to tragedy, from comedy to news, from cartoons to documentaries.... It can contribute to bringing people closer, to reconciling enemies, to favoring an ever more respectful dialogue between diverse cultures."

[John Paul II, *Address to the Festival for the Third Millennium,* December 1999]

Contents

HOLY WEEK/TRIDUUM

EASTER

SUNDAYS OF ORDINARY TIME

Foreword

The first film I ever saw was *King Kong*, and I was terrified. Perhaps that's why, as a child, I didn't see more than a dozen movies—none of them memorable.

So I experienced a big *"Aha!"* when I began seeing more movies as a young adult. A serious literature student, I was especially taken by fiction's capacity to illuminate our human condition, to pry open an understanding of self and others using the leverage of feelings and emotional involvement. I started approaching cinema as literature, and soon found myself captured by *Johnny Belinda*, entranced by *The Seventh Seal*, inspired by *La Strada*, moved to compassion by *A Taste of Honey*. And I had a running argument with a friend over *West Side Story*: could a musical be more than "just entertainment"?

When I began teaching high-school English in Chicago, I formed a student film club that met monthly to view and discuss movies. Despite the lack of such social "sweeteners" as music and dancing, the monthly screenings drew standing-room-only crowds. Looking back, I now realize that we were really engaging in the human search for meaning, also known as spirituality.

Eventually, I decided to make movies my profession, and after film school I found myself in Assisi, working on Franco Zeffirelli's movie, *Brother Sun, Sister Moon*. I watched Zeffirelli's attempt to engage a broad audience in St. Francis' spiritual search. And something inside me clicked. Connecting faith and cinema! After all, the Church uses sacraments that reach all of the senses; it uses drama to catechize, and the visual beauty of stained glass and the power of music to tell its story. So why not the movies? We believe in a God who took on human flesh in all its physical and emotional characteristics. In short, we believe that Christ is God *Incarnate*.

An incarnational approach to the movies is what this book is all about. Father Peter Malone and Sister Rose Pacatte show us how anyone who watches movies can explore spiritual meaning not only through movies as literature, but also through storytelling as entertainment. The resulting dialogue not only leads to greater discernment in our movie viewing, but also to a keener understanding of the Gospel—our measure of modern-day parables.

With *Lights, Camera...Faith!* we can take our encounter with the Sunday Scriptures to the movies. This title makes a significant contribution to the renaissance of books and on-line discussion groups, which a whole new generation of viewers is using to unwrap its movie experience in order to glimpse the divine. *Lights, Camera...Faith!* may be a link in bridging the gap between religious belief and popular culture. The question is not *whether* we should watch movies, but how to relate the movies we *do* watch to our religious convictions. It's my hope that this book will launch a new wave of discovery and dialogue within the community of Christian disciples.

Frank Frost, Ph.D., a graduate of the University of Southern California film school, has served on special juries at the Venice Film Festival and the Monte Carlo Television Festival, and is a co-founder of the annual National Film Retreat. He makes his living today as a documentary television producer.

Introduction

The Story

A what?

A Movie Lectionary.

*A movie **what?***

Lectionary…you know, the book of scripture readings for the celebration of the Eucharist.

But, what do you mean? A book with the liturgical readings and *movies?*

Perhaps I'd better just tell the story!

It may have been a chance remark at the end of a meeting about movies, but Frank Frost, a friend and television producer, said to me, "Why don't you find a movie that links to the Sunday Gospel? It might make a good homily."

Easier said than done. Not that trying to find movies that might correspond to Gospel themes isn't an enjoyable pastime! But once you've found a movie, what do you do with it? Practically speaking, how could a parish group, a homilist, or your average movie buff use a movie and the Sunday Bible readings?

While mulling over this, I happened to come across the title *St. Paul at the Movies* by Robert Jewett, a biblical scholar whose specialty is St. Paul. He also enjoys the movies. Jewett created a conversation between Paul and the themes of his letters, and some contemporary movies like *The Shawshank Redemption, Tender Mercies, Tootsie,* and *Star Wars.* The dialogue that occurred intrigued me. Perhaps here was the key: a dialogue between the Sunday readings and a movie that would in some way challenge people to engage in the conversation between faith and culture. And so was born *Lights, Camera… Faith!*

The Format

Each chapter of *Lights, Camera...Faith!* is simple and accessible.

Synopsis: Not all readers may have seen every movie included in this book, though it is strongly recommended to see a movie before using it in a homily or with a group. The synopsis offers details that may be helpful in recalling movie characters, plot, and sequence.

SYNOPSIS

Commentary: Each movie commentary provides interesting information about the movie itself: actors, directors, producers, related films, etc.

COMMENTARY

Dialogue with the Gospel: This is the core of each chapter: how the movie and its themes relate to the liturgical readings. Some movies and Gospel passages harmonize quite well. Other pairs do not correspond as clearly—for the most part, movie makers probably did not intend a scriptural message! Therefore, each dialogue begins with a short *Focus* to point the reader in the right direction.

DIALOGUE WITH THE GOSPEL

Key Scenes and Themes: To enrich the dialogue, I highlight several sections of the movie that would be worth discussing thematically, or showing as a clip during group discussions, liturgy preparation, or course presentation if the scenes are sequential.

KEY SCENES AND THEMES

For Reflection and Conversation: Practical, thought provoking comments and questions provide a focus for living the Gospel message in one's daily life.

FOR REFLECTION AND CONVERSATION

Prayer

Prayer: My editor had the rather beautiful idea of adding a short prayer to bring the reflections to a conclusion.

The subtitle **A** *Movie Lectionary,* rather than **The** *Movie Lectionary,* is intentional. It would be possible to match the same readings with 72 other movies. In that sense, this lectionary is a set of samples; you might like to start constructing your own version as well!

Most of the movies used here have been released during the last fifteen years and are available on videocassette or DVD. However, some earlier movies have been chosen because of their relevance to the Gospel. They, too, should be available, at least on cassette.

How to Use **Lights, Camera...Faith!**

Individuals who appreciate deeper meanings in movies may want to watch the film, read the scriptures, and use both for personal reflection and prayer.

Homilists will find suggestions for sermon preparation.

Young Adult groups will discover new ways to bring the Gospel message to bear on contemporary culture.

Parish study and discussion groups might find that watching a movie or sections of it will lead to discussion, further reading and viewing, and a deeper entry into the Liturgy of the Word.

Professors and students of film and media criticism will find a useful text for discussing the phenomenon of faith in film.

Again, it is recommended that a movie be seen before using it. The nature of some movies may suggest working with a film clip, since not every movie is suitable for wide audiences. Some themes demand greater maturity than that of adolescents; there may be certain movie sequences that are too strong or explicit regarding language, sexuality, or violence for some audiences. *Lights, Camera...Faith!* is not meant to be a "viewing guide." Checking with a publication that provides this type of information will be useful, although such guidelines often differ in their opinions.*

Each of the movies represented in *Lights, Camera...Faith!* has been chosen because in some way the movie portrays the real-life struggles of people—human struggles that beg a human response—and connects these struggles to the Christian story found in the Sunday liturgy's scripture readings. While not every movie may work for you, I do hope that the majority will.

—PETER MALONE, MSC

---

*From an international point of view, such publications might seem arbitrary in their comments. While objective norms of truth and morality certainly exist, sometimes what is objectionable to one culture is not to another; "infrequent coarse language" in one culture seems "far too frequent" in another. Modesty and nudity norms differ from country to country. One culture deplores violence; another has a greater tolerance for visual violence. (See *Movie Ratings Chart* at the end of this book.) These are the hazards when movies are shown internationally.

The Beach

U.S. / U.K., 2000 / 119 minutes

Actors: Leonardo DiCaprio, Virginie Ledoyen, Guillaume Canet, Tilda Swinton, Robert Carlyle

Writer: John Hodge

Director: Danny Boyle

The Beach

Imperfect World

Richard, a young American looking for adventure, arrives in Bangkok. At his dingy hotel he encounters Daffy, an insane man who, before killing himself, gives Richard a map with directions to an island with a perfect beach. Richard shows the map to a young French couple, Etienne and Françoise. They decide to travel to the island together. On the way, Richard meets some fellow Americans, tells them about the island, and gives them a copy of the map.

Richard and companions sail to a nearby island, but must swim to their final destination because no one is legally permitted there. They first discover a marijuana plantation patrolled by armed guards, and then, as they search for the perfect beach, they encounter a man who is a member of a commune.

Richard and his companions join a group of Western dropouts presided over by an Englishwoman named Sal. While the beach is perfect and life seems tranquil, emotional and power tensions lurk beneath the surface. Sal asks the newcomers if they have told anyone about the island. Richard lies about copying the map. Françoise becomes involved with Richard, but he is blackmailed into a sexual relation-

SYNOPSIS

ship with Sal while on a supplies-buying mission. It is during this mission that the Americans recognize Richard and he must admit he has lied to Sal.

A shark attack kills one commune member and wounds another. There are signs that the Americans are trying to find the beach. Richard is forced to do sentry duty; he is alienated from everyone. The isolation induces hallucinations, and Richard finds his own "heart of darkness." Guards shoot the American intruders and give Sal an ultimatum: kill Richard or everyone must leave. Sal pulls the trigger, but the gun has no bullets. Everyone leaves the island except Sal.

COMMENTARY

The Beach draws on the modern desire to find a place where all is in harmony with nature, far from the rat race and responsibility.

Alex Garland's original novel, popular with young people, projects a spirit of adventure while focusing on the frequent insecurity and dangers of international backpacking.

The movie is beautiful to watch and, like the book, draws younger audiences. The movie combines the spirit of *Robinson Crusoe, Swiss Family Robinson,* and *Cast Away* with that of a naïve young man trying to live in harmony with nature in the modern world and to be part of something, a community.

As shown in William Golding's *Lord of the Flies,* human beings are not perfect and, when isolated, tend toward destruction. In sequences reminiscent of *Apocalypse Now,* Richard discovers his dark side, reverts to a primal savagery, and the utopia comes to an end.

DIALOGUE WITH THE GOSPEL

Focus: Advent is a time for acknowledging the need for repentance and redemption. The Liturgy offers visions of a perfect world while alerting us to the fact that in our present reality all is not well, a situation mirrored in The Beach.

Life in the commune might be described as a kind of Advent situation. The members have opted out of life for idealistic reasons, and Richard rejoices that there is no communal ideology. At first, the group is blissfully unaware of the consequences of giving the map away. By ignoring the realities of human nature and conflict, the members make themselves vulnerable to human limitations. As a result, their commune and spirit first crack and then split wide open. They need a benevolent and wise leader. The one they have, Sal, is self-centered and shortsighted.

The vision of an ideal society is reinforced in the Advent hope of the first two readings: the rooting out of all war by turning weapons into tools for harvesting and peace in Isaiah and hints of the second coming of Jesus and a moral and "enlightened" world in Paul's Letter to the Romans (cf. 13:11–14).

Today's Gospel reflects our world realistically, the mixture of good and evil, a world that needs redemption. Jesus' Advent warning is about readiness. The people of Noah's time were not awake and "suspected nothing" of what was to befall them. The community on the beach was just as unaware. Jesus urges us to be ready for his coming.

KEY SCENES AND THEMES

- Richard, eager and naïve; meeting Daffy; the map; sharing the news of the beach with the French and the Americans; Richard's idyllic hope that the beach will be perfect.

- Life in the commune, harmony with nature, the secrets, how members opt out of the world's pressures; the seeds of evil and darkness; Sal's power, her seduction and punishment of Richard and the consequences.

- Richard's isolation and increasing madness, imitating the violence of the guards; the massacre and the confrontation in the hut; his return home.

1. Richard and the band of narcissists he joins have a lot of growing to do and they learn the hard way. How does one grow as a person and develop spiritually in a world where pleasure and fun are all that matter and where people, when inconvenient, are disposable?

2. The prophet Isaiah offers a vision of peace on the holy mountain where the Lord "will instruct us in his ways that we may walk in his paths." Richard and the members of the commune seek peace on a perfect beach where the only real imperative is to keep its location a secret. What things would be necessary in order to gain inner peace?

3. Young people want to be "branded" by popular clothing and products in order to belong. Richard, Etienne, and Françoise go through a tattooing process when the commune accepts them. At the end of the film, Richard says, "It's not where you go, but how you feel when you are part of something.... If you find that moment it lasts forever." Talk about how the Advent promises invite us to be "part of something": the divine plan of God's love.

Prayer

Lord, may you offer us visions of joy and peace. May we also be alert to the realities of our world, a world of sin and pain, and, the need for your redeeming presence. Come, Lord Jesus. Amen.

The Apostle
U.S., 1997 / 134 minutes
Actors: Robert Duvall, Miranda Richardson,
Farrah Fawcett, Billy Bob Thornton
Writer: Robert Duvall
Director: Robert Duvall

The Apostle

Sincere Repentance

Eulis Dewey, known as "Sonny," is a traveling evangelist in the American South and has a popular following. He grew up attending church services in black communities and has absorbed their spirit. He is a persuasive preacher and, no matter what his sins, he is a true believer. But then trouble begins.

SYNOPSIS

He is voted out of the church that he co-founded because of his inconsistent behavior. His wife, Jessie, is involved with a younger minister. Sonny arrives at a baseball game and attacks the minister with a baseball bat; the minister later dies. Sonny leaves town and ditches his car in a lake. He then prays that God will call him to be an apostle. He re-baptizes himself. He calls himself "The Apostle E.F." and moves to Louisiana to begin a new ministry.

He works as a short-order cook and becomes a radio preacher to support himself. He remodels an old church and calls it: One Way Road to Heaven Holiness. Jessie hears him on the radio and reports him to the police. In the meantime he has confessed his crime to a fellow-preacher. He knows he has sinned. When the police arrive, E.F. is in the throes of a powerful sermon. He surrenders.

5

Robert Duvall once attended a revival meeting and was fascinated by it. He also felt that evangelical believers and preachers were not fairly treated by the media. So he wrote the screenplay for *The Apostle,* directed it, and gained an Oscar nomination for his performance.

The story is a look at the inner spiritual workings of a man who loves God and struggles with that love and his own humanity. It is not, as some reviewers have suggested, a critique of revivalist religion and the faith of those for whom this religious expression is a joy and comfort. Duvall is sensitive in his portrayal of Sonny, a man who has a gift for preaching, loves prayer and his ministry.

Sonny is a mixture of goodness and sin, although in his capacity to pray and uplift, he is also a Christ-figure (in film, one who in some way represents Christ-like virtues and characteristics). In his amazingly honest portrayal, Duvall does not minimize his character's sinfulness. He plays Sonny's complex figure, at once violent, guilty, and pursued by faith.

There are some fine supporting performances from Farrah Fawcett as Sonny's estranged wife and Miranda Richardson as the radio station secretary he befriends and lusts after. An important aspect of the plot plays beneath the final credits.

DIALOGUE WITH THE GOSPEL

Focus: These Advent readings focus on the preacher par excellence, John the Baptist. It is in his image that modern evangelicals rouse up ordinary people who come to revivals to hear passionate preaching about sinfulness, repentance, and penance.

John the Baptist can be seen as a model for the evangelical preacher, challenging people to acknowledge their sins and repent. Sonny Dewey is certainly a preacher in this evangelical mode.

The first reading from Isaiah speaks of the ideal time when people have repented and are filled with the gifts of the Spirit (Sonny describes himself as filled with the Holy Ghost), and reconciliation and peace have been achieved. These are Advent longings.

John the Baptist is something of a wild and strange man, apocalyptic in bearing, who proclaims his message of purification with a threatening turn of phrase. While Advent is a time to acknowledge sinfulness, it is always in view of hope in the coming of Jesus. John breathes fire and proclaims the coming of Jesus at the same time.

Sonny's background and call are imaged in that of the Baptist. However, Sonny is a man of contradictions, full of passion and violence. In his desperation for forgiveness, he starts again by re-baptizing himself. His beliefs are firm, his convictions solid. But, finally, as the police catch up with him, he has to follow his own preaching, not "flying from the retribution that is to come."

KEY SCENES AND THEMES

- The black communities' religious influence on Sonny; Sonny's preaching ability, his faith and prayers; Sonny's passions and violence, his attack on another minister.

- Sonny's re-baptism, his new sense of evangelistic ministry, his new name; Sonny's new church, new friends and associates; Sonny supporting himself as a cook and a radio preacher.

- Sonny's confession and its consequence; his final fervent sermon; Sonny giving himself up.

FOR REFLECTION AND CONVERSATION

1. Sonny is a good man with many flaws. He is tormented by his call to preach the Gospel and his inability to follow what he preaches in his own life. How differ-

ent is Sonny's struggle from our own to "walk the talk" of the Word, to practice what we preach?

2. Who is a free person in this tale of fervor gone astray? Do any of the characters act and make choices freely? How can we respond to God in freedom, confronted with personal weaknesses and the situations of everyday life?

3. Though full of violence, guilt, and sin, Sonny is ever aware of God pursuing him. In the closing sequence, we are doubly convinced of Sonny's sincerity and the hope that with God, we can repent and always begin again. Recall times in your own life when God has pursued you, inspired you to repentance and hope, and helped you to begin again.

Prayer

Jesus, John the Baptist prepared people for your coming by challenging them to look at their sinfulness and to repent. Help us to reflect on our own sinfulness and respond honestly to you in this Advent season. Amen.

Jesus' Son
U.S., 1999 / 110 minutes
Actors: Billy Crudup, Samantha Morton, Denis Leary,
Dennis Hopper, Holly Hunter
Writers: Elizabeth Cuthrell, Oren Moverman, David Urrutia
Director: Alison Maclean

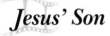

Jesus' Son

Unintentional Healer

SYNOPSIS

A not-so-bright but very good-natured young man tells the dark story of his years as a drifter and drug addict in the early 1970s. We never know his real name because he is now known by an expletive given him by a drug dealer. The young man's story is episodic and broken, and not without moments of dark humor. He continually interrupts his narrative to explain his relationships with friends and the dangers he found himself in when he fell in love with Michelle, a drug-addict, who led him to become one himself.

He encounters various crises, including the accidental shooting of Michelle's boyfriend whom he tries to save. He wanders the roads aimlessly and demonstrates a kind of fore-knowledge of future events.

He and a friend find work in a hospital, and their drug use makes this a bizarre experience. Then he and Wayne, another friend, strip a house of its copper wiring. They both overdose on drugs afterward. Wayne dies, but Michelle saves the young man. Michelle becomes pregnant with his child, has an abortion, and ultimately dies from an overdose.

The young man spends six months in rehab and then goes to Phoenix to work in a nursing home filled with people society would rather ignore: the deformed, the senile, the mentally and the emotionally ill. A nurse urges him to touch the patients, and he is able to calm them, but is oddly unaware of this gift. On his way home one night, he eavesdrops at the window of a young Mennonite woman. Her singing soothes him and he repeatedly returns to listen. Looking through her window one night, he sees that she is blind, reaches through the window and touches her. She regains her sight.

He befriends a crippled woman who thinks she is the cause of the illnesses and deaths of her numerous husbands and lovers. When he invites her to dance at a party, she leaves her cane behind. The young man becomes a means of healing.

COMMENTARY

Jesus' Son won the International Catholic Cinema Organization's award at the 1999 Venice Film Festival. The jury called it a film of healing. It is the journey of a morally confused, aimless, but good young man who gradually grows into a man of compassion. He literally and spiritually touches people and changes their lives, though restoring sight to the blind woman is the most dramatic moment of the film.

Alison Maclean, whose previous film was the New Zealand made *Crush,* directed *Jesus' Son.* The movie is based on a series of best-selling short stories by Denis Johnson. The film recreates the marginal drug culture of the early 1970s in the American Midwest. The early part of the narrative is told in a fragmented, non-linear way, a broken stream of consciousness, with "chapter headings" shown on screen.

Billy Crudup (*Without Limits, The Hi-Lo Country*) shows versatility in the central role as a young man who is good yet weak, intellectually slow yet genuine. Often, his face resembles paintings of Jesus. Denis Leary and Dennis Hopper make brief cameo appearances, and Holly Hunter contributes a forceful supporting performance as the woman with the cane.

Jesus' Son is perhaps of more interest to fans of independent and art house cinema because of its dim, often unsettling presentation. While it is definitely mature fare, the film has humor and warmth, especially in the nursing home scenes. *Jesus' Son* can be said to make compassion and grace visible through someone the viewer would least expect.

Focus: Healing the sick is an Advent sign of the coming of the Savior because healing is about hope.

DIALOGUE WITH THE GOSPEL

Hope is the Advent theme of the first reading from Isaiah 35: the desert will be rich in beauty and all human beings will be healed; they will find themselves whole and be filled with joy and gladness because God comes to save us.

The Gospel takes up this theme as John the Baptist announces that the coming of Jesus fulfills Isaiah's text. Jesus confirms this for John's disciples.

Jesus also takes this opportunity to remind his listeners that they cannot predict what a prophet will look or sound like except that he will be neither weak nor pampered. While John was a great prophet, any disciple who follows Jesus—no matter if he or she is considered the least—is greater than John.

The confused young man who feels like *Jesus' Son* when he is high on drugs is nevertheless a good and kind person. He is open to grace and change, and he continually questions the meaning of life and death. Rough and ready, he is a gently wild prophet who transforms people's lives, and yet needs transformation himself. He brings a beauty to his world, unaware that he also brings healing: the blind see, the lame walk and dance, and the hopeless and neglected receive love and attention. The young man might now truly be called Jesus' Son. He is a meaningful Advent sign.

* The young man's world: his so-called friends; falling in love with Michelle, but his dependence on her for

KEY SCENES AND THEMES

drugs; the deaths and the young man's helplessness, being part of a lost world.

* The young man's move toward another way of life; conquering his addiction; his encounters with the nursing home patients; the young man learning how to touch and be touched.

* The young man's unawareness of his healing power; his touching the blind Mennonite woman; the crippled woman and doomed relationships, his dancing with her, her leaving the cane behind.

FOR REFLECTION AND CONVERSATION

1. This film depicts drug addiction and alcoholism as tragic human problems, and the scenes that show the young people taking drugs are harrowing and extreme. What does it take for the young man to stop using drugs? How does he find his way? How does a film like this compare with one like *Traffic?*

2. The young man thoughtlessly accompanies his girlfriend for an abortion, but comes to regret it too late. Later he hitches a ride with a family and the car crashes. He rescues the baby. How does this scene develop the film's dramatic emphasis on the young man's growing awareness of the gift of life over death, both for himself and for others? Talk about the ways a film like *Jesus' Son* can provide a "place" to communicate about the dignity of human life from the moment of conception.

3. The nurse at Beverly Nursing Home tells the young man that one of his duties is to touch the patients because they need to have contact with someone. She teaches him how to touch and soothe people. How

can we reach out and touch someone? In what ways is this film an Advent sign prompting us to reach out during this graced time to choose healing for self and others?

Prayer
Jesus, in this Advent time, show us the healing and grace-filled signs of your coming to our world. You are the fulfillment of all our hopes. Amen.

Where the Heart Is
U.S., 2000 / 120 minutes
Actors: Natalie Portman, Ashley Judd, Stockard Channing,
Sally Field, James Frain, Keith David, Dylan Bruno,
Joan Cusack
Writers: Lowell Ganz, Babaloo Mandel
Director: Matt Williams

Where the Heart Is

Awaiting the Child

SYNOPSIS

Novalee is an unmarried pregnant teenager who likes to take photographs. She and her boyfriend, Willy Jack Pickens, leave Tennessee to drive to California for work. He abandons Novalee at a Wal-Mart in Oklahoma. For six weeks she hides out in the huge store by night, and by day sits in the park and visits the library. She makes friends with Sister Husband, a recovering alcoholic, and with Forney, the reclusive town librarian. One night, Forney sees her sneak into the Wal-Mart and then jumps through a glass window to help her as she goes into labor. Due to the strange circumstances, the new mother and infant become celebrities. The "Wal-Mart Baby" is named Americus. Meanwhile, Willy Jack ends up in jail and then tries to make it as a country singer.

People who have seen Novalee on television send her mostly supportive letters, though some revile her. The president of Wal-Mart sends her $500. Novalee and Lexi, a nurse's aide, become friends. Novalee's neglectful mother visits her in the hospital and then steals her money under the pretext of finding them a place to live. The kindly Sister Husband, a God-fearing Bible woman with a live-in boyfriend, takes

14

Novalee and the baby in. Forney, who cares for his sick sister, is devoted to Novalee and Americus.

Novalee gets a job at Wal-Mart and eventually becomes a freelance photographer as well. A few years later, Sister Husband is killed in a tornado that suddenly strikes the town. Sister leaves Novalee her land, insurance, and stocks. Novalee builds a home and takes in Lexi and her children. Novalee spends one night with Forney and though he loves her, she says she doesn't love him. When his sister dies, Forney goes back East to finish college.

Novalee wins a photography contest. She reads about Willy Jack who lost his legs in a train accident during an alcohol and drug binge. She visits him in the hospital, where he talks about his regret over his many lies. Novalee comes to realize she lied to Forney. She goes to visit Forney at school and tells him she loves him, and they are married in the Wal-Mart.

Where the Heart Is, a slice of Oklahoma life, focuses mainly on the relationships of its female characters. It is a very emotional, earthy, fairly realistic tale with a hopeful message.

COMMENTARY

Natalie Portman (*Leon, Anywhere But Here, The Phantom Menace*) is one of America's most talented up-and-coming actresses. Stockard Channing, as Sister Husband, shows what hometown generosity can be like. With care and feeling, Ashley Judd plays Lexi, who could perhaps be Novalee's older alter ego. Keith David is a photographer who encourages Novalee's abilities. Britain's James Frain plays the devoted librarian. Joan Cusack provides a cameo as Willy Jack's hard-bitten agent. Sally Field gives a very brief, effective performance as Novalee's irresponsible mother.

From the onset, *Where the Heart Is* affirms life when Novalee asks Willy Jack to feel the beating of their unborn baby's heart. We follow the lives of the women through their pregnancies and the birth of their children. Their relationships with men are difficult and they make poor, even tragic choices. The movie criticizes righteous types who think they are better than others. For those who have not had many opportunities in life, this film offers encouragement amid life's hurts and confusions.

DIALOGUE WITH THE GOSPEL

Focus: Mary experienced the suspicion and rejection of others in Nazareth when she became pregnant. Novalee, the pregnant teenager in Where the Heart Is, *shows how hard it is for a young, inexperienced, and unwed girl to be with child.*

Mother and child have always been a symbol of life and hope. The reading from Isaiah (which dates from a time more than 700 years before the coming of Jesus) offers the sign of a mother and child to King Ahaz, who has no faith. The child is a sign of life and blessing, showing that "God is with us."

While Novalee's life is quite different from Mary's life in Nazareth, there are some striking similarities. This movie is about a struggling mother and her love for her child. Novalee is hurt and feels abandoned. She has no resources to fall back on, is not prepared for the experience of giving birth, or for raising a child. Novalee gives birth in a huge chain store because there is nowhere else for her to go. She finds comfort in the goodness of strangers who bring gifts, like the Magi. Forney, the unobtrusive librarian, is something of a Joseph-figure who assists at the birth of the child and becomes a foster father to Americus.

We need insights like these to remind us of the social and religious difficulties that Mary faced, and that today's unmarried and pregnant teens also face. The Gospel challenges our Christian commitment to compassion.

Where the Heart Is mirrors the Advent symbol of Mary and Jesus, the mother and child who bring the promise of hope into a needy world.

KEY SCENES AND THEMES

- The young and pregnant Novalee in love with Willy Jack, abandoned in a parking lot, and having to sleep in Wal-Mart for six weeks (keeping strict accounts of the items she used); Forney finding her and taking her to the hospital; the townspeople rejoicing in the birth of her child.

- Sister Husband: her generosity, her non-judgmental and encouraging attitudes; her struggles with alcoholism and celibacy; her death and the gift of her house and stocks to Novalee.

- Forney: the quiet man who protects and cares for his sister; his hard life; his love for Novalee; his constant care for Americus; his experience of Novalee's rejection; the joy of the wedding and the three becoming a happy family.

FOR REFLECTION AND CONVERSATION

1. The theme of the "heart" is woven throughout the film: the scene when Novalee asks Willy Jack to feel the baby's heartbeat in her womb, the words of the song about the beat of a heart, the unconditional love of the people of Sequoia for Novalee and the baby. How does each of the characters show a selfless love in the movie? Talk about how Willy Jack grows and changes.

2. Novalee receives at least one letter condemning her for being an unwed mother, written by a couple from Mississippi. They arrive at Sister Husband's home car-

rying a Bible so they can "save" Novalee. They kidnap the baby and place her in the crib of the town's Nativity scene. How does this episode fit into the moral universe created by the film? What does it mean?

3. Novalee, Sister Husband, and Lexi all have a number of affairs, while at the same time retaining their own particular image of and relationship to God. Does their behavior have a social or religious explanation? How? How does each of these women view God, and how is this reflected in their own self-image? What is my image of God, and how does this influence *my* own self-image?

Prayer

Mary, we remember today what it was like for you to be a young mother. Be with all mothers who experience anxiety. May they share your hope and trust in God. Amen.

The Lion King

U.S., 1994 / 85 minutes

Voices: Jonathan Taylor Thomas, Matthew Broderick, Jeremy Irons, James Earl Jones, Madge Sinclair, Rowan Atkinson, Nathan Lane, Ernie Sabella, Whoopi Goldberg, Cheech Marin, Moira Kelly, Robert Guillaume

Writers: Irene Mecchi, Jonathan Roberts, Linda Woolverton

Directors: Roger Allers, Rob Minkoff

The Lion King

Born to Be King

SYNOPSIS

A baby cub, Simba, is born to the Lion King, Mufasa, in Africa's "Pride Lands." All the animals of the jungle assemble to honor the cub and he is anointed the future king. His uncle, Scar, is jealous and wants to kill both Mufasa and Simba.

Mufasa trains his son not to stray from the Pride. But when Scar persuades him to go beyond the boundaries of the "Pride Lands," Simba does not want to seem afraid, and his father has to rescue him. Scar then enlists the help of scavenging hyenas that cause a stampede, and once again Simba is trapped. When Mufasa saves Simba and tries to climb the cliff to safety, Scar causes Mufasa to fall to his death. Scar makes Simba feel guilty over his father's death and advises him to run away.

Pumbaa (a warthog) and Timon (a meerkat) find and befriend Simba. He grows up with them, longs for his father, and learns responsibility. When Simba and his best friend, the lioness Nala, chase Timon in the jungle, Simba learns that Scar has taken over as king. The hyenas have plundered the land and wasted the kingdom so that the animals are starving. The old baboon, a counselor/prophet, finds Simba, shows him his true self, and the image of his father within him. Simba returns, confronts Scar, and brings the kingdom to prosperity. Simba and Nala's cub is born and presented to the animals as the future king. The circle of life continues.

COMMENTARY

The Lion King is the Disney Studio's most successful and popular animated movie to date. It is also a highly successful Broadway musical. The animation, especially the variety of animals, is stunning.

The story contains the right mix of family themes, royalty, adventure, danger, multiculturalism, comic characters, and music. The songs by Tim Rice and Elton John, as well as Hans Zimmer's score, were Oscar winners.

DIALOGUE WITH THE GOSPEL

Focus: The family of lions in The Lion King *parallels the Holy Family: the roles of Mary and Joseph as parents and the special destiny of Jesus as the Savior of his people.*

Since its release in 1994, primary school teachers especially have been able to use *The Lion King* to suggest aspects of the nativity of Jesus. Simba's birth at the opening of the movie and his presentation to the animals recalls the adoration of the shepherds and the magi, and their acknowledgment of Jesus as the Prince of Peace.

Other themes are Mufasa as a role model; the mother lioness who remains in the background, watching, pondering (as in Luke's Gospel, Mary is one who contemplates things in her heart); Simba growing up, being educated, living in exile, and becoming responsible.

The first reading from the prophet Isaiah speaks of an oppressed people living in darkness who need a savior. They long for the child to be born who will save them and who will be a true king, a Wonder-Counselor, a Prince of Peace. In fairytale style, Simba exemplifies all these aspects of the true prince, the warrior who saves his people, the restorer of order. This is similar to the last sentence of the reading from the Letter to Titus (cf. 2:11–14): "he sacrificed himself for us in order to set us free from all wickedness and to purify a people so that it could be his very own...."

- Simba's birth as the royal prince, the old baboon presenting him to the animals, Simba reverenced and anointed as future king—a parallel to Jesus' birth; Mufasa as father-figure (like Joseph), Mufasa's love for his son, his training and guiding of Simba.

- Scar and the kingdom of darkness: the hyena troops stripping and impoverishing the land, the oppression; "a people in darkness wanting to see the light."

- Simba looking at the stars and wanting to see his father; the baboon/prophet; Simba's seeing his father within himself; Simba gaining strength to return to save the animals.

1. The theme song of *The Lion King* is "The Circle of Life." It is sung as the lion family celebrates Simba's birth and as the old baboon, the prophet-figure, arrives to anoint the infant Simba in a ceremony of initiation into life, the animal kingdom, and his "family." How do the song and the imagery evoke nature's cycle of life, family life, and the sacramental life that we begin through the Sacrament of Baptism?

2. Simba is the "prince," born with the calling to be king; but he fails, runs away, and then, with the help of his friends, remembers who he is and comes to his senses. What parts of the film suggest other Gospel passages besides the Nativity narratives (e.g., the Prodigal Son, Luke 15:11–32)?

3. "Hope is a good thing—maybe the best thing, and no good thing ever dies" (Stephen King in *The Shawshank Redemption*). As Simba was the hope for the "Pride Lands," so Jesus is our hope. How does Jesus bring light into your life? How can we bring the Gospel of hope to those around us?

Prayer

Jesus, we celebrate your coming into our world today. Bring your light into our darkness. May we live good and religious lives in this present world while we wait in hope for your coming in glory. Amen.

Jimmy Stewart and the cast of *It's a Wonderful Life.*

It's a Wonderful Life

U.S., 1947 / 121 minutes, B & W

Actors: James Stewart, Donna Reed, Thomas Mitchell, Lionel Barrymore, Gloria Grahame, Henry Travers, Beulah Bondi

Writers: Frances Goodrich, Albert Hackett, Jo Swerling, Frank Capra

Director: Frank Capra

It's a Wonderful Life

What If?

George Bailey grows up in a warm family atmosphere in Bedford Falls. His father is a kindly, unsuccessful manager of a building and loan company who extends easy credit to his customers. George dreams of leaving Bedford Falls. He wants to plan things; to build modern cities, airfields, and bridges; and change the world. He falls in love with Mary.

George's brother has left town and when their father dies, George also has the chance to leave. But he decides to stay because the harsh Mr. Potter takes over the Bailey firm. George believes that he can influence Mr. Potter to continue treating customers well, as his father did.

Mary and George get married. Over the years, George builds up goodwill among the townspeople and creates a housing estate for them. But he never leaves town to follow his dreams. Time passes, his family grows, but he feels trapped. When a large deposit is missing from the building and loan, George has to find money to cover losses. (George does not know that his good-natured Uncle Billy had mistakenly given Mr. Potter the day's deposit wrapped up in a newspaper.) George is in despair and is harsh to Mary and his children. He contemplates killing himself for the insurance money.

SYNOPSIS

Clarence, an angel, is sent to help him see the real meaning and value of his life. Clarence shows him what Bedford Falls might have been like had he not lived: a town of squalor and corruption. Coming to his senses, George runs home to Mary and his family to celebrate Christmas.

COMMENTARY

It's a Wonderful Life is probably the most referred to film in the history of cinema; it is either shown or mentioned countless times in other movies (even *The Gremlins* mischievously watch it). Though it was not warmly received in 1947, it has gained a reputation over the decades. In a sense, *It's a Wonderful Life* has become the American Christmas movie.

The film's pedigree is almost perfect. A Frank Capra movie, it immerses its audience into social problems of the times. Through the goodwill of the characters and plot, the film creates a hero who can break through great obstacles with integrity, like Gary Cooper in *Mr. Deeds Goes to Town* and James Stewart in *Mr. Smith Goes to Washington*.

Hollywood golden era veterans Frances Goodrich, Albert Hackett, and Jo Swerling wrote this film, by adapting a story that Philip Van Doren Stern originally wrote on a Christmas card.

DIALOGUE WITH THE GOSPEL

Focus: It's a Wonderful Life *has become one of America's favorite films, the quintessential and perennial Christmas movie. The film asks the audience to appreciate their blessings. Through the angel, Clarence, the movie promises peace to people of goodwill.*

The readings for the Mass at Dawn on Christmas are about blessings: the hopes of a Savior from Isaiah, the kindness and love of God in Titus (cf. 3:4–7), and the revelation to the shepherds in Luke. The readings are full of comfort, joy, and hope.

The climax of *It's a Wonderful Life* comes at Christmas— for George Bailey and his family, a time of crisis. The present and the future are threatened if George kills himself.

George was and is a man of blessing for the people of Bedford Falls. He has dedicated his whole life to them, and has sacrificed all of his personal hopes and ambitions for them. But he believes his life has been dull and ordinary, certainly not very wonderful at all.

It takes God's special intervention for George to look at his life, accept it, and see the wonder of it. It is in the spirit of that first Christmas that the apprentice angel, Clarence, gently persuades George that his life has meaning as he takes him on a journey to the past and the future, similar to Scrooge in *A Christmas Carol*. The reading from Titus describes George's blessings, if only he can open his eyes and see.

- The young George Bailey as the decent man: in his family, in the town, in his work; George's personal anguish over his choice to remain in Bedford Falls.

- George feeling that life is passing him by; George's ambitions, his lack of awareness regarding all his actual achievements.

- The crises: Uncle Billy's mismanagement, Potter's exploitation; Clarence as the apprentice angel, his saving and befriending George and guiding him through past and future; George running home to be reunited with his family.

KEY SCENES AND THEMES

1. Christmas movies seem to follow the pattern of Charles Dickens' archetypal Christmas story, *A Christmas Carol*, written in 1843. Some essential ingredients include a family with burdens, forays or glimpses into past holiday memories before any problems existed,

FOR REFLECTION AND CONVERSATION

images of the future, and someone to help resolve the difficulties, making Christmas once again full of family warmth, happiness, and peace. How does *It's a Wonderful Life* fulfill the conditions for a "traditional" Christmas story? What is the source of the Christmas joy that gives rise to a successful Christmas tale?

2. This film focuses on George's personal journey from despair to awareness to hope. How can contemporary people identify with George's plight? How can Clarence's message about what would have happened if George had never lived be applied to situations today?

3. Angels are among us in many ways if we but listen and look to the signs of goodness around us: the people we meet, the books we read, the songs we hear, and stories we see on television and in movies. In what ways can we contemplate divine mysteries and human goodness in daily life?

Prayer

Lord, on this day you sent us Jesus, your Son, as a gift of peace to the world. May he be a gift to those who are anxious, who suffer in this season of joy. Amen.

E.T.: The Extra-Terrestrial

U.S., 1982 / 118 minutes

Actors: Henry Thomas, Drew Barrymore, Dee Wallace, Peter Coyote

Writer: Melissa Mathison

Director: Steven Spielberg

E.T.: The Extra-Terrestrial

Come Down to Earth

Elliot lives with his older brother, younger sister, and their mother in a pleasant neighborhood in California. One night, he senses a "presence" in the house and discovers a mysterious creature. The creature likes Elliot. Elliot decides to protect him by hiding him in the house, but his brother and sister soon find him. Elliot calls the alien, this extra-terrestrial being, E.T.

SYNOPSIS

E.T. adapts to life in the family despite having to hide, but he wants to find a way to make contact with his world, to "phone home." Eventually the children have to tell their mother about E.T. In the meantime, the authorities are searching for the extraterrestrial. Their leader is a scientist called Keys.

Elliot does his best to protect E.T., but the extraterrestrial is captured and examined.

E.T. languishes, and it is only when Elliot gives his blood for his friend during an operation that E.T. revives.

The children and their friends escape with E.T. in a van. However, E.T. knows that it is time to leave and goes to a mountain to meet his spacecraft. E.T. invites Elliot to go along. Keys and Elliot's mother, along with the children's friends—

29

who ride their bikes through the sky—arrive at the site. Elliot decides he must stay with his family, and E.T. promises to always be with them.

COMMENTARY

E.T. was one of the surprise movies of the 1980s, and it is still one of the most popular and financially successful movies of all time.

Steven Spielberg, who made *Close Encounters of the Third Kind* in 1977, had already shown an interest in space and extraterrestrials. *Close Encounters* presented an optimistic perspective about aliens and other worlds beyond this one, in contrast with other films that portrayed aliens as enemies.

Spielberg wanted to make a movie for children and chose the Peter Pan story for the background. He commissioned Melissa Mathison (*An Indian in the Cupboard, Kundun*) to adapt the story using outer space as the backdrop. When Mathison was interviewed later, she said that while she was watching *E.T.* being filmed, she realized its similarities to the Gospels.

Henry Thomas is Elliot and a young Drew Barrymore is his sister Gertie. The voice of E.T. was supplied by Debra Winger and technically modified for the now-familiar rasp.

DIALOGUE WITH THE GOSPEL

Focus: The Word was made flesh. Christians have always tried to understand what this means: that the Divine entered our world, became one of us, and shared our humanity with us. Movies like E.T. *help us to imagine a little something about the Incarnation of Jesus.*

The Gospel parallel with *E.T.* is quite strong. *E.T* comes from "out there," in space, beyond this world, and dwells among people. At first E.T. is shy, and then becomes part of a family and shares human experience. Gradually, the humans, first the children, and then the adults, are able to get to know and appreciate E.T.

Government authorities are also searching for E.T. so they can test the little alien. E.T. goes through a dying process when he is captured. When Elliot donates his blood as they travel in the ambulance, E.T. revives; he appears in a white shroud, his red heart beating.

E.T. then goes back to his home using words very much like those from the ending of St. Matthew's Gospel: Be good, I will be with you always.

When the film was released, people joked that after the O.T. (Old Testament) and the N.T. (New Testament) came E.T., the Extra Testament. Mathison and Spielberg did not set out to create something theological. Rather, they tapped into stories and myths present in many cultures about incarnations. Scriptural parallels are obvious, however, and add "super-natural" significance to the filmmakers' *E.T.* creation. Theology has always used analogies and stories to help understand something of the mysteries of God. Here, popular culture provides the audience with a moving and imaginative opportunity for theological reflection.

KEY SCENES AND THEMES

- E.T. coming to earth: being isolated and his desire to go home, E.T. hiding outside and Elliot's discovery; Elliot's taking E.T. into the house.

- The scientists' search: their motives, their suspicion and hostility, the equipment, their hunting down and capturing E.T.

- Elliot giving his blood for E.T., who revives; E.T. in the shroud-like sheet with a burning heart; the farewell; E.T.'s final words; Elliot's decision to stay with his family; E.T.'s final "ascension."

1. Steven Spielberg's films return to the theme of lonely children again and again. E.T. is also alone, but freely offers friendship and love to other lonely children. How is this theme a subtext of *E.T.: The Extra-Terrestrial?* How is it expressed and played out? How does the relationship between the children and E.T. parallel with the life and mission of Jesus?

2. At first glance, aliens and extraterrestrials may not seem to match the celebration of Christmas, yet alien figures abound in the Gospels. The Romans were aliens to the Israelites; Joseph and Mary would soon leave for Egypt to become aliens in a foreign country. In the movie, Elliot and his siblings welcomed E.T. the alien, despite the fact that he was so different from them. How do mainstream films usually treat people who are "different," whether by race, social status, country or culture of origin, gender or age?

3. God can speak to us in many ways if we are open and willing to listen. How did God speak to you through the story of *E.T.* today, the Feast of the Nativity of the Lord?

Prayer

Jesus, help us to understand and appreciate what your Incarnation means. You came to live a human life like ours to give us an example of courage and love. Be with us always. Amen.

The Family Man

U.S., 2000 / 126 minutes

Actors: Nicolas Cage, Téa Leoni, Jeremy Piven,
Josef Sommer, Saul Rubinek, Don Cheadle,
Mary Beth Hurt

Writers: David Diamond, David Weissman

Director: Brett Ratner

The Family Man

The Essentials...

SYNOPSIS

Jack Campbell bids farewell to his girlfriend Kate, and leaves for England and a successful banking career. He forgets her. Thirteen years later he is an expert in corporate takeovers and has become very persuasive in the boardroom.

On Christmas Eve, Campbell walks home in the snow. Unexpectedly, he helps a storeowner deal with a customer who claims at gunpoint to have a winning lottery ticket. But it is Jack who is the "winner" when the man with the gun turns out to be an angel, who offers Jack a glimpse of what his life with Kate might have been.

Jack wakes up on Christmas morning with Kate and two children. He has been married for thirteen years and works for his father-in-law as a tire salesman. He tries to adapt to a more friendly and loving family atmosphere, something he is not accustomed to, and uses his ingenuity to cover the gaps in his knowledge. He yearns for his old life, and even visits the company office. Ultimately, he realizes that he loves Kate and now appreciates what it means to have a family.

When the angel returns him to his old life, he is unwilling to remain there. He calls Kate and finds she is a successful businesswoman on the verge of going to Paris. They have coffee and Jack describes the life that could be theirs....

The Family Man is a pleasing Christmas movie characterized by sentiment and goodwill with a touch of sharp realism. The writers have surely seen *It's a Wonderful Life* several times, as this is a twist on that now familiar story of someone realizing what a difference his life has made.

The hero is an unlikely Nicolas Cage. His Jack is a "hotshot" tycoon, a company and people manager who discovers that deep down, he really does have a generous heart. Street-smart Don Cheadle is a modern alternative to Capra's angel, Clarence, (or Dickens' "Ghost of Christmas Past"), offering Jack a glimpse of a different life had he married Kate and not become a financier.

Cage is good at acting bewildered as he copes with a family and with feelings of love. His career as a salesman might have been humdrum, but he would have been happy.

The Family Man is also very similar to *Me, Myself, I,* an earlier movie which is a female version of this familiar story, with Rachel Griffith as a woman who finds herself living the family life she might have had.

The Family Man is about integrity and having a heart.

Focus: Joseph was the Gospel's ideal "family man," a man who sacrificed whatever plans and dreams he might have had for the love of Mary and Jesus.

Matthew's Gospel offers us a portrait of Mary and one of Joseph as well. His role as foster father and legal guardian of Jesus is given high significance. The first reading from Sirach emphasizes the role of father in the Jewish family: protector, wise guide, and teacher. The Letter to the Colossians (cf. 3:12–21) gives Paul's vision of the qualities of the Christian family.

The title, *The Family Man*, points to the role of father in today's society. The ideal situation is a father who is a partner with his wife in providing support, protection, wisdom, and guidance to his family. Jack Campbell gave up these family opportunities to be a successful businessman, but now has a chance to reconsider his choice. There is a kind of similarity between Joseph in the Gospel and Jack. Joseph, who was certainly anticipating family life with Mary, had his expectations shattered by her unexpected pregnancy. In a dream, Joseph listened to an angel, God's messenger, and discovered how he would be both a father to Jesus and a husband to Mary. For Joseph, it was to be a challenging role, especially when faced with having to save Jesus from Herod, and later, bringing him home to Nazareth, where Jesus would grow into manhood.

Jack has a dream/vision of his future, too, and in that dream a message comes to him about what his life could be like, different from the one he expected. Jack's dream is only "what if…?" Yet, the message and the challenge of his "angel" are enough for Jack to run the risk of exchanging power, success, and wealth for the love of a wife and family.

On the Feast of the Holy Family, the Church takes the opportunity to offer us a vision of ideal family relationships. Idealized and optimistic movies like *The Family Man* offer us images of that vision.

KEY SCENES AND THEMES

- The opening airport scene: Jack leaving Kate and making choices only for himself; the movie's ending scene: Kate making her choice for Jack and a family.

- Jack waking up to a new life: to love for Kate; the experience of having children; Jack's initial awkwardness and unwillingness; the ordinary domestic experiences that change his mind.

- Jack's transformation: his change of attitude and heart toward his old life, toward the prospects of the new; Jack's visit to the office; Jack meeting Kate; their discussion over a cup of coffee.

FOR REFLECTION AND CONVERSATION

1. *The Family Man* focuses on the life of Jack, a would-be father of a family, the choices he makes, and what might have been. But what about Kate, the wife and mother, and the children? What is the family ideal presented in this film? Which episodes best demonstrate this? In what ways does it fit the Christian profile for "family"?

2. Many Christmas movies use the "Scrooge" plot device: what happened, what's happening, and what might happen, if the main character will only have a change of heart. Does Jack grow and change in the film? In what ways?

3. *The Family Man* is not only about what Jack does for his family, but what his family does for him. The essence of the message of today's feast is that family members can contribute to one another's holiness. In what ways do I try to make my family happy and holy?

Prayer

On the Feast of the Holy Family, we pray to you, Jesus, Mary and Joseph, to grace families with the love and harmony that were yours. Amen.

Superman: The Movie

U.S., 1978 / 150 minutes

Actors: Christopher Reeve, Gene Hackman, Marlon Brando,
Susannah York, Margot Kidder, Valerie Perrine, Glenn Ford,
Phyllis Thaxter

Writers: Mario Puzo, Robert Benton, David Newman, Leslie Newman

Director: Richard Donner

SECOND SUNDAY AFTER CHRISTMAS
Sirach 24:1–4, 8–12; John 1:1–18

Superman: The Movie

The Father Sends His Son

This chapter focuses on the first fifty minutes of the movie only—its "prologue." After that, the film's tone changes completely, turning into a comic-strip action adventure. Which, of course, is what the movie is....

Jor-El, a prominent citizen of Krypton, warns the leaders of the planet that it is about to self-destruct. The ruling council makes Jor-El promise not to alert anyone else because they are afraid of causing a panic.

Jor-El and his wife, Lara, are concerned for their infant son Kal-El, and they prepare a special spacecraft for him to travel from Krypton to earth. The infant is sent off as the planet explodes and his parents are killed.

The journey to earth takes many years (in Krypton time). During this time Kal-El grows into a young boy and gains all the knowledge he will need for his life on earth through a kind of narrative infusion of his father's voice, which continues during his time in the Arctic "desert."

His spacecraft crash-lands near Smallsville, U.S.A., just as Mr. and Mrs. Kent are driving along a rural road. They get a flat tire and are amazed when a child appears and effortlessly lifts the truck that has fallen on Mr. Kent. The Kents

SYNOPSIS

adopt the boy and name him Clark. He lives a quiet life with them and grows up with amazing powers. It is obvious that he is from another world. When his adopted father dies, Clark goes to the Arctic on a journey of self-discovery. He contacts his biological father in time and together they study the cultures of Krypton and the earth. Clark returns to the U.S. to begin his public life.

COMMENTARY

Superman: The Movie was released in 1978, the year after the first *Star Wars* film. Audiences around the world were enthusiastic about both of these movies and several sequels followed both.

Superman: The Movie uses a mixture of writing and cinematic styles and devices. The prologue, written by Mario Puzo and featuring Marlon Brando as Jor-El, begins on Krypton, following the child's journey to earth and his adoption by the Kents. Clark Kent's life in Smallsville and in the Arctic parallels the "hidden life" of Jesus.

Christopher Reeve is a genial hero (both as Superman and as Clark Kent), and Gene Hackman is well cast as the arch-villain Lex Luthor. David Newman, Leslie Newman and Robert Benton wrote the second part of the movie. Richard Donner, who went on to make *Maverick* and the extremely successful *Lethal Weapon* series, directed *Superman: The Movie*. John Williams wrote the music for *Superman* and its sequels, as he did for all the *Star Wars* films.

DIALOGUE WITH THE GOSPEL

Focus: The first part of Superman: The Movie *is written with attention to both the theology of the Incarnation and the words of St. John's Gospel about the relation of the Son to the Father. The movie provides imaginative and plausible parallels with the Gospel.*

Puzo must have been very familiar with the New Testament. This is obvious because so many of the elements of his Superman "prologue" relate directly to the Prologue of St. John, and some of Jor-El's dialogue is straight out of the Last Discourse in John.

The Prologue to St. John's Gospel is a mystical hymn. It provides material for meditation on the nature of God as well as the mystery of the Incarnation. It takes us back to the person of the Divine Word, one with the Father and the Spirit in the Trinity, who came to earth and lived as a human being. This hymn owes something to Greek philosophy with its concept of the Logos, the word of Wisdom spoken by God, which enters into human wisdom.

Puzo imagines Krypton as a kind of heaven (although the comparison ends when Krypton self-destructs). Jor-El is a God/Father figure who sends his son into the world from above, giving him wisdom and explicitly declaring that he and his son will always exist together. When the son is "made flesh" and arrives on earth in a crib-like vessel, he lives a hidden life until his appointed time comes.

KEY SCENES AND THEMES

- Jor-El and his wife saving their child, preparing him for the journey; Jor-El's explanation that he will always live in the child and the child live in him; the parallel with the Gospel texts.

- The spacecraft's journey to earth; Jor-El infusing his knowledge into the mind and memory of his son.

- The landing on earth, the small child's smile at the Kents, their desire to adopt him, the boy lifting the truck and the Kents' amazement; the "hidden life" in Smallsville and the Arctic; Clark Kent growing in years, stature and wisdom to prepare for his public life.

1. Superman's early life can be seen as a metaphor for the Incarnation. He is sent to earth and empowered to use his gifts for the good of others. How does the prologue of this film contrast with the mystery of the Incarnation?

2. *Superman: The Movie* does not address deeper questions of faith or the historical truth regarding Jesus. At the same time, Superman is a kind of mythical or cultural Christ-figure who reminds us of Jesus because he saves the community from harm. He performs "miracles" so that good can conquer evil and justice can prevail. What other scenes or episodes in the film point to Superman as a "Christ-figure"?

3. Superman was loved by his parents and by the Kents. The Father's love has been revealed to us in the Incarnation, the birth of Jesus, the Word made flesh. How can our lives reveal the love of God in concrete ways to those with whom we live, work, and worship?

Prayer

Lord, your coming to earth to be one of us and share our lives is one of the great mysteries of our faith. Strengthen that faith and give us hope in your promise to help us in the struggles of our lives. Amen.

The Fisher King

U.S., 1991 / 137 minutes

Actors: Robin Williams, Jeff Bridges, Mercedes Ruehl, Amanda Plummer

Writer: Richard LaGravenese

Director: Terry Gilliam

The Fisher King

A Quest for Meaning

SYNOPSIS

Jack Lucas is a ruthless radio personality who not only disparages his audience, but also spews out extreme ideas. One day, a listener follows Jack's rhetoric literally and massacres a group of diners in a yuppie restaurant. Full of guilt, Jack opts out of life. He moves in with Anne, his girlfriend, and works in her video store.

One night, when Jack is drunk, he heads to the river to kill himself. Some thugs accost him and try to set him on fire, but he is saved by a group of homeless people. Their leader is Parry, who believes he is a "knight." Jack discovers that Parry is a former professor of medieval history, who was placed in a mental hospital following his wife's tragic death. Parry now lives in a fantasy world.

To atone for his own sins, Jack helps Parry by giving him money. Jack watches over the awkward and unaware Lydia, the woman Parry is infatuated with as his "fair maiden." Jack listens as Parry tells him the fable of the "Fisher King." Parry shows Jack a picture of a cup owned by a billionaire. Parry envisions it to be the Grail. Parry also talks to invisible little people and is haunted and pursued by a giant Red Knight.

Jack and Anne set up an encounter between Lydia and Parry in the video store. All goes well and the two couples go out for a meal together.

Jack begins to feel better and wants to go back to work. He leaves Anne. Parry is mugged and the incident causes him to relive the trauma of his wife's murder; he goes into a catatonic state. Jack visits Parry in the hospital and then decides to retrieve the Grail; through it he is able to revive Parry. Anne and Jack are reunited, and Parry and Lydia are together. They have fulfilled the fable of the "Fisher King."

COMMENTARY

Director Terry Gilliam was the American cartoonist member of the U.K. Monty Python group that directed *Monty Python and the Holy Grail.* Gilliam also directed the mythic fantasy, *Time Bandits.* Some of his other films include *Brazil, The Adventures of Baron Munchausen, Twelve Monkeys,* and *Fear and Loathing in Las Vegas.*

Robin Williams draws on his capacity for mania and pathos as Parry, the would-be modern knight deeply affected by grief and trauma. Mercedes Ruehl won the Oscar for Best Supporting Actress for her performance as Anne. Jeff Bridges, who was nominated for an Oscar as Best Supporting Actor in 2001 for his role in *The Contender,* gives a gritty performance as the world-weary and self-absorbed media personality. Amanda Plummer has no trouble handling the role of an eccentrically direct and accident-prone Lydia.

Robin Williams recounts the story of the "Fisher King": A young prince with great ambitions sets out on a quest for the Grail, but when he reaches for it his hand is burned. The prince then becomes a frustrated and self-deprecating King. When the court Fool offers the King a cup of water, the King recognizes the cup as the Grail and he finally obtains the object of his ambition. Jack is the contemporary Fisher King whose life has been stunted and contaminated. Parry is the

Fool who offers his help so that Jack can discover that he is holding the Grail in his hands.

> *Focus: The Feast of the Epiphany is a celebration of Jesus' revelation to the world. It is also a commemoration of the Magi's fulfillment of their quest. All their hopes and their dreams are realized when they find the Child.*

DIALOGUE WITH THE GOSPEL

The Fisher King is an old myth about a hero's quest, which the film interprets for modern audiences. A parallel can be drawn in some ways between Jack and the mythological king. He is the seemingly doomed Fisher King who does not realize he is on a journey in search of grace and wholeness. The Magi were also on a quest for wisdom and for the child who would show them the meaning of their search. Parry, a would-be knight, is on his own quest for a Grail, which symbolizes God's vessel of grace.

Parry tells Jack the story of the Grail as they lie on the grass in Central Park looking at the night sky. The first reading from Isaiah reminds us that light shines in and through the darkness. New York City is a place of darkness for both Jack and Parry. The idea of the Grail gives Parry hope and it ultimately becomes an active goal for Jack to achieve, even though it is only a billionaire's trophy kept in a case in his mansion.

The Magi search for the King. They are unable to take a direct route because they don't know the way. They seek help from the treacherous Herod and study the words of the prophecies in order to find Jesus. Jack and Parry are also on an indirect journey to their Grail. They are beset by doubts and Parry fears being pursued by the demonic Red Knight, but they finally obtain the "Grail." When the Magi reach their goal, they offer gifts. Jack and Parry have gifted each other. Jack atones, Parry is healed, and both receive grace.

**KEY SCENES
AND THEMES**

- Jack's arrogance in his talk show; mocking the listeners, taunting Edwin to destroy the yuppies and his horror when it happens; Jack about to be burned and rescued by Parry, a knight in shining armor.

- Parry's visions of the Red Knight, his calm after the vision; Parry telling Jack the Fisher King's story; the story's parallel with the Magi's quest.

- Jack's response to Parry's catatonic state; his embracing the quest to retrieve their "Grail"; the quest fulfilled; the grace-experience at the quest's end: atonement and forgiveness, love and reconciliation.

**FOR REFLECTION
AND
CONVERSATION**

1. Jack's words on his radio show lead to tragedy; viewers of this film are reminded of the influence that entertainment and information media have on audiences and individuals among them who may be vulnerable. Jack embarks on a personal quest for meaning and peace, but what about his responsibility as a media personality? In a democratic society, how are free speech and responsibility we have for the consequences of free speech balanced?

2. Burdened by guilt and sorrow, Jack and Parry seek the Grail. It becomes a symbol of love, forgiveness, and peace. In the process of their search, the two men gift each other with redemption. We see this especially toward the end of the film when Parry is in the hospital, and in the closing moments of the final scene under the stars. But what about the women in their lives? How do they contribute to the redemptive process? Are they redeemed as well in the film? Why or why not?

3. Epiphany means the "showing" or the manifestation of God. It can also mean a personal moment of enlightenment when something suddenly becomes clear. What are the moments of epiphany in *The Fisher King*? How do we respond to epiphanies or moments of truth in our own lives?

Prayer

Lord God, you revealed Jesus to the world. The Magi journeyed on a quest to find you. Reveal yourself to us as we search for you in our daily lives. Amen.

Robert Duvall and Tess Harper star in *Tender Mercies*.

Isaiah 42:1–4, 6–7; Matthew 3:13–17

Tender Mercies

U.S., 1983 / 89 minutes

Actors: Robert Duvall, Tess Harper, Betty Buckley, Ellen Barkin

Writer: Horton Foote

Director: Bruce Beresford

Tender Mercies

Heartfelt Conversion

SYNOPSIS

Mac Sledge is a washed-up Country Western singer well on the way to killing himself with alcohol. He is divorced from his wife Dixie, a successful singer who has forbidden Mac to see his daughter Sue Anne. Ten years later, Mac wakes up broke and broken after a particularly wild drinking binge. He asks Rosa Lee, a Vietnam War widow with a young son named Sonny, for a job. She runs a small motel in an isolated part of Texas. She hesitates, makes him promise not to drink, and then mercifully hires him. The three slowly and awkwardly develop a trusting relationship. Mac starts writing songs again. The bonds between Mac and his new family are strengthened. Rosa Lee and Mac marry.

Mac discovers that his estranged wife is performing in a nearby town and goes to visit her and his daughter. Mac wants to offer Dixie's agent a new song he has written. His ex-wife meets him with resentment, accusations, threats, and warnings to stay away from Sue Anne. Rejected by Dixie and the agent, Mac's old demons rise up and he almost leaves his new home and family.

Rosa Lee and her prayerful reflection about God and his tender mercies comfort the angry Mac. Sonny, Rose Lee and Mac attend church together. Soon Mac and Sonny are baptized.

After visiting her father Mac, Sue Anne dies in a car accident. Mac attends the funeral. When he returns, Mac questions the meaning of life's tragedies. Meanwhile Sonny has talked with Rosa Lee about his father's death in Vietnam. The film ends when Sonny goes out to play ball with Mac, as Rosa Lee watches them serenely from the house.

God has wrought his tender mercies.

COMMENTARY

Tender Mercies is a somewhat autobiographical screenplay from Horton Foote, the author of a number of plays and movies about Texas: *1918, On Valentine's Day, The Trip to Bountiful*. He also adapted *To Kill a Mockingbird* for the screen. The blend of toughness and gentleness in all of his work is enhanced by his own knowledge of the simplicity of the life and people of rural Texas.

Tender Mercies was the first American movie of Australian director Bruce Beresford, and it was nominated for several Oscars. Beresford won Best Screenplay written directly for the screen and Robert Duvall won Best Actor. Beresford went on to make many movies in the U.S. (*Crimes of the Heart* and *Double Jeopardy*), and in Africa and Australia *(Paradise Road)*. Foote and Beresford engage in religious themes directly and sincerely, portraying the experience of the American South with reverence. Duvall has built a most respectable acting career since his role in *To Kill a Mockingbird* (1962). He received Oscar nominations for *The Great Santini, Apocalypse Now* and *The Apostle*, which he also directed. Duval composed his own songs for *Tender Mercies*.

Tess Harper made her acting debut in this film. Actress singer Betty Buckley plays Mac's wife, and Ellen Barkin his daughter.

Focus: Mac Sledge is redeemed by the love of Rosa Lee and her son. This love helps him to repent of his past life and, like those converted by John the Baptist, he is baptized. Once baptized, he shares in the life of Jesus.

The image of God from the first Servant Song of Isaiah is one of gentleness. God is the gentle father to the beloved son-servant. Whatever pain a sinner may experience, the Servant will not break or crush the person, nor extinguish any wavering flame of hope or life. In the reading from the Acts of the Apostles (cf. 10:34–38), the aftermath of the dream of Cornelius is a vivid reminder that God wants all people to hear the good news and to be saved, no matter who they are.

Mac Sledge is an outsider and a failure, as a man and in his career. In the opening scene of *Tender Mercies* there is nowhere left for Mac to go. For Mac, Rosa Lee is the servant of God who does not crush him, but she takes him in, gives him a job, and enables him to gain some self-respect and begin again. He hears her pray for God's tender mercies.

Mac has no more sense of expectancy for new life than the crowds at the Jordan did when they sought baptism from John. They repented. Mac repents, although he later comes close to falling into despair as he encounters his wife and daughter. In finding love and family though his relationship with Rosa Lee and Sonny, Mac also finds God.

Sonny wants to be baptized. Mac has decided to be baptized as well, which is a symbol of his new life and repentance. When Jesus is baptized the voice of the Father is heard, "This is my beloved son." When Mac is baptized, he begins his life anew, which includes a loving wife and family. Thus, Mac becomes God's beloved son, a receiver of tender mercies.

- Mac the alcoholic with nowhere to go, his drinking binge, waking up broke; Mac: a failed husband, father, and singer; his transformation and new life at the motel; Mac's work and self-respect; the love of Sonny and Rosa Lee, Mac finding a family; his writing songs again; his conversion and redemption experience.

- Rosa Lee and Sonny's lives, their struggles, their life at the motel; their welcoming Mac into their lives and home; Rosa Lee's prayer, Mac hearing her talk about God's tender mercies; Rosa Lee's church-going, hymn-singing, and her prayer for Mac.

- Sonny and Mac baptized: the ritual, the symbols, the prayers, and the new life.

FOR REFLECTION AND CONVERSATION

1. As a film, *Tender Mercies* is not that different from the country songs Mac writes, observes film critic Roger Ebert. Bad things happen, and in the end so do good things. After Sue Anne's death Mac tells Rosa Lee, "Is there a reason for what happened?...Sonny's dad died in the war and my daughter was killed in an automobile accident. Why? You see...I don't trust happiness. I never did. I never will." How does Mac lose his life and then get it back? Does he ultimately learn to trust happiness?

2. When Mac is rejected by Dixie, he almost loses hope. In a scene symbolic of his confusion and perhaps anger, he buys a bottle of whisky and starts driving in all directions at an intersection of a rural road, as if guided by a broken compass. How realistic is the human story *Tender Mercies* tries to tell? How does its small-budget look succeed in keeping our focus directed on the human drama of Mac, Rosa Lee, and Sonny, as they become a family united in love, trust, and faith?

3. Visual representations in magazine photos, film, and
    television tend to "normalize" the behavior they de-
    pict. For example, the use of cigarettes, drugs, alco-
    hol, guns, and sex become acceptable ways to release
    tension and postpone having to deal with problems,
    or they become the tragic means to resolve problems.
    Why is it important to talk about the context of alco-
    hol, drug and tobacco use, as well as sex and violence,
    in entertainment and advertising media? What are the
    consequences of alcohol use in *Tender Mercies*? Why
    does Rosa Lee make sobriety a condition for Mac to
    live and work at the motel?

Prayer

*Jesus, at your baptism in the Jordan, the Father revealed you as his
beloved Son. Grace us with your life-giving spirit as we share in your
baptism through our baptismal promises. Amen.*

Cookie's Fortune

U.S., 1999 / 118 minutes

Actors: Glenn Close, Julianne Moore, Liv Tyler, Chris O'Donnell,
Charles S. Dutton, Patricia Neal, Donald Moffat, Ned Beatty

Writer: Ann Rapp

Director: Robert Altman

Cookie's Fortune

Woe to Hypocrites

SYNOPSIS

Cookie is a wealthy southern widow who lives in Holly Spring, Mississippi. She has a friendship with Willis, the family's loyal African-American handyman who was close to her deceased husband. Forlorn over her husband's loss, Cookie decides to shoot herself. Camille, her greedy, proud, self-righteous fool of a niece, finds her body and suicide note, but she eats the note and arranges everything to look like a robbery and murder. The police investigate and arrest Willis as their prime suspect. Camille feels some remorse, but her fear of a family scandal is greater, and she says nothing about the truth.

It is Easter and Camille is busy rehearsing the church play—her own adaptation of Oscar Wilde's *Salome*—with her browbeaten sister Cora in the lead role. It also stars Camille's lawyer and the young police officer in love with Cora's wayward daughter Emma, who has recently returned to town.

As the police continue to investigate Cookie's death, they interrogate various people around town and obtain blood samples. The results surprise them. It becomes evident that Camille is somehow involved. She is arrested during the play, and other family secrets are revealed. Cora knows that Cookie's death was a suicide, but she has promised Camille to say it was a murder. She cannot be persuaded to change her testimony despite Camille's frantic attempts from her jail cell to bully her into telling the truth.

Robert Altman is well known for telling stories *(Nashville, A Wedding, The Player, Short Cuts)* that involve a large ensemble of characters interacting as the camera moves, showing one, then another, until a satisfying cinematic mosaic is created. This time his story takes place in a small southern town and, though lighter than usual, the variegated effect is the same.

As always, Altman assembles a splendid cast headed by veteran Patricia Neal as the pipe-smoking Cookie and Charles S. Dutton as Willis. Glenn Close gives another of her "wicked witch" performances. In *Cookie's Fortune,* she is a superficial southern gentlewoman and pillar of the parish, as well as a scheming controller who has deeply hidden secrets. Julianne Moore is the somewhat dim, browbeaten sister and Liv Tyler plays her daughter Emma.

The small town atmosphere is well created and the characters have depth. Altman's deft irony and comic touch make subtle moralizing easy.

Focus: At the beginning of Lent, Jesus advises us on how to do penance through prayer, fasting, and charity. He also warns us that it is hypocritical to trumpet our alleged virtue, as Camille does so effectively in Cookie's Fortune.

The initial warning from the Sermon on the Mount in today's Gospel tells us to be careful not to parade good deeds to attract notice. This is precisely what Camille does in her hometown of Holly Spring. She presents herself as a model of godliness and expects people to pay homage to her. Only her sister Cora knows the truth about her bogus façade, but Camille browbeats her into submission.

Jesus also tells us that by doing good things to attract attention we will lose all recompense from our heavenly Father, because we already have our reward. Camille engineers everything to create and maintain her reputation and wealth, and to keep her personal secrets buried. Her machinations eventually catch up with her and she is exposed. Camille is jailed for a murder she did not commit because she manipulated the death scene to look like a homicide. After all, Camille says, "Suicide is undignified."

Jesus says almsgiving should not be trumpeted. Camille goes through the motions of being generous to Cookie's friend Willis, to whom Cookie has left her fortune, but not before she pockets Cookie's supposed jewels.

Jesus says praying should be private, done in secret. Camille, who shares a room with Cora, prays in a self-serving manner. She produces the Easter play to enhance both her own self-esteem and her reputation in the community.

The first reading from the prophet Joel calls for repentance. By the time Camille is jailed, she is indeed repentant, but it is too late. Her previous instructions to Cora to cover up the truth of Cookie's suicide are fulfilled to the letter. Camille is in a dreadful state, caught up in a web of her own making. *Cookie's Fortune* is an ironic fable with which to begin Lent.

KEY SCENES AND THEMES

- Camille and Cora's relationship as sisters, their mutual dependence; Camille dominating Cora, Cora's dependence.

- The play: Camille's choice of *Salome,* Camille's control and direction, her oppressive manner; the church and Camille's righteousness; her night prayer, her hypocritical manner of praying.

- The revelation that Camille is Emma's mother; Cora remaining unmovable regarding the fabricated story; Camille trapped in a prison of her own making.

1. Camille's false religiosity and superficiality provide much material for reflection. She masks her true self under the guise of righteousness. Why does she decide to hide the truth about Cookie's death? Why is this important to her? What other secrets does Camille cover up?

2. It's very disturbing that Camille is willing to allow a family friend to be suspected, accused, and jailed for a crime she knows he did not commit, just so that her family's name and her image can remain untainted. Camille's actions make the viewer wonder how vanity could justify such gross injustice. How can *Cookie's Fortune* be read as a commentary on personal and societal integrity? And what does it say about racial bias in our culture and legal system?

3. *Cookie's Fortune* is the story of Camille's pride and fall told in minute detail. We also see how Cora finally emerges from under her sister's thumb and the cover of lies in order to acknowledge the truth about her own life. Lent is a time for unmasking hypocrisy. It is a time to tell the truth about ourselves, and even the social structures that are part of our lives. What truth can we acknowledge during this Lenten season so that we can take responsibility for the consequences of our choices?

FOR REFLECTION AND CONVERSATION

Prayer

Lord, on this Ash Wednesday guide us to true prayer, fasting and charity, so that you will see what is in our hearts as we begin this Lenten journey with you. Amen.

Arnold Schwarzenegger in *End of Days*.

End of Days

U.S., 1999 / 122 minutes

Actors: Arnold Schwarzenegger, Gabriel Byrne,
Robin Tunney, Kevin Pollak, Rod Steiger, CCH Pounder,
Miriam Margolyes, Udo Kier

Writer: Andrew W. Marlowe

Director: Peter Hyams

End of Days

Overcoming Temptation

SYNOPSIS

A baby girl is born in 1979, but she is immediately taken away from her mother by a group of satanic worshippers, who dedicate her to the devil with the plan of making her his bride in 1999 to inaugurate his next thousand-year reign. In the Vatican, some officials think the child should be killed, but the pope wants her protected, believing that faith will prevail against evil.

As crowds in New York prepare to celebrate the new millennium, an evil power is unleashed and takes over the body of a Wall Street banker. He becomes an instrument of Satan, and a berserk priest tries to shoot him. Jericho Cane (*J.C.*) is an alcoholic former cop turned security man, who is grieving for his dead wife and daughter. While Jericho and his partner, Bobby, are investigating the priest, they discover the prophecy of Revelation 20:7 ("When the thousand years are over Satan will be released from his prison"), which leads them to the now 20-year-old girl, Christine York (*Christ in New York*).

Attempting to stop their interference, Satan takes over the police and then Bobby. Satan overcomes Jericho and hangs him from a building in the form of a crucifix, but Jericho survives. A group of clerical assassins tries to kill Christine in order to avert Satan's plan, and there is a showdown with Satan in a runaway subway train. Against all odds, Jericho saves Christine.

Satan confronts Jericho about his lack of faith, telling him, "You walked away from the light just like I did." Satan tempts Jericho to share his diabolical power in order to get his wife and daughter back. Though Jericho has lost his faith, he comes to terms with it against a backdrop of the Crucifixion scene. To save Christine and the world, he gives up his life. The new millennium starts without Satan's thousand-year reign.

COMMENTARY

End of Days will not be on everyone's best film list. It was intended as a big action thriller for the end of 1999 and the beginning of the third millennium. It consists of comic-strip action and characterization and relies on a myriad of special effects, which culminate in the appearance of a gigantic, fiery, dragon-like Satan.

While it is geared to multiplex audiences, the film is a blend of over-literal interpretations of Scripture (notably the Book of Revelation) and a cinematic use of Christian iconography specifically from Catholic tradition. Satan is, of course, quite diabolical as played by the quietly persuasive Gabriel Byrne. Jericho Cane's temptation scene is an imaginative parallel of Jesus' temptation in the desert. Arnold Schwarzenegger is the ambiguous Christ-figure who has lost his faith in God, yet protects the devil's victim.

This is a pop-religion and pop-heroics film which critics mocked, but it was seen by large audiences just the same. Despite the film's limitations, there are actually several points worth reflection.

DIALOGUE WITH THE GOSPEL

Focus: In a time of profound testing, a security man, Jericho Cane, is tempted to join the devil, reminiscent of the way Jesus was tempted and tested in the desert.

Jericho Cane is set up as a Christ-figure, though one in need of redemption. Christine, a female Christ-figure for the times though unwittingly destined to be part of the devil's plan for a thousand-year reign, ultimately leads Jericho to redemption.

The first reading from Genesis is the story of the Fall and the serpent's role in the temptation of Adam and Eve. The movie relies on the conviction that we exist in a fallen world, that the serpent still seduces people, and that we need redemption. The reading from St. Paul (cf. Rom 5:12–19) also takes up the age-old theme of sin and is one of the key passages about Jesus as Redeemer: "divine grace coming through the one man, Jesus Christ." The devil worshippers who have literally chosen to serve Satan represent this theme of sin's presence in the world.

The Gospel is that of the temptation of Jesus. The *End of Days* screenplay has a featured sequence where Jericho Cane is tempted by the devil. He is not offered bread, but the possibility of getting his family back. Satan cruelly shows him—and us—the brutal killing of his family while Jericho was not there to protect them, making us feel the strength of the temptation as well. Satan also tempts Jericho to trust him and to share his power in the millennial reign. He knows that Jericho has lost his faith. Jericho prays for faith before the crucifix above the church altar. When his faith returns, he gains the strength to save Christine and the world.

- Revelation 20:7, "When the thousand years are completed Satan will be released from prison" and its literal interpretation in the film; the presence of Satan and evil in the world; Satan in a suave and beguiling human form; Satan's monstrous form.

- Jericho Cane protecting Christine, being impaled on the wall as on a cross: Jericho Cane as a Christ-figure.

KEY SCENES AND THEMES

- The temptation scene: the church, the icons, Jericho's struggle with his faith; Satan's tempting offers; Jericho's refusal; Jericho abandoning force and violence and surrendering to God in faith; Jericho willing to be pierced through for Christine and the world.

FOR REFLECTION AND CONVERSATION

1. Today's responsorial psalm is the sinner's prayer acknowledging sin, asking for compassion and cleansing from guilt. The psalmist also prays for a new, clean heart so that he will once again know the joy of salvation. Jericho Cane feels such intense guilt over the death of his wife and daughter that he is ready to take his own life at the beginning of the story. How does Jericho's attitude change? How does the message that God is with us and can sustain us come to light in this film (even when the action is so extreme it's almost comical)?

2. Traditional beliefs about the devil are well articulated in this film, such as the devil being happiest when we deny he exists, or when Satan says rather sadly to Jericho: "You walked away from the light just like I did." What do we really know about the devil and evil based on Christian teaching and tradition? How does Christ redeem us from the glamour of evil and sin, from Satan and all his works and empty promises? How does the movie demonstrate that in the face of temptation strength is available to us?

3. Jericho lives in the hell of his alcoholism. His partner and colleagues know he drinks to drown his sorrow and to escape feelings of guilt over the death of his wife and daughter. The devil capitalizes on his vulnerability. If Jericho's choices were not determined by the role in the film, what faith alternatives could

have helped him in his time of need? In what ways are we vulnerable to the temptation to despair? What faith choices can we make when faced with guilt, shame, and despair?

Prayer

Jesus, you were tempted and tested in every way that we are, but you did not turn away from your Father. Help us when we struggle with temptation to be faithful to you. Amen.

Phenomenon

U.S., 1996 / 110 minutes

Actors: John Travolta, Robert Duvall, Forest Whitaker, Kyra Sedgwick

Writer: Gerald DiPego

Director: Jon Turteltaub

Phenomenon

Transforming Light

SYNOPSIS

George Malley is a simple, pleasant, and popular man who lives in a small town where he fixes cars and experiments in growing vegetables in his garden. He turns 37 and after his birthday celebration, he is knocked unconscious by a bright light in the sky that falls towards him and explodes. When he comes to, he is transformed. His I.Q. soars and he develops telekinetic powers. He begins to speed read and to discuss deep issues. He learns Portuguese instantaneously and is able to translate for the local doctor when he is treating a non-English speaking patient. The townspeople are puzzled because George has always been so ordinary.

A scientist interviews and tests him. George is apprehended by the FBI who are suspicious about his amazing knowledge and contacts. Meanwhile, his friends support him; so does Lace, a furniture maker with two small children whom George begins to court.

Eventually his physical condition deteriorates and the FBI keep him in custody in a hospital. He escapes and returns to Lace, and we discover the reasons for his extraordinary intelligence before he dies. She mourns for George. A year later the whole town and his friends gather to celebrate his birthday as his memory and spirit live on.

COMMENTARY

Phenomenon is one of those films that can really be called "nice," meaning that it appeals to a wide audience, makes us laugh and cry, and leaves us feeling good. Jon Turteltaub also directed *Cool Runnings, While You Were Sleeping, Instinct,* and *Disney's The Kid.*

It would not be surprising to learn that the screenwriter was reading the Gospels while writing *Phenomenon.* Filmmakers are often intrigued by the person of Jesus: his actions, his message, and especially the impact of his death and resurrection on the world, and that his spirit still lives.

DIALOGUE WITH THE GOSPEL

Focus: When George is transformed by his encounter, we are reminded of the transfiguration of Jesus when he appeared in glory. Jesus' companions are amazed, as are George's friends. Soon, George will die and leave his goodness as a heritage for his friends, again reminding us of Jesus.

In the Gospels, the Transfiguration is a foretaste of Jesus' post-resurrection glory, a revelation of Jesus' oneness with the Father. The Transfiguration offers us images of ancient prophets: Moses the lawgiver and Elijah the prophet, who appear with Jesus on the mountain.

In today's first reading, the Lord tells Abram that "all the communities of the earth shall find blessing in him" because he is the chosen of God. In *Phenomenon*, George Malley is portrayed as a good, down-to-earth man in his relationships with the people of his community. When a marvelous light transforms his natural abilities, he becomes a blessing to the people: he translates for a doctor so a sick person can be healed, he finds a boy who was lost.

Today's Gospel tells us about Peter, James, and John who witness the Transfiguration and see Moses and Elijah speaking with Jesus. These apostles want to celebrate the moment without truly understanding what they are experiencing, and it is soon over. The effects of George's transformation are short-lived as well and until the end of his life, no one in the community understands why he has developed such amazing powers. George's goodness and intelligence radiate from him and he helps others while he can.

KEY SCENES AND THEMES

- George's birthday party, his strange experience, the transforming light; the "grace" he now experiences: playing chess, telekinetic powers, speed reading and keen understanding; learning Portuguese, helping the doctor.

- The search for the boy, its impact on George—draining him of power; George's interactions with his friends and the townspeople, their amazement and questions.

- George's interaction with Lace and her children, Lace's eventual support; George's death and her grief, Lace feeling the wind in the trees; the community bonding as they celebrate George's memory.

FOR REFLECTION AND CONVERSATION

1. In the Book of Genesis, God tells Abram to "look up at the sky and count the stars...." Abram's life is changed by this encounter. At first we think that George is changed by a supernatural phenomenon when he looks at the night sky. How are both of these experiences out of the ordinary? What did each phenomenon mean, in its own context?

2. That George is an ordinary man is emphasized over and over in the movie. We see him working in his garden and at the garage, attracted to a young woman, and friendly with the townspeople. How does the film

present George's uncomplicated and generous personality? How does this correspond to the Christian ideal of "ordinary holiness"?

3. After George is transformed, what do we, as the audience, expect to happen? Why? How do our expectations regarding the resolution of a film's story contribute to our enjoyment of it, or to the inspiration we may or may not experience when the last credit rolls?

Prayer

Lord God, as we journey with Jesus towards his suffering and death during this time of Lent, reveal him to us so that we too may glimpse his glory. Strengthen us in faith and hope. Amen.

The Bridges of Madison County

U.S., 1995 / 135 minutes

Actors: Meryl Streep, Clint Eastwood

Writer: Richard LaGravenese

Director: Clint Eastwood

The Bridges of Madison County

Secrets

SYNOPSIS

When Francesa Johnson dies, her son and daughter discover that she has asked to be cremated and to have her ashes scattered on the water from a local bridge. Her children are surprised by her request. They find information in a safety deposit box that leads them to a letter Francesca had written to them a few years earlier. Just as their mother intended, they discover her journals, so they can begin to know who she really was as they read…

…Francesca's husband and children leave for the Illinois State Fair and she is happy to have a few days to herself. A traveling photographer, Robert Kincaid, is on an assignment for *National Geographic* to take pictures of the bridges of Madison County, Iowa. He stops at Francesca's house to ask directions to the Roseman Bridge and she goes with him to show the way. They are attracted to one another and begin an affair that fills the four days.

Robert asks her to leave with him. Francesca refuses for the sake of her family; it would cause a scandal that would hurt them deeply. He understands and leaves. They never forget one another and, when her husband dies, she tries to contact Robert only to find that he died some years before and that his ashes were sprinkled from a nearby bridge. He has left his camera equipment to Francesca and has published a book of photos dedicated to her.

Francesca's children accede to their mother's wishes after they read her journals.

From a very popular, brief bestseller by Robert Waller, Richard LaGravenese *(Fisher King, Unstrung Heroes, Living Out Loud)* has created a very moving screen adaptation. Meryl Streep gives yet another excellent performance and Clint Eastwood, cast against type, gives a sensitive performance as well. He also directed the film.

The basic plot synopsis is simple: a brief affair ensues between a lonely middle-aged Iowa farm wife and an aging traveling photographer. However, the film offers more. It begins with Francesca's death, and we, like her children, know the end before the beginning. The audience shares her children's discovery of their mother's letters and journals. Together we learn the meaning of her desire to be cremated and to have her ashes scattered off a bridge as Kincaid's were. Knowing the outcome ahead of time prompts the audience to consider the moral perspective of this brief encounter, the relationship, the separation, and when her husband dies, Francesca's attempt to get in touch with Kincaid. This film lets us glimpse the breadth of humanity, and offers much for reflection.

Focus: The woman at the well has her secrets. Jesus' kindness and his lack of judgment enable her to speak, to confess, to express her longings as he listens and then promises her new life. She is finally known. She goes off to tell the villagers that Jesus has told her everything she has ever done. Francesca Johnson of Madison County is one of many variations, old and new, on the Woman at the Well.

The Gospel account about the Woman at the Well is one of the most popular Gospel stories—and one of the longest. This is the portrait of a woman whose unfortunate relationships have scandalized her neighbors. Yet, she possesses a loving and searching heart and engages sincerely in the extraordinary opportunity of meeting Jesus at Jacob's well. In this Gospel, we likewise observe Jesus in what seems an unlikely encounter. He meets a foreign woman alone at a well and engages in discussion, even moral debate, with her. We sense his joy as her understanding of him grows. The sketch of the disciples is less than flattering, as they seem suspicious of Jesus for speaking with a foreigner—and a woman at that. They fail to appreciate the meaning of the encounter and of the moment.

Francesca Johnson is not exactly the woman at the well; she is basically a good woman who has sinned but who ends up choosing others over self. Her infidelity to her husband is a secret shared only with her journal and, after her death, with her children. In fact, her decision to end the affair was both to avoid a scandal that would harm her family and to do the right thing.

Like the woman at the well, she needs deeper love to be known for who she is. Kincaid is a stranger and can offer her only the passing warmth and passion of an affair, yet this enlivens her and reveals to her what love can mean. The stranger is also transformed, and what could have been just a casual experience becomes the love of his life. *The Bridges of Madison County* is a moral fable about relationships, sexuality, temptations, choices, and long-term decisions. It's about an illicit affair and its consequences. It's about how a woman's difficult decision to honor her commitment allows her to grow in ways she never imagined.

KEY SCENES AND THEMES

- Francesca's children reading her will, their discovery of the journal, the secrets of their mother's life; their questions surrounding the burial, the cremation, the scattering of ashes; Francesca's four-day affair seen in the broader perspective of values and morals.

- Francesca and the journals: the story from her point of view, the therapeutic value of writing, Francesca wanting her children to read her journal so as to know her; Francesca at home: at meals, with the family, working; Francesca's relationship with Richard: his silence, the daily phone calls, Richard's not kissing her, the taken-for-granted tenderness, their leading an ordinary life.

- Robert's experience: the possibility of a relationship, the temptation; Robert and Francesca talking together, sharing intimacy and quiet, passion and love; their ultimate decisions; the future: discussing possibilities, the relationship's long-term effect; the farewell and the aftermath.

FOR REFLECTION AND CONVERSATION

1. Many pastoral ministers think extramarital affairs are one of the biggest problems facing church and family life today. Rather than condoning or condemning the affair, this story focuses on the loneliness of a woman who has lived faithfully, but without creativity, color, and zest. How do image and sound tell Francesca's story? How do these cinematic elements draw us in emotionally so that we can identify with her situation?

2. At the beginning of the film, as Francesca's children read her letter aloud, she finally allows her real voice to be heard: she wants to be known for who she is. She does not want to be lost in routine or to be taken for granted. How might Francesca's character be

understood as a voice for other women? How is Francesca like the woman at the well in today's Gospel?

3. The film revolves around Francesca, but Robert is the catalyst for the action. We see some major star power in this movie, and despite Clint Eastwood's screen presence, Meryl Streep's Francesca prevails. In these decades when women are striving for balanced rights with those of men, what has happened to masculine identity? What is the role of men presented in the Gospels? What does this mean for the Church and the world today?

Prayer

You listened, Lord, to the woman at the well. You came to know her. You shared her life story, especially her pain. You offered her new life, which transformed her. You and the woman listened to one another. Help us to listen, to care, and let ourselves she known and transformed. Amen.

The Miracle Worker

U.S., 1962 / 106 minutes

Actors: Anne Bancroft, Patty Duke, Victor Jory, Inga Swenson

Writer: William Gibson

Director: Arthur Penn

The Miracle Worker

Discovering "Fullness of Life"

When she is nineteen months old, Helen Keller becomes deaf, blind, and dumb because of an illness. As she grows up, her family indulges her and, lacking all discipline, she becomes unmanageable. They write to Boston's famous Perkins School for the Blind hoping to find help.

SYNOPSIS

The school sends one of its students, Annie Sullivan, who is partially blind. She assesses the situation, realizes that Helen is intelligent but needs structure and discipline in order to learn to communicate meaningfully. Annie and Helen clash and some of their frustrated struggles are violent.

Annie Sullivan persuades the Kellers to allow Helen to live with her, apart from the family for a while. They move to the garden house. Gradually, Helen accepts Annie and learns to do basic things for herself. But the key skill Helen begins to develop is language.

Annie teaches Helen to spell with her fingers, as she herself once learned, and hopes that Helen will then connect this spelling and words with real objects and concepts. But it is not an easy process and there are more struggles. One day, after Annie and Helen return to the family home, Helen throws a jug of water over Annie. Annie makes Helen refill the jug. Feeling the water, Helen starts to make the connection and her amazing life as a communicator begins.

COMMENTARY

The Miracle Worker is the celebrated movie—one of four film or television versions and a stage play—about a teacher, Annie Sullivan, and her blind and deaf student, Helen Keller. Helen Keller went on to become one of the most celebrated American personalities of the twentieth century. Her breakthrough in language made it possible for disabled people to learn communication skills in a new way, and ultimately to realize their right to an education.

Anne Bancroft and Patty Duke acted in William Gibson's play on Broadway before they made the movie version. They won Oscars for Best Actress and Best Supporting Actress in 1962.

The film is both austere and melodramatic under the direction of Arthur Penn (who went on to direct *Bonnie and Clyde* in 1966). Watching *The Miracle Worker* is a highly emotional experience.

The film is not really the story of Helen Keller but of Annie Sullivan. She is the "miracle worker." Annie and her beloved brother Jimmy were orphaned as children and placed in a Massachusetts workhouse, a terrible solution to poverty based on the early British welfare experiments, that did more harm than good. Her brother died from the terrible conditions and neglect. The film shows Annie Sullivan's heroism and pays tribute to the extraordinary success of her perseverance and life's work.

When the play/film was remade for television in 1979, Patty Duke played the part of Annie Sullivan and Melissa Gilbert, star of *Little House on the Prairie*, played Helen Keller. The television remake (2000) starred Allison Elliott (*The Spitfire Grill*) as Annie.

Focus: Annie Sullivan, the miracle worker, is an image of Jesus who gives sight to the man born blind. While Helen Keller does not receive her sight, she receives the gift of communication that opens the way for her to live a long and full life.

On this Sunday in Lent, the Gospel is another lengthy story from John: that of the man who was born blind. Even though his parents appear in the Gospel, the man is left to his own devices when challenged by the authorities. *The Miracle Worker* reminds us that disabled people have a long history of being abandoned and cruelly treated. Their disability was often seen as a punishment for their own sins or the sins of those who came before them. Another variation of this scenario is parents who blame themselves when a child is afflicted by an illness or is developmentally challenged.

The man born blind receives his sight. Helen Keller does not, but she is the recipient of a miracle nonetheless. Helen learns how to be human and how to communicate from someone who was once treated little better than an animal. Helen, like Annie before her, is freed from the limits of her affliction to become a mature and giving person.

Annie Sullivan can be seen as a Christ-figure. While she is not able to give Helen the visual sight that Jesus gave to the man born blind, she enables Helen to communicate and to understand. She is a life-giver who patiently struggles against the criticism of family and authorities, as Jesus had to when complaints arose about the blind man's healing. Annie uses "tough love," thus empowering Helen Keller to be an example for others with disabilities to lead fuller lives. Jesus came that we might have life and have it to the full.

- Helen Keller's early illness; her animal-like behavior: spoiled, frustrated and violent, Helen loved yet feared;

Helen's response to Annie Sullivan, the meal; Helen learning to use her face and hands for communication.

- Annie Sullivan's relationship with her brother, the workhouse, the school, her difficulties with her eyes; Helen's antics and Annie's patience; the manual alphabet, the understanding of water.

- The Kellers' reaction to their daughter, their hopes in Annie Sullivan; the parents' impatience and incomprehension regarding how to treat Helen; their sacrifices and their reward when Helen recognizes them.

FOR REFLECTION AND CONVERSATION

1. In film and in history Annie Sullivan's life was extremely difficult, even cruel. She managed to rise above her harsh beginnings for the most part and gave her life for another. How effectively does the film teach about Annie Sullivan's life and work and about her student, Helen Keller? What do the film and today's Gospel reading teach about the value of the human person?

2. Water figures strongly in both today's Gospel and the film, as it does in other movies, literature, and the liturgy. Water is a symbol of cleansing, grace and the communication of new life. What does the water episode communicate about thought and language in the movie? What did water mean to Annie Sullivan? to Helen? What did it mean to the man who had been blind from birth?

3. The Keller family is at its wits' end when Annie Sullivan arrives, as we see in the scenes where Helen is tormenting the family at meals. When Annie unlocks the

girl's ability to communicate, Helen and her family begin to live fully. How can communication help relationships and families to grow?

Prayer

Jesus, you are the light of the world. Give the grace of your light to those who long to see and to communicate. Amen.

Awakenings

U.S., 1990 / 116 minutes

Actors: Robert De Niro, Robin Williams, Julie Kavner, John Heard, Penelope Ann Miller, Ruth Nelson, Anne Meara, Max von Sydow

Writer: Steven Zaillian

Director: Penny Marshall

Awakenings

Life That Will Never Die

SYNOPSIS

Based on the life of Dr. Oliver Sacks and his book by the same title, this film recounts medical experiments with the drug L-dopa in a New York City hospital in the summer of 1969.

Dr. Sayer gets a job in a hospital where some of the patients are in a catatonic state. With the support of a nurse, Sayer studies the records of the patients and finds that they had all suffered from encephalitis in the 1920s. Sayer, in a controversial move, gives L-dopa to Leonard Lowe with the permission of his devoted mother. Leonard awakens and comes to life. Donations enable the drug to be given to the other patients who also "wake up." Eventually, the drug is unable to sustain their awakening and the patients return to their semi-comatose state.

The experiment, however, has a life-giving effect on the shy Dr. Sayer and on the hospital staff.

COMMENTARY

Nominated for three Academy Awards, *Awakenings* is a gently told tale with emotional power. Paced according to the shy but ingenious personality of Dr. Sayer, the film shows how a concerned scientist and a devoted doctor can intuit

76

and discover ways of bringing people to life. The central character, Leonard, was a bright child who went into his trance-like existence because of encephalitis lethargica, or sleeping sickness. On reawakening, he discovers the exuberance of life as an adult. He breaks free of his mother as any child would, is attracted to a visitor who reads to her father and is eager, despite his regression, for his case to be studied in order to assist others.

Robin Williams lived with Dr. Oliver Sacks for some time to prepare for his role. In *Awakenings*, Williams gives an almost subdued performance. Robert De Niro seems to relish the demands of the role of Leonard and plays it with depth and feeling. The director, Penny Marshall, also did *Jumping Jack Flash*, *Big*, and *A League of Their Own*. *Awakenings* is a fine drama about the human spirit.

> *Focus: Jesus brings Lazarus back from the dead. Dr. Sayer brings Leonard and the other patients back from the "dead." This awakening can be seen as an image of Jesus' miracles, the raising of Lazarus, and Jesus' own resurrection.*

DIALOGUE WITH THE GOSPEL

Apart from breathing, being fed and cared for, Leonard Lowe is dead. Aside from some devoted relatives, he and his fellow patients live hidden from the world's sight. The patients are a contemporary equivalent of the deceased Lazarus.

In the case of the encephalitis patients, no one asks that they be raised to life, but that they receive decent care. Leonard's mother and the young woman who comes to read to her father might be considered parallels to the devoted Martha and Mary. We can empathize with the grief of the sisters over Lazarus' death and the grief of the relatives in *Awakenings*.

However, it is Dr. Sayer who resembles Jesus because he is moved with compassion by the plight of his patients and feels compelled to do something for them. They have waited thirty or forty years for their awakenings. Dr. Sayer does not expect to actually bring these people back to life, but in fact, that is what he does.

Yet, L-dopa gives them only a temporary life. We see them as they regress into their living death. Lazarus was raised to life with great joy. We are reminded that he too will have to go through his death experience again. Life, for the first or the second time, is only temporary.

Still, life is a wondrous gift. Later on in John's Gospel (cf. 12:2–3), there is a banquet where Lazarus and his friends celebrate. Martha again waits at table and Mary does something special; she anoints Jesus' feet with precious ointment. The raising of Lazarus is a foreshadowing, a sign of Jesus' rising from the dead, a hope for an everlasting new life.

KEY SCENES AND THEMES

- Leonard's "dying" and coming to life again; Leonard as a child at school, Leonard unable to write; Leonard watching his friends from the window; the gradual succumbing to a death-like state.

- Dr. Sayer's skill and care: his understanding and fortitude as his patients come to life; Leonard's new quality of life, his becoming an adult; his succumbing again to the condition, his speech, his jerky movements; Leonard to be filmed in order to help others; the value of Leonard's "Lazarus-like" experience.

- Dr. Sayer overcoming his shyness, inviting Eleanor for a cup of coffee; Leonard helping him toward his own awakening.

FOR REFLECTION AND CONVERSATION

1. All of today's Scripture readings are about going from death to life. *Awakenings* is about people waking out of a sleep-like death, from Robert De Niro's Leonard to the woman who catches a ball mid-air, to Dr. Sayer

awakening to the possibilities of human relationships. How is *Awakenings* a metaphor for the reawakening of the spiritual life? In what scenes is this especially true?

2. Leonard's story is especially meaningful in a Lenten context. He awakens, grows as a person, sacrifices his privacy to help people, and learns to love. As Dr. Sayer helps Leonard to wake up, Leonard does the same for Dr. Sayer. What is the view of the human person and human relationships projected in *Awakenings*?

3. Dr. Sayer and his staff try so hard to "cure" the patients. At first, their efforts seem completely successful. But in the end the patients, some of whom have become Dr. Sayer's friends, return to their catatonic state. What keeps a person going even when their best efforts seem to fail? What sustained Dr. Sayer?

Prayer

Jesus, when Martha was saddened by the death of her brother, you consoled her with the revelation that you are the Resurrection and the Life. You also gave Lazarus the gift of new life. In this time of Lent, give us new life and hope in your resurrection. Amen.

PALM SUNDAY

Isaiah 50:4–7; Matthew 26:14—27:66

The Insider

U.S., 1999 / 159 minutes

Actors: Al Pacino, Russell Crowe, Christopher Plummer, Diane Venora, Lindsay Crouse, Philip Baker Hall, Michael Gambon, Gina Gershon

Writers: Michael Mann, Eric Roth

Director: Michael Mann

 *The Insider*

Life and Death Convictions

SYNOPSIS

Research scientist Jeffrey Wigand is fired from his job at Brown and Williamson, a major U.S. tobacco company. He knows too much and the company is afraid he will go public. He is concerned about his family, paying for his daughter's medical care, and covering expenses.

Lowell Bergman, *60 Minutes* producer, receives documents concerning some tobacco industry statistics. He is advised to ask Wigand to help explain the information.

As Bergman works with Wigand, it becomes apparent that Wigand has inside information. But to keep his severance package from Brown and Williamson, Wigand will not talk. He was pressured into a confidentiality agreement before leaving his job. Bergman gets Wigand subpoenaed to testify at a big tobacco trial in Mississippi. Once his testimony is public record, Wigand can go on *60 Minutes* without violating his agreement with Brown and Williamson, thus keeping his family's health coverage, etc. Wigand then agrees to do an interview with the famous Mike Wallace on *60 Minutes*. He reveals that cigarettes were known to be a delivery system for nicotine and that big tobacco companies have perjured themselves in sworn testimony.

Wigand's family is terrorized and he receives death threats. Though protected by bodyguards, the situation is too much for his wife. She takes the children and leaves him. His reputation is damaged when unrelated personal information is made public. The interview on *60 Minutes*, with Wallace's concurrence, is cancelled because another company, which proposes to buy CBS, fears its financial interests will be compromised if the segment airs. Wigand is devastated because it seems his sacrifice of family and reputation has been for nothing. Bergman leaks the network's actions to the press, which berates CBS. The interview is finally aired, and Wigand is cleared. Bergman leaves CBS, disillusioned that the company would compromise journalistic integrity.

COMMENTARY

The Insider received six Oscar nominations, including Best Director for Michael Mann and Best Actor for Russell Crowe. Though the film received strong critical acclaim, it did not have the expected box office response.

The film is a serious dramatic look at a whistleblower exposing big tobacco and whose action led to increased legal battles concerning the effects of tobacco.

Michael Mann, the co-writer and director, is better known for action movies like *Manhunter*, *Last of the Mohicans*, and *Heat*, as well as for the television series *Miami Vice*. Al Pacino starred in *Heat*. Here, Pacino gives a superbly edgy performance as the *60 Minutes* producer, obsessively committed to his work and to being a man of his word. This is in contrast to Christopher Plummer's smoothly egoistic portrayal of Mike Wallace, and Philip Baker Hall as a CBS executive.

Russell Crowe, who went on to win a Best Actor Academy Award in 2001 for his role in *Gladiator*, gives a fine performance as Wigand, who is also obsessive and often abrasive, but who wants to do the right thing, believes in integrity, and is willing to suffer for it.

DIALOGUE WITH THE GOSPEL

Focus: On this Palm Sunday we read St. Matthew's account of Jesus' suffering and death. The character of Jeffrey Wigand, the insider, offers a parallel of someone who suffered, risking life and death for his beliefs.

Today's Gospel is strong on the sayings of Jesus, the "thinking person's" Gospel. It is a Gospel filled with teaching, sermons, and principles presented without frills. There is a direct statement on truth which says that our word is to be "yes" for "yes," and "no" for "no."

In the Passion account, Judas betrays Jesus and then the High Priest questions Jesus' testimony. He is interrogated by Pilate and compared with the brigand, Barabbas. Jesus received death threats during his ministry and now people jeer at him. He is tortured. Jesus receives some recognition when Pilate decrees that his title, King of the Jews, be put on the cross.

Jeffrey Wigand is not a religious person. He is an ordinary man with a drinking problem, an educated executive with failings. He loves chemistry and comes to enjoy his new life as a teacher. He opts for personal integrity when the industry he works for comes under fire and then lies publicly to protect itself. Wigand chooses plain truth and plain speaking. This truth and integrity cost him his family, career, good name and personal safety. He decides that he values truth over all else so that others may live.

Christ-figures are not perfect representations of Christ, but in some way they do resemble the Jesus of the Gospels significantly and substantially. The makers of *The Insider* did not intend to portray Jeffrey Wigand as a Christ-figure. However, Wigand's experiences can be considered in the light of Jesus' integrity and his passion and death.

- Jeffrey Wigand after he is fired; his personal dilemmas and anxieties, his relationship with wife and family; the reason for his being fired; his future prospects.

- The encounter with Lowell Bergman, Wigand's need for trust; the preparation of the interview for *60 Minutes*, the confidentiality agreements, the tobacco executives' filmed testimony, the consequences for witnesses.

- The collapse of Wigand's world; the interview cancellation; the death threats and the need for security; Wigand's wife leaving, the conspiracy to blacken his name; the interview finally airing; Wigand being able to live with himself regardless of his sufferings.

1. The responsorial psalm refrain today is "My God, my God, why have you forsaken me?" (cf. Ps 22:8–24) When Jeffrey's wife and daughters leave him, past secrets are revealed, and his life is threatened, it is easy to imagine this being his prayer. Why does Wigand decide to be interviewed on *60 Minutes* despite the fact that his life is collapsing all around him? How does the film portray his dilemma and his courage?

2. Fr. Elwood "Bud" Kieser, CSP, founder of Paulist Productions, established the Humanitas Awards in 1974 to recognize writing that enriches the human condition. In 2000, the scriptwriters for *The Insider* were awarded a Humanitas Prize because, as Fr. Kieser told a TV interviewer who could not "see" God in the film, "Even though the word [God] was not there, the real-

ity was. When people love unselfishly, God is present."
How does the script for *The Insider* enrich the human
condition? Compare the film with others that have
inspired you because someone was willing to lose everything to help others.

3.   Besides the story of Jeffrey Wigand blowing the whistle
on big tobacco and cigarette addiction, *The Insider* is
about journalistic integrity on the part of producers
and networks. How critical are we regarding what we
see, hear, and read in entertainment media? Talk
about ways you can make questioning the media and
media practices an everyday skill.

Prayer

*Jesus, in our own way, we share in your suffering and death. Give
us your courage and strength to do what is right no matter what is
asked of us. Amen.*

Moira Kelly, Martin Sheen and Heather Camille in *Entertaining Angels*.

Entertaining Angels: The Dorothy Day Story

U.S., 1996 / 114 minutes

Actors: Moira Kelly, Martin Sheen, Heather Graham,
Lenny Von Dohlen, Melinda Dillon, Brian Keith

Writer: John Wells

Director: Michael Ray Rhodes

Entertaining Angels: The Dorothy Day Story

Struggling with Faithfulness

SYNOPSIS

Twenty-year-old Dorothy Day is a reporter and a suffragette. She is also part of a New York socialist group that includes artists and writers like Eugene O'Neill. The freethinking group meets to drink and talk about current events and social issues. Dorothy becomes pregnant and has an abortion. She moves away from Manhattan to Staten Island. Forster, a member of the group, follows her. They live quietly together and Dorothy falls in love.

During this time, Dorothy encounters a homeless man and a friendly nun. Curious, she follows them to a church that has opened a soup kitchen for the poor. Despite her own skepticism, her friends' comments, and Forster's hostility, she often goes to the kitchen to help. She begins to read Catholic books. Once again she becomes pregnant and has a daughter; Forster refuses to marry Dorothy.

Dorothy and her daughter are baptized and move back to Manhattan. Peter Maurin, an eccentric and charismatic Frenchman, urges her to start feeding the poor and caring for street people. Together, they begin the Catholic Worker

87

Movement and Dorothy founds a small paper, *The Catholic Worker.*

During the 1930s, Dorothy becomes even more socially active. She opens hospitality houses and tries to improve the lives of the poor. More people join her to help in her work. Some Catholics condemn her as a communist. The Cardinal asks her to remove "Catholic" from the name of her paper so that he won't be embarrassed, but she refuses. When a depressed girl from the shelter kills herself, Dorothy's co-workers tell her that they really can't manage and that she is egotistical. She prays desperately, admits her limitations to her friends and workers, but is determined to go on. They stay to help her.

COMMENTARY

Fr. Ellwood "Bud" Kieser, a Catholic priest, produced *Entertaining Angels* for Paulist Pictures. Kieser first produced *Insight,* a television series that aired between 1966 and 1983; he then began making movies. He is best remembered for *The Fourth Wise Man* and *Romero,* and for introducing the Humanitas Awards for screenwriting which enhances the human condition. Kieser died in 2000.

John Wells' screenplay uses a 1963 prison incident to create a framework for telling Dorothy Day's story from the time she is twenty, as the U.S. entered World War I, until she is about forty. Dorothy Day lived through the aftermath of the Vietnam War and died in 1980. Her cause for beatification was officially opened in March 2000.

The movie uses familiar biopic (a cinematic biography) conventions such as stringing together selected incidents to create the narrative. Emotional struggles are emphasized to engage audience empathy. Dorothy led a very unconventional life by Catholic standards. Her pre-conversion past and abortion, her decision not to marry and to remain a single parent are interesting because she used these unusual circumstances to follow Christ by helping the poor and homeless. She is a twentieth-century example of lay holiness. Dorothy Day was a feisty woman of compassionate energy who worked tirelessly for justice through the Catholic Worker Movement.

Focus: Dorothy Day, like the apostles, was someone who did not have faith at first. She gradually accepted the gift of faith and grew in it by serving others. She spent almost her entire adult life living Jesus' commandment of love. She personally cared for indigent and homeless people in many ways, from preparing and serving meals to washing their feet.

DIALOGUE WITH THE GOSPEL

The Exodus reading today is about deliverance from servitude and hardship. Dorothy Day gave her life to overcome oppression and free the poor. Her work continues today in the Catholic community that she co-founded and through *The Catholic Worker* newspaper.

Traditionally, Holy Thursday celebrates the institution of the Eucharist and the priesthood. The washing of the feet is a powerful reminder of our Christian call to service. There is a sequence in *Entertaining Angles* where Peter Maurin washes the feet of a poor man and gives the man his own shoes. Dorothy then washes Peter's feet. John's Gospel tells us about Jesus as servant, and his service is symbolically understood in the washing of the feet.

A continual challenge to Dorothy Day concerns the nature of her service and her motivations. When visiting her, the Cardinal asks if she is doing her own will or God's will, and just how long she can continue this life of sacrifice. Her friends and co-workers confront her inconsistencies. She takes her examination of conscience to church and shouts at God, but grounded in faith, she repents and returns to her friends in humility.

Jesus says he is giving an example that all may follow. Sister Aloysius works cheerfully with the poor people and she gives Dorothy Day a Christ-example. Peter Maurin challenges

Dorothy and gives her an example of service. In turn, Dorothy gives the same example to many others.

This is Jesus' new commandment: to love one another is to serve. "What I just did was to give you an example: as I have done, so you must do." This was the life of Dorothy Day. An exasperated volunteer agreed to go on working when she wanted to quit because Dorothy had said, "You never know...you might be entertaining angels."

KEY SCENES AND THEMES

- Dorothy's lifestyle as a reporter; her pregnancy and the father's response; the abortion and the aftermath; Dorothy's later pregnancy and her desire for the child.

- Sister Aloysius's cheerfulness, her direct manner in asking Dorothy to assist with the poor, to come to church, to read; the conversion experience and Peter Maurin's influence.

- The nature of Dorothy Day's holiness, Dorothy's speech to the Catholic group, the Cardinal's visit; Dorothy's service to street people with their demands and weaknesses; Dorothy's desperate visit to the church, shouting at God; her finding peace and her "confession" to the group.

FOR REFLECTION AND CONVERSATION

1. Dorothy Day seemed to start out on the wrong foot. As a young woman, she led a bohemian lifestyle, engaged in sex outside of marriage, and had an abortion. Through the good example of others, as the film shows during her sojourn on Staten Island, Dorothy changed her life. How does the film portray Dorothy's life and conversion? How far did she take her newfound life and commitment to Christ and the Church?

2. There are many good lines in the film. For example, when the Cardinal of New York visits Dorothy, he tells her that both her work and her questioning of the Church's status quo regarding social issues embarrass the Church. "That's funny," she responds. "I thought we were *being* Church." Then the Cardinal tells her that people are calling her a communist. Her reply is that when they feed the poor, the Catholic Workers are saints, but when they ask why the people are poor, they are communists. What do you think the film is saying about how we can both live and be "Church" for others?

3. *Entertaining Angels* is a film that shows how Dorothy Day and her companions tried to live the Sermon on the Mount every day by serving others. On this Holy Thursday we are reminded to blend our beliefs and actions into one life lived for God. How does the Eucharist remind us of this? How central is the Eucharistic celebration in our lives?

Prayer

Jesus, help us to hear and act on your new commandment to love one another as you love us. Through the intercession of Dorothy Day, may we learn to serve the marginalized of our society. Amen.

The Miracle Maker

Russia/Wales, 2000 / 91 minutes

Voices: Ralph Fiennes, Rebecca Callard, William Hurt,
Julie Christie, David Thewlis, Miranda Richardson, Ian Holm,
Richard E. Grant, James Frain, Ken Stott, Alfred Molina

Writer: Murray Watts

Directors: Stanislav Sokolov, Derek Hayes

The Miracle Maker

Through the Eyes of a Child

SYNOPSIS

Sepporis is a town near Nazareth. It is A.D. 30, the ninetieth year of the Roman occupation of Palestine. Tamar, the daughter of Jairus and Rachael, is ill with a persistent fever. Her father brings her to a doctor who says she cannot be cured. On the way home, Jairus meets his friend Cleopas and tells him the sad news. Meanwhile, Tamar sees a man rescuing a woman from a beating and recognizes that he is special.

Soon after, Jesus explains to his mother that he must be about his Father's work and he must leave his work in the carpenter's shop. She recalls his birth, the visit of the Magi and the time he was lost in the Temple. Jesus is baptized by John, and then tempted in the desert. When he encounters Andrew and preaches from Peter's boat, Peter and Andrew draw in a huge haul of fish. Jesus heals Mary of Magdala of seven demons and defends her when she comes to Simon the Pharisee's house. Jesus teaches the disciples and the crowds, and heals the paralytic. Tamar and her mother witness these events and marvel.

The Pharisees and Herod are hostile. Pilate rules in the name of Caesar. Barabbas the rebel is a friend of Judas, who joins Jesus with great hope. Jesus enjoys visiting his friends,

Mary and Martha. He later raises Lazarus, their brother, from the dead. At Jairus' request, Jesus goes to heal Tamar and cures the woman with the hemorrhage on the way. Jairus and his family become disciples of Jesus.

Jesus enters Jerusalem triumphantly, clears the Temple, tells the story of the Good Samaritan, and urges his disciples to be like children. Judas is disappointed that Jesus will not rise up against the Romans. Jairus, Rachel, and Tamar are present at the Last Supper, and Tamar comforts Jesus just before his agony in the garden. Judas betrays Jesus. Jesus is brought before the High Priest, Herod, and then to Pilate. They find no reason to condemn him. However, the people plead for Barabbas' release. Jesus is condemned, and on the way to Calvary Tamar once again comforts him. Jesus is crucified.

After he dies, his body is taken down and buried, but Mary finds him later in the garden. Peter sees Jesus, too; he is risen! Jairus and Cleopas walk with him on the road to Emmaus. Jesus then ascends to heaven.

COMMENTARY

The Miracle Maker is another development in the long history of movie versions of Jesus' life. It combines three-dimensional clay-model animation, conventional two-dimensional animation, and computer effects. The two dimensional animation represents the flashback portions of the story, Jesus' teachings, and his parables. The music and sound effects add another dimension of realism to the film. *The Miracle Maker* adheres to the Gospel narratives, and the visuals are embellished with heavily researched historical and religious details of the times.

The three-dimensional model animation was produced in Russia. A Welsh company, known for its animated short movies of Shakespearean plays, produced the two-dimensional animation sequences. The voices, with the exception of William Hurt as Jairus, are British.

The models combine touches of realism with a sense of theater. The costumes reflect the Jewish culture and historical period, and the lavish settings give a feel for the times and the land of Jesus.

Ralph Fiennes' voice of Jesus presents him as a strong-minded, genial young man with a touch of humor. Fiennes articulates the parables and teachings beautifully and clearly, bringing emotion to such scenes as the agony in the garden. This is a very accessible and credible Jesus.

The writers decided to put Tamar and her parents at the dramatic center of the story. By making them disciples and recipients of a miracle, and allowing us to see Jesus through Tamar's eyes, the writers created a storytelling device that works effectively for audiences of all ages. This decision reflects a thoughtful approach to the film's construction that satisfies and inspires viewers.

DIALOGUE WITH THE GOSPEL

Focus: The Miracle Maker *is a straightforward, visually enhanced, and integrated experience of the Gospels told through the eyes of a child and her parents.* The Miracle Maker *forms the basis for an on-going dialogue with the life and teachings of Jesus, especially with the events Good Friday, in appealing and meaningful new ways.*

The Miracle Maker tells the entire public life of Jesus; approximately one-fourth of the movie focuses on the last week of Jesus' life, especially Good Friday and Jesus' passion and death. Tamar is present in the narrative from the beginning of Jesus' public life. She demonstrates a child's ability to grasp the essence of Jesus' Divine presence and power and to relate to him in uncomplicated, authentic ways. This cannot be said of her father Jairus, who is afraid to approach Jesus for religious reasons, fearful of what the officials might think. In the end, he is able to overcome his fear and asks Jesus to cure his daughter.

Tamar and her family are there when Jesus enters Jerusalem on Palm Sunday, at the Last Supper, on the way of the cross, and the Crucifixion. Experiencing Good Friday through their eyes helps viewers imagine what it might have been like if we had been present, and how we might have reacted or responded to the events unfolding before us.

The film concludes quickly with several appearances of the resurrected Jesus. It shows Jairus and Cleopas as the two disciples on the road to Emmaus. Tamar bears witness to Jesus at the Ascension, saying that the Kingdom of God has come and that Jesus is with us still.

KEY SCENES AND THEMES

- Jesus and healing: driving the devils out of Mary, forgiving and healing the paralytic, the woman with a hemorrhage, curing Tamar, and raising Lazarus.

- Judas: his rebel background with Barabbas, his disappointment after Jesus' entry into Jerusalem; the kiss in the garden and his realization of what he has done.

- The agony in the garden, the passion, the court trials, Peter's denials; the carrying of the cross, Jesus commending himself to the Father and dying; the resurrection and Emmaus appearances.

FOR REFLECTION AND CONVERSATION

1. The first reading from Isaiah is almost a "picture" of Jesus on Good Friday, written six centuries before Christ. *The Miracle Maker* is a sophisticated moving picture created almost two thousand years after the events it depicts. In what ways does *The Miracle Maker* compare to other films about the life of Christ as they represent the events of Holy Week, in particular *Ben-Hur* or Zeffirelli's *Jesus of Nazareth*?

2. The Letter to the Hebrews speaks of the prayers and tears of Christ asking God to deliver him from suffering and death. How do the animation techniques and plot devices work to effectively show Jesus' suffering, death, Resurrection and Ascension?

3. *The Miracle Maker* shows how loving parents need a miracle for their sick daughter, Tamar. So many parents are willing to give up everything for their children, especially when they are ill. What does the story of Jairus, Rachel and Tamar teach families today?

Prayer

Jesus, this is the day that you said your final "yes" to your Father to give yourself completely in death for love of us. Help us to be thankful to you for the completeness of your love. Amen.

Girl, Interrupted

U.S., 1999 / 125 minutes

Actors: Winona Ryder, Angelina Jolie, Brittany Murphy,
Whoopi Goldberg, Vanessa Redgrave, Jeffrey Tambor,
Jared Leto, Clea Duvall, Mary Kay Place

Writers: James Mangold, Lisa Loomer, Anna Hamilton Phelan

Director: James Mangold

Girl, Interrupted

Buried So as to Rise

Susanna Kaysen, a young woman with a reputation for promiscuity, has just attempted suicide. Her parents, conscious of what people might think, place her "voluntarily" in a mental institution. Before her suicide attempt, Susanna had become acquainted with a young man afraid of being drafted into the army and dying in Vietnam; perhaps this has contributed to her obsession with death. In the institution she lives with a group of disturbed young women. One is a pathological liar, another is bulimic, some are extremely insecure. Lisa, who has been a patient in the institution for eight years, is a dominating and strong person.

SYNOPSIS

Susanna follows the institution's regulations, tolerating the continual "checks" and regular visits with her therapists. Lisa, who continually confronts the staff and incites rebellion among the patients, fascinates Susanna. A few of the women go on a night raid of the psychiatrist's office, where Susanna reads her file and discovers she has been diagnosed as a borderline personality.

When Susanna starts making trouble, she begins seeing Dr. Wick on a regular basis. Lisa urges Susanna to escape with her, and they flee to the apartment of a former patient named Daisy. Daisy's abusive father pays her living expenses, but she is disturbed and desperate for love, although in denial. Lisa bluntly and mercilessly taunts her and Daisy kills herself. Susanna is distraught and returns to the institution, while Lisa continues her escape.

Susanna blames herself for not preventing Daisy from taking her own life. This becomes a pivotal moment of growth for Susanna. Lisa is brought back to the institution, and after a harrowing encounter, Susanna is able to speak honestly with her. Susanna begins to recover and wonders why she has wasted a year of her life.

COMMENTARY

Susanna Kaysen's autobiographical *Girl, Interrupted* was published in 1994. It was very successful among women and teenage girls who were able to identify and empathize with the author. In the book, Kaysen recounts her two-year experience in an institution in the late 1960s.

Winona Ryder stars in the film and was its co-executive producer. When she was about twenty years old, she spent time in an institution, and this experience helped her to bring an intensity and fragility to her performance as Susanna.

The movie has a very strong cast including Angelina Jolie, who won both a Best Supporting Actress Golden Globe and an Oscar for her role as the tormented Lisa. Whoopi Goldberg is Valerie, the tough but sympathetic nurse, and Vanessa Redgrave plays Dr. Wick.

The movie shows us a small group of emotionally and mentally ill women who veer back and forth between their dysfunctions and the consequences, their erratic behavior and happy moments, co-dependence, and mutual hostility. The film gives us an inside look at a comfortable enough environment, yet shows the institutional limitations to the women's freedom: the regular inspections, references to hydrotherapy, psychotherapy sessions, and the constant lack of privacy. Susanna's socially conscious parents are embarrassed by their daughter. They do not engage with her and do not know how to cope when her life spins out of control.

Girl, Interrupted is a biopic that joins other films about the experience of women in mental institutions, such as *The Snake Pit, The Bell Jar*, and *I Never Promised You a Rose Garden*.

Focus: According to our Creed, Jesus died and was buried. Then he was raised to new life. The story of Susanna Kaysen is the story of a girl whose life was interrupted when she was "buried" by her despair and was institutionalized. Then she was raised to a new life.

DIALOGUE WITH THE GOSPEL

Towards the end of her time in the mental institution, Susanna says that she has wasted a year of her life, though obviously this is not the case. She attempted suicide and was dead to herself. Through her encounters with the other women in the institution and the staff, by confronting the aggressive Lisa and herself, Susanna comes to life again.

During the Triduum, we contemplate the Paschal Mystery. On Good Friday, Jesus dies and is buried in the tomb. We experience the theme of dying and rising through water at the Easter Vigil. Our reflections lead us to realize that some of our brothers and sisters actually share a burial experience similar to that of Jesus, as did Susanna and her companions.

This dying and rising to new life is the theme of St. Paul's Letter to the Romans (cf. 6:3–11). He speaks of the Rite of Baptism, of being buried with Jesus, and that by rising with Christ we shall live with him, nevermore to die. Susanna was buried into death when she tried to take her own life and found herself in a mental institution. When Susanna regains her health and her life, she experiences a kind of resurrection. Her book, published twenty-five years later, and the movie released after more than thirty years (with Susanna Kaysen as an associate producer), show that she has indeed "arisen."

**KEY SCENES
AND THEMES**

- Susanna and her uncomprehending parents, her sense of denial, her memories of her family; Susanna's relationship with Toby, her discussion of suicide with him; the reasons behind her suicide attempt.

- The therapy sequences: Susanna's sessions with Dr. Wick, her discovery of the file, her reaction to her diagnosis.

- Lisa's escape, Lisa taunting Daisy in Daisy's apartment, Susanna finding Daisy's body; Susanna's recovery; Lisa's return, the final confrontation; Susanna and Lisa discussing true freedom.

**FOR REFLECTION
AND
CONVERSATION**

1. How does the film *Girl, Interrupted* show that emotional and mental illnesses are real? How does the film compare to other films that have dealt with the same topic, such as *I Never Promised You a Rose Garden* or *One Flew Over the Cuckoo's Nest*? What social purpose do films such as these serve? How are they a commentary on who determines when someone is mentally ill, and the criteria used to determine this?

2. Ultimately, Susanna chooses life over death. What seemed like her way out becomes unacceptable because she sees death "up close and personal." This is not the path to happiness and meaning. What can we do to promote the culture of life in society?

3. Like other young people who feel their lives are meaningless, Susanna bottomed out. Her suicide attempt and her relationship with her parents and boyfriend show that she wasn't aware of any reason to continue living. What happens in the film to show Susanna's

return to life? If asked why I get out of bed every morning, how does my faith in the risen Christ transform my response?

Prayer

Jesus, sometimes we feel buried by our lives and we long to rise to new life. You have shown us the way. Give us the grace and strength to follow you. Amen.

EASTER SUNDAY

Acts 10:34, 37–43; John 20:1–9

The Hurricane

U.S., 1999 / 146 minutes

Actors: Denzel Washington, John Hannah, Deborah Unger, Liev Schreiber, Vicellous Reon Shannon, David Paymer, Dan Hadaya, Harris Yulin, Clancy Brown, Rod Steiger

Writers: Armyan Bernstein, Don Gordon

Director: Norman Jewison

The Hurricane

Victory over Darkness

SYNOPSIS

Rubin Carter's New Jersey childhood reads like a menu of difficulties: petty theft, trouble with the police, a confrontation with a pedophile who is a public figure. Rubin is placed in juvenile detention. He escapes and joins the army in an attempt to do something with his life, but is arrested on his return from service.

When Carter gets out of jail, he becomes a champion boxer, nicknamed "The Hurricane." He marries and starts a family. He loses a championship because of racial prejudice. When some people are murdered during a hold-up, he and a young man, John Artis, are questioned and released. However, the police rig the evidence and frame the two men for the murders. Barely escaping the death penalty, they are sentenced to life imprisonment.

Carter takes a stand for independence in the prison and refuses to wear a uniform or to be pushed around. He develops his inner life in order to survive, and manages to write and publish his autobiography. In the meantime, many people, including celebrities, have taken up his cause. But appeals to higher courts fail.

In Toronto, a young student named Lesra is living with a group of socially active people. He reads Carter's book, writes to him, and is allowed to visit Carter. A friendship begins. The group from Toronto decides to appeal Carter's case. They move to New Jersey and begin investigations, which over a ten-year period reveal inconsistencies in testimony and documents. The police harass them as they work to prove Carter's innocence.

In a final move, Carter pushes his case forward one last time, even though this means the loss of all future appeals. The judge rules in Carter's favor. Rubin "The Hurricane" Carter is finally released from prison, twenty years after being convicted for a crime he didn't commit.

COMMENTARY

The Hurricane is based on the autobiography of Rubin Carter, *The Sixteenth Round*, as well as the book, *Lazarus and the Hurricane*, by Sam Chaiton and Terry Swinton, two members of the Toronto group who helped free Carter from prison. Bob Dylan and Jacques Levy's ballad, "Hurricane," written during the early stages of Carter's appeal process, is featured on the sound track.

Denzel Washington has a great screen presence. He realistically portrays a man who is innocent of a crime, but trapped by prejudice and the inconsistencies of the American justice system. Washington deftly reveals how Carter almost gives up, but finds the inner strength to go on.

Norman Jewison directs *The Hurricane* with skill and commitment to Carter's story. Jewison's forty-year career spans a wide range of movies including *Fiddler on the Roof, Jesus Christ, Superstar, Agnes of God, A Soldier's Story, Moonstruck*, and *In the Heat of the Night*, an influential movie about racial issues in the 1960s.

The Hurricane spans over twenty years of Carter's adult life. Most of the action takes place in the prison and courtrooms. Vicellous Reon Shannon is very good as Lesra, the young man who began the final effort to free Carter. The members of the Toronto group are not as strongly portrayed, however. *The Hurricane* is a fine, human, "inspirational" movie.

DIALOGUE WITH THE GOSPEL

Focus: Rubin Carter's sufferings as a victim of society can be a reminder of the sufferings of Jesus. Like Jesus, Carter has an experience of "resurrection" and a new "risen" life.

The story of Hurricane Carter is one of continual dying and rising. If it is true that we share in the sufferings of Christ and he in ours, then Rubin Carter has shared in these sufferings more than many others. He was already an urban victim in his childhood, as confirmed by his years in juvenile detention. After a time of brief hope and achievement in the army, he is again imprisoned, only to find when he is free that the police still want him behind bars.

Like the young man, John Artis, who chauffeured him on the night of the murders, Carter is "the wrong man." Twenty years of imprisonment as an innocent victim compound the injustices of his life. He is tempted to let go, seemingly unable to find the strength to go on. Then, in the midst of death, he finds inner light and peace. In this way, he shows something of the pattern of Jesus and his suffering.

With the help of friends and strangers, and with their loving support, Carter is raised from the death of unjust imprisonment. He experiences resurrection.

Carter's subsequent "risen" life has been devoted to the cause of the unjustly imprisoned. In this way, he is mirroring something of what St. Paul says to the Colossians (cf. 3:1–4) in the second reading: He has been brought back to life and looks for the things of heaven here on earth.

- Rubin Carter: his childhood, the championship, Rubin as a victim of racial prejudice; Rubin in prison, his making a life for himself after much suffering.

- Carter studying the law, his appeals and their failure; the importance of his spirituality, his inner centeredness and humanity; his writing and publishing an autobiography.

- The phone call; Rubin's admission of weariness; the final court appeal and the judge's finding; Rubin's vindication and release: a symbol of hope.

KEY SCENES AND THEMES

1. When Denzel Washington received the Best Actor Golden Globe award of 2000 for his portrayal of Rubin Carter in *The Hurricane,* he said that as God is love, so Rubin Carter demonstrates that love in his life. How does the film show Carter's resolve to maintain his dignity in prison? How does his decision to use this time for personal growth help him to survive?

2. A young black teenager, Lesra, who was just learning how to read, bought a discarded copy of Carter's autobiography for twenty-five cents. It was the first book this young man ever read, a seemingly inconsequential fact, which led to Carter's eventual release from prison. What does this film say about the power of a good book?

3. What is the basic message of this film and how does it contribute to the ongoing debate about law enforcement's racial profiling and legal representation for the poor? The prosecutor sought the death penalty

FOR REFLECTION AND CONVERSATION

for Rubin Carter and John Artis. If they had been executed, two innocent men would have died. Is it truly possible for the death penalty to be reconciled with the teachings of Jesus?

Prayer

Jesus, after all of your human suffering, you still trusted in your Father. He raised you to new life in love, a life of grace in which you invite us to share. Grant us the gift to persevere in love in our daily lives. Amen.

Message in a Bottle

U.S., 1999 / 130 minutes

Actors: Kevin Costner, Robin Wright Penn, Paul Newman, John Savage, Robbie Coltrane, Illeana Douglas

Writer: Gerald DiPego

Director: Luis Mandoki

Message in a Bottle

Enduring Love and Grief

SYNOPSIS

While jogging along a beach, Theresa finds a bottle containing a letter. Theresa, a divorced mother, works for a newspaper in Chicago. When her editor publishes a piece about the message in a bottle, two other letters surface and are sent to her. Theresa traces the letters' author to a North Carolina boatman, Garrett Blake. Despite her editor's reservations, Theresa goes to visit the lonely man. Though she had intended to, Theresa does not tell Garrett about the recovered letters. They are attracted to one another. Theresa meets Dodge, Garrett's father, who is practical and wise.

Theresa discovers that the messages were written to Garrett's dead wife, Catherine. She was an artist whose family still resents Garrett and blames him for her death. Garrett visits Theresa in Chicago and gets along well with her son. By chance, Garrett discovers that Theresa knows about the letters he wrote to his dead wife. Worse yet, Garrett learns that his story has been in the newspaper. Feeling hurt and used, he returns home.

Garrett makes peace with his wife's family and builds a boat in her memory. Theresa comes to the launch, but when she sees that the boat is named "Catherine," she thinks Garrett will not be able to let go of Catherine's memory. There is no real reconciliation between them, and Theresa leaves. Garrett sails out to sea to throw overboard another bottle with a message to Catherine, but dies trying to rescue a family in a storm. Theresa is comforted when Dodge gives her Garrett's final letter, found in the bottle, which remained in the pocket of his recovered slicker. The letter is his final farewell to his wife, telling her about his joy in loving two people, first Catherine and now Theresa.

COMMENTARY

Message in a Bottle is a traditional Hollywood romantic love story. It focuses on a boat builder, Garrett Blake, played by Kevin Costner, whose wife has died. Costner plays an ordinary man who loved his wife and lost her in death. The character contrasts with his heroic roles in *Dances with Wolves* and *Robin Hood.*

Robin Wright Penn gives a sensitive performance as the journalist. The audience's ability to engage in the story depends on the extent to which they identify with her. Paul Newman plays Costner's father with crusty humor and wisdom.

The material runs the danger of cliché and easy sentimentalism, though the film adds its own twist to the formula. In *Message in a Bottle*, the cast combines credibility and feeling to make the movie a satisfying experience. The cinematography is beautiful, almost too lavish for the plot.

Luis Mandoki directed the film, adding it to his other films such as *White Palace, Born Yesterday,* and *When a Man Loves a Woman.*

DIALOGUE WITH THE GOSPEL

Focus: Facing another's death is a profound experience, especially if the one who dies was deeply loved. Thomas had to touch Jesus' side so that he could believe in his death and his resurrec-

tion. In Message in a Bottle, *Garrett has to learn that love and death mean to let go in order to rise to a new life.*

The second reading from the First Letter of Peter (cf. 1:3–9) tells of the new life experienced through Christ's Resurrection. It emphasizes that no matter our trials in life, faith will sustain us.

Previously in John's Gospel, Thomas brashly wants to go with Jesus to Lazarus' home in order to die with him. In answer to Thomas' desire to know Jesus' true identity, Jesus reveals himself as the Way, the Truth, and the Life. Both stories speak of Thomas' deep regard for the Lord. Now, we hear about Thomas' distress over Jesus' death. We see the delight of the other apostles because Jesus has risen, an event Thomas only heard about, but did not witness.

Garrett's messages in bottles reflect his distress and guilt about what he did not do for his beloved wife before she died. The messages are an attempt to communicate with her, to express his abiding love for her. Above all, the messages are a testimony to his inability to accept her death. In a somewhat different perspective on life and death, Garrett shares the distress of Thomas. Garrett wants to tangibly communicate with Catherine before he can let her go.

Jesus invites Thomas to touch his pierced side, so he can relieve his doubts and believe. Garrett, too, must touch the reality of Catherine's death before he can let go of his doubts about himself. Only then can he come alive and truly love Theresa. Here the formulaic plot takes a twist. When Garrett finally sees the truth and believes in himself so he can love again, he gives up his life to save others.

- Theresa jogging and finding the bottle, her wanting to know more, the article and the discovery of other messages.

KEY SCENES AND THEMES

- Garrett: his declaration of love, his grief; the nature of life, of separation and death, of sorrow and regrets, of reconciliation and asking forgiveness; Catherine's family: their anger, her brother, the painting; the reconciliation and building the boat as Catherine's memorial.

- Garrett discovering the truth, his hurt and alienation from Theresa; Theresa at the boat's launch; Garrett sailing to sea, the family in distress, the rescue, Garrett's drowning; the final message in the bottle.

FOR REFLECTION AND CONVERSATION

1. Garrett is a man emotionally at sea because his wife, Catherine, has died. What techniques does the film use to show Catherine's presence and Garrett's grief? How do the messages in a bottle work to communicate Garrett's love and grief? How were the messages in the film symbols of enduring love?

2. Theresa worked for a news organization. Even though she was not directly responsible for publishing Garrett's story, what were the ethical issues involved that would have assured Garrett's privacy? How might the story have been different if she had been truthful with Garrett from the beginning?

3. Several events occur in the story that require reconciliation before people can go on with their lives in peace, especially the relationship between Catherine's family and Garrett. What function did Catherine's paintings serve as the story unfolded? What did the building of the boat mean? Why was this something Garrett had to do? How can we live our daily lives in reconciliation?

Prayer

Lord, you let Thomas touch your wounds and he learned to believe in you. You even call blessed those who do not see you and yet believe. Help all of us who experience the death of loved ones to be comforted, to let go, and to rise to a new life. Amen.

The Prince of Tides
U.S., 1991 / 132 minutes
Actors: Barbra Streisand, Nick Nolte, Kate Nelligan,
Melinda Dillon, Blythe Danner, Jeroen Krabbe, Jason Gould
Writers: Pat Conroy, Becky Johnston
Director: Barbra Streisand

The Prince of Tides

Healing Memories

SYNOPSIS

Tom Wingo tells his story of growing up on the coast of South Carolina in a dysfunctional family. As a child, he lives with his brother, sister, cultured mother, and violent father who is a captain of a shrimp boat. His parents never get along and when they finally divorce and his mother remarries, it affects the grown children. Tom has his own family, but his marriage is strained. Tom's twin sister is a poet and when she attempts suicide, her doctor, Susan Lowenstein, asks Tom to come to New York. By helping Dr. Lowenstein understand his twin sister, Tom comes to an understanding of himself.

When Tom and his siblings were children, they and their mother were violently attacked and raped by two escaped prisoners. Tom's brother kills them and later drowns. Tom has masked his feelings and suppressed the memories of this horrific event, as has his sister. His mother pretends nothing ever happened.

Once Tom is freed from the burden of his memories and guilt after telling his story to the doctor, he has an affair with her. Dr. Lowenstein's son and Tom develop a friendship that upsets the boy's father. It is obvious that Dr. Lowenstein's marriage is on the rocks. Tom realizes that his relationship

112

with the doctor does not have a future and that he needs to return to his family and home in order to be reconciled and to truly begin again.

The Prince of Tides is the film adaptation of a novel by Pat Conroy *(Sounder, The Water Is Wide, The Great Santini, The Lords of Discipline,* and *Beach Music).* Conroy co-wrote the screenplay with Becky Johnston.

Nick Nolte leads the cast in an award-winning performance as a tentative man who is full of rage. Barbra Streisand stars as the psychiatrist, Dr. Susan Lowenstein. The supporting cast includes Kate Nelligan in an Oscar-nominated performance as Tom Wingo's mother, Melinda Dillon as his sister, and Blythe Danner as his wife. Jeroen Krabbe plays the role of Dr. Lowenstein's husband.

The film introduces us to the stunning beauty of South Carolina's Low Country and contrasts it with the city of New York. The film centers on the need for people to come to terms with personal pain, dark family secrets, and the truth. Anyone who has ever experienced or had an interest in psychiatry or the inner workings of the mind will want to see this film. The same goes for those who value talking to a skilled impartial person who knows how to listen without judging. *The Prince of Tides* is not an easy film to watch because of its graphic darkness. But it will enrich those who are looking for the possibility of catharsis and wholeness through honesty.

Focus: Jesus is the extraordinary listener and healer of the distraught disciples on the road to Emmaus. The Prince of Tides is a movie about listening and healing as a man gradually reveals the secrets and sadness of his life.

During the Easter season, we celebrate one of the most famous journeys in history: the Emmaus walk. While it ends in joy, it begins in deep disappointment and hurt. The two disciples talk about the unexpected painful events they have just lived through. The journey becomes a healing walk as Jesus helps the unsuspecting disciples to acknowledge their shattered hopes and expectations. Jesus talks to them about God's mystery of salvation by explaining the Scriptures. They finally recognize Jesus in the breaking of bread. Filled with joy, they return to Jerusalem to begin a new life of discipleship. The journey to Emmaus is the only resurrection appearance Luke narrates, indicating its importance to his audience.

Today's liturgy provides us with an opportunity to take our own Emmaus walk toward self-awareness regarding sin and self-generated expectations. This awareness leads to repentance and the ability to see how close God is, walking with us in our lives.

The Prince of Tides is the story of Tom Wingo's Emmaus walk. He is lost in his pain. He remembers his father with anger, regards his mother with bitterness, is disappointed in his marriage and achievements, and all the while has suppressed the trauma of a childhood attack on him and his family.

Tom's companions on his walk are his traumatized sister and the psychiatrist who is helping her. Tom comes to trust Dr. Lowenstein to the extent that he finally feels free to acknowledge the past himself, and to weep. His passing sexual relationship with Dr. Lowenstein is unethical, and Tom realizes its futility. He emerges from the entire experience in New York as a different person, a freed man. He is enabled to walk back to his life with new vision, new hope, and renewed love.

KEY SCENES AND THEMES

- Tom Wingo's memories: the happy portrait of the children with their mother, the island explorations; the traumatic event of his parents' divorce; the children diving into the water to escape the fights and pain.

- Tom: his age and experience, the strong yet vulnerable white American male, his contrasting relationships with his wife and children; Tom as coach: out of work, his shattered expectations, his self-image and fears.

- Tom telling Dr. Lowenstein his buried secret, the glimpses of the prisoners, the rape and the violence; the business-like attitude of Tom's mother, her zealous cleaning and disposing of the bodies; a secret; Tom telling this story and weeping; his hope for reconciliation and a future.

1. What were the circumstances that brought Tom Wingo to New York and led to the final healing of his memories and life? How did the film show the differences between life in New York and life in South Carolina? How did the cinematic elements of the film contrast with Tom's interior reality?

2. "Lord, you will show us the path of life" (cf. Ps 16:1–11) is today's responsorial psalm. Tom Wingo and his sister both had to walk very difficult paths for inner healing. We experience this pain with Tom, especially as we relive the torturous events of his early life. How was his journey to New York and to his past an Emmaus walk? How was this experience a time of healing for Tom's wife and mother?

3. The relationship between Tom and Dr. Lowenstein is immoral and Tom comes to realize that it cannot lead to life. He must return home and conclude his healing journey by reconciling with those closest to him

FOR REFLECTION AND CONVERSATION

and taking up his responsibilities. In what ways can today's Gospel reading and the film encourage us to confront what may not be right in our lives? How can we seek healing and reconciliation in order to live life to the full, and to feel the presence of the Lord burning within us as we travel through life?

Prayer

Jesus, you walked with your friends to Emmaus and you listened to their sadness and their story. Accompany us on our way, hear us, and enable us to experience a grace-filled healing. Amen.

Erin Brockovich

U.S., 2000 / 132 minutes

Actors: Julia Roberts, Albert Finney, Aaron Eckhart,
Marg Helgenberger, Peter Coyote

Writer: Susannah Grant

Director: Steven Soderbergh

Erin Brockovich

Compassionate Leadership

Erin Brockovich, a former beauty queen, now twice divorced with three young children, searches unsuccessfully for a job. When her outspokenness in court prevents her from winning compensation for a car accident, she demands a job from her surprised lawyer, Ed Masry.

SYNOPSIS

Her co-workers look askance at her because of her revealing wardrobe and loud mouth. They think she flaunts her sexuality. Nevertheless, she perseveres in the low level job Masry gives her and discovers anomalies in a case she is researching. Erin visits the plaintiffs and finds that the effects of the local gas company's industrial pollution in the water supply have been covered up and that over 600 people have ailments because of it. She deals with the victims personally and they feel she is a friend.

Erin immerses herself in the case and this opens up new channels for her intelligence and talents. Her self-esteem grows. Erin's biker friend, George, looks after her children, but tensions arise between them because of her absence and preoccupation with her investigations. Ed Masry supports her and they build up a case despite hostility and threats from the electric company. To have the best chances to win, Masry

117

and Erin go into partnership with a larger firm. The new lawyers look down on Erin for her lack of professional know-how. She dramatically proves them wrong.

Erin and Ed get the signatures of the 600 plaintiffs and win a settlement of over $300 million. Erin has a new life and continues to work on similar cases with Ed Masry.

COMMENTARY

Julia Roberts has no need to prove that she is adept at light comedy. In this Academy Award-winning role she carries the entire film as its dramatic lead, and she excels. Albert Finney, nominated for an Academy Award for Best Supporting Actor as Ed Masry, gives one of his best performances and is a perfect match for Roberts' prickly character. Their interaction adds irony and humor to a story marked with tragedy, loss, and greed. Aaron Eckhart (who first hit the screen as the archetypal misogynist in the film, *In the Company of Men*) plays the tough, good-hearted biker-construction worker who is able to bring domestic warmth to Erin's children.

The movie was directed by Steven Soderbergh, whose varied and unpredictable career has produced *Sex, Lies and Videotape, King of the Hill, Out of Sight, The Limey,* and *Traffic.*

Erin Brockovich is a David and Goliath story that parallels other true stories brought to the screen: *A Civil Action* (1998), about industrial pollution, and *The Insider* (1999), about big tobacco. *Erin Brockovich* was nominated for five Oscars, including Best Picture, Best Director, and Best Screenplay.

Erin discovers her own personal worth when she realizes that with her energy and compassion, and some aggression, she has the people skills necessary to help those in need. Some of the laughs in the film come at the expense of professionals who are not people-oriented.

DIALOGUE WITH THE GOSPEL

Focus: The story of the Good Shepherd is well known. At first, Erin Brockovich may seem to be a surprising image of Good Shepherd leadership. Yet, in her dealings with people, she pos-

sesses Good Shepherd qualities: she knows her clients, genuinely cares for them, and generously sacrifices herself for them.

There is an impressive scene toward the end of the movie when Erin and Ed meet the lawyers of their partner firm. The setting is formal: the lawyers' power-dressing, authority, dominance, and high professional expectations create an intimidating climate. The female lawyer patronizes Erin. Judging Erin by her appearance, she is sure that her files are poorly kept. When her competence is challenged, Erin confounds everyone by firing off the names, phone numbers, and details of each plaintiff from memory.

The way Erin relates to her clients is the way she exercises leadership. She mirrors the words of Jesus in today's Gospel about the Good Shepherd: hers is the voice that is known by the sheep that follow the shepherd. Jesus says the sheep run away from the stranger. This is exactly what the clients do when a lawyer from the partner firm interviews them after Erin has already gathered their information and become their friend.

Erin Brockovich's good shepherd leadership style can serve as a model and a challenge to religious leaders who may tend to be "strangers" when relating to their flocks. The need for quality pastoral leadership is reinforced by the other readings. Peter's enthusiastic words in the Acts of the Apostles persuade the crowds to be baptized. The pattern of Jesus' leadership is also sketched in the reading from the First Letter of Peter (cf. 2:20–25).

KEY SCENES AND THEMES

- Erin's immediate impact: her appearance, her manner, her way of speaking, her clothes; Erin's job interviews, the ways she is perceived and treated; Erin's love for her children, her desire to have them with her.

- The staff's disdain at work, Erin's clashes with Ed; Erin's curiosity about the case's anomalies; her intense pursuit of the irregularities, its effect on herself and her children; her relationship with George and her previous husbands.

- The family visits: her interest and sympathy, her listening; the people's trust, her increasing credibility and the ability to help; the clash with the "hot-shot" lawyers, Erin proving herself; Erin's son reading the document and realizing his mother has been helping others.

FOR REFLECTION AND CONVERSATION

1. Some of the more humorous moments in this film involve comments on Erin's personal appearance and wardrobe. If anything, the movie proves that appearances can be deceiving. Erin thinks she looks good and is satisfied with her appearance, while others think she looks cheap and treat her accordingly—at first. How is Erin able to help people despite the way she dresses? Who cannot see past her external appearance in the film; who is able to see her identity and dignity as a person? Why?

2. We find out early in the film that Erin has three children and is twice divorced. She has no marketable skills and no child support. When the new man in her life wants her to stay home, she refuses and he leaves. What are some of the forces at work in society and culture that create situations like those which surround Erin? Was Erin right to fight for a job and become independent so that she could be a good shepherd to her children too? What is the Christian view of the role of women in society today?

3. Besides the parable of the Good Shepherd, this film reminds us of the story of the unjust judge whom the persistent widow nagged until she got justice (Lk 18:1–8). Erin wore Ed Masry down until he finally showed compassion and gave her a job. Masry didn't always consult her about the case, and she never failed to call this to his attention; in fact, she demanded that he respect her as a colleague. In the end, Masry trusted and rewarded her. Is it possible to have compassionate leadership in the workplace? How?

Prayer

Jesus, Good Shepherd, help all leaders to imitate you in gentleness of style while being firm and supportive of people's rights. Amen.

Shadowlands

U.K., 1993 / 131 minutes

Actors: Anthony Hopkins, Debra Winger, John Wood,
Edward Hardwicke, Joseph Mazzello, Peter Firth

Writer: William Nicholson

Director: Richard Attenborough

Shadowlands

"Surprised by Joy"

SYNOPSIS

Oxford, England, 1952. C.S. Lewis, known as Jack, is an Oxford don, a Professor of English, and a bachelor. He is also well known for the children's stories he has written, *The Chronicles of Narnia*. He lectures and lives a comparatively reclusive and academic life and shares a home with his brother Warnie.

Jack receives a letter from an American poet, Joy Gresham. She and her son Douglas visit Oxford and Jack invites them to stay for Christmas. Douglas does not enjoy the visit. They return to the United States and Joy and her husband divorce.

Joy and Douglas later return to England and she attends one of Lewis' lectures on Christianity. Lewis agrees to a civil marriage to enable her to stay in England. Though they do not live together, the arrangement stirs up the quietly complacent life of the dons.

One day Joy collapses and is diagnosed with cancer. Lewis goes every day to London to see her and gradually realizes he loves her. He proposes to Joy and they are married "before God" by a vicar in the hospital. Joy and Douglas move in with Jack and Warnie. Later, Jack and Joy go on a honeymoon trip to the Golden Valley. When they return, Joy dies.

122

Lewis is distraught, but gradually returns to his university life. He and Douglas deepen their relationship and become friends.

COMMENTARY

Shadowlands has come to the big screen from a made-for-television movie written by William Nicholson and starring Joss Ackland as Lewis and Claire Bloom as Joy. Nicholson then adapted *Shadowlands* for the stage in an award-winning play starring Nigel Hawthorne. Nicholson adapted *Shadowlands* yet again for the big screen's director, Richard Attenborough *(Gandhi, Cry Freedom, Chaplin, A Chorus Line).*

Attenborough creates the atmosphere of Oxford in the 1950s with an eye for detail. Anthony Hopkins gives a moving, finely nuanced performance as Lewis. The role highlights the personality of the reclusive don who is comfortable with his life. Jack comes alive during academic discussions in the dining hall or at the pub.

Jack enjoys lecturing and is demanding on his students. He is an essayist and novelist who wrote on the relationship between literary language and medieval courtly love along with Christian allegories. His studies penetrate literature, always seeking to understand the mystery of God in the experience of suffering. Hopkins' portrayal of a comfortable celibate attracted to his opposite personality type is both touching and restrained. It is matched by the vigor and vulnerability of Debra Winger, who plays Joy.

Focus: Jesus says he is the Way, the Truth, and the Life. C.S. Lewis discovers this for himself, as dramatized in Shadowlands.

DIALOGUE WITH THE GOSPEL

C.S. Lewis was an Anglican layman and one of the best exponents of the relevance of Christ's self-definition and of Christianity during the twentieth century. *Shadowlands* gives the audience the opportunity to see and reflect on elements that were part of Lewis' faith. As a professor of literature, he appreciates truth and beauty both in poetry and in fantasy. As a Christian, he explores the mystery of God.

In the film, the intellectual Jack easily accepts Jesus as "the Way" and "the Truth," and eloquently lectures on suffering, calling it "God's megaphone to rouse a deaf world." But he must learn that Jesus is not merely the answer to questions. Jesus is also "the Life." As Jack imperceptibly begins to fall in love with Joy, his heart feels new stirrings. We see Joy gradually bringing him out of his ivory tower to share her life; and through her, he learns "the life" of love.

With Joy's help, Jack discovers that the way to learn Jesus as "the Life" is through our intense living of ordinary human events: love, joy, pain, and sorrow. A heart that allows itself to feel will more easily relate to Jesus as "the Way, the Truth and the Life." Finally, when Joy dies, Jack experiences *in fact* what he had written of *in theory:* the mystery of suffering. His life has been transformed.

KEY SCENES AND THEMES

- Lewis: a man of intelligence and truth; Lewis lecturing, conducting tutorials, engaging in academic discussions.

- Lewis' surprise at meeting Joy; his inviting Joy and Douglas for Christmas; Lewis showing Douglas the wardrobe.

- Joy's return and the marriage of convenience; Joy stirring Lewis from his impersonal academic lifestyle; Joy's illness, the hospital wedding and the honeymoon; Joy's death: its effect on Lewis' life, faith, and spirituality.

FOR REFLECTION AND CONVERSATION

1. As Jack's understanding of the mystery of suffering grows, he speaks about prayer: "I pray because I am helpless and because the need flows out of me all the time." What other parts of his life, writings, and talks

does the film focus on to help us follow Jack's human and spiritual journey?

2. When Joy is in pain, Jack tells his brother that when someone you love suffers, you want to take on that suffering. This shows how much Jack's understanding of Jesus' example and of Christianity has grown. What does Jesus, the Way, the Truth, and the Life, mean to us in the circumstances of our daily life? How well have we integrated Jesus' teaching into our own lives?

3. Today's readings and *Shadowlands* are all about living the Christian life, and not just believing it. When Joy dies, a friend tries to comfort Jack by saying that only God knows why. Jack responds with a question that many people have: "I know God knows why, but does he care?" Does Jack find an answer to his question? How might we respond to the same question?

Prayer

Jesus, you reveal yourself as our Way, our Truth, and our Life. May we experience this fullness of your life in ours, as we come to a fuller understanding of who you are. Amen.

Denzel Washington and Kevin Kline star in *Cry Freedom*.

Cry Freedom

U.K., 1987 / 158 minutes

Actors: Kevin Kline, Denzel Washington, John Hargreaves,
Penelope Wilton, Alec McCowan, Zakes Mokae, Ian Richardson

Writer: John Briley

Director: Richard Attenborough

 *Cry Freedom*

South African Martyr

This is the story of Donald Woods, a liberal South African newspaper editor and what happened when he became interested in the work and impact of the antiapartheid black consciousness activist, Steve Biko. The story takes place from 1975–1977.

Woods publishes an article criticizing Biko without ever having met him. Challenged to interview Biko, Woods travels to King William's Town where Biko is under a banning order that restricts his movements, visitors, and activities. Despite the ban, Biko manages to show Woods a clinic, as well as the crowded township. Biko begins to explain his ideology, and the two men become friends. Woods is inspired and influenced by Biko's ideas about apartheid. He publishes articles reflecting Biko's perspective.

As a consequence, the police threaten Woods. Two of the black journalists from his paper are arrested. In the meantime, Biko ignores the ban and is arrested on his way home after speaking to students. When Biko dies in custody, it is alleged that he had been on a hunger strike. Woods secretly visits the morgue and sees that Biko's body has been severely beaten. Woods photographs the body.

SYNOPSIS

127

Donald Woods campaigns for an investigation, but is banned, put under a five-year house arrest, and forbidden to write. At great risk, he uses his time to write a book about Biko. His youngest daughter is burned by the contents of a parcel received in the mail. To get the manuscript published and in order to escape further harm to his family, he flees the country secretly, disguised as a Catholic priest. His wife and children follow a few days later and they meet in Lesotho. From there, they go to London.

COMMENTARY

This is the second time writer John Briley *(Molokai: The Father Damien Story)* and director Richard Attenborough have collaborated on a film. Both won Oscars for their work on *Gandhi* in 1982.

Cry Freedom portrays the last months in the life of the South African antiapartheid martyr, Steve Biko, and Donald Woods, editor of the *East London Daily Dispatch*. Woods led the campaign to reveal the truth about Biko's death and then wrote a book about him *(Biko)*.

The story revolves around issues of apartheid and justice, told from a white, South African perspective. Some critics see its only flaw as the (debatable) overemphasis that is given to the escape of Woods' family during the last hour of the film. The filmmakers hoped that their movie would influence the social and political peace process. In 1988, the South African government reacted strongly to the film and banned it. The rest of the world, however, paid attention and the pressure on the South African government increased. In 1990, Nelson Mandela was freed from prison, an action that led to the dismantling of apartheid in South Africa. Hope was becoming a reality.

Steve Biko's spirit was also a spirit of truth. About fifteen years after his death, the South African Truth and Reconciliation Commission began its hearings, an important experience of soul-searching for all South Africans.

Cry Freedom is a worthy successor to other Attenborough biopics such as *Chaplin, Shadowlands,* and *Gandhi.* Kevin Kline is persuasive as Donald Woods, and Denzel Washington received an Oscar nomination for his charismatic performance that effectively launched his career to stardom.

Focus: The Holy Spirit, the Advocate, is sent to inspire and to be the Spirit of Truth. Social martyrs like Steve Biko inspire others with their spirit and strength.

DIALOGUE WITH THE GOSPEL

The Holy Spirit descends upon the Samaritans in the first reading from the Acts of the Apostles. The Holy Spirit, called "the Advocate" in John's Gospel, is the gift of Jesus to his disciples. The Holy Spirit is the Spirit of Truth that the world can never see or know. The gifts of understanding, and the grace to live God's commandments, are given to those who receive the Spirit.

Steve Biko inspired a generation of fellow countrymen and women, and the world community. He is considered a martyr because he died for his belief in the fundamental dignity of all people, shown in the film's scene of his interrogation and beating. Biko took risks to build the morale of the oppressed when he defied the banning order and spoke clandestinely to a crowd at a soccer stadium, when he met with Donald Woods at the pub, and when he traveled to other townships. These risks ultimately led to Biko's arrest and death.

Like Jesus in today's Gospel, so Biko accomplished the work he was called to do. His heroism enabled others to continue his work after his death. Biko told Donald Woods his story and shared his beliefs with him, thus entrusting his tradition to his followers through Woods' writing. The Woods' dramatic escape from South Africa is an episode of modern history that *Cry Freedom* presents very well. Today, wherever people are oppressed, Biko's legacy inspires courage.

Steve Biko can be seen as a Christ-figure who, though not perfect, courageously manifests the actions and virtues of Christ in a notable way. As Christ died a just man for the sake of the unjust, giving us life in the Spirit, so did Steve Biko.

KEY SCENES AND THEMES

- Steve Biko: the man, his persecution by the authorities, his guiding Woods in the township and in understanding his ideas; Biko's arrest, torture and death.

- Donald Woods' critique, meeting Biko, his eyes opening to conditions in South African townships; Woods' change of mind and heart; his writing and campaigns; the house arrest; the journey and escape.

- The flashbacks to Biko's arrest and torture; his death; the scenes of children in Soweto and Biko's activism to overthrow apartheid.

FOR REFLECTION AND CONVERSATION

1. Though a political liberal, Donald Woods never took the time to meet with Biko until challenged to do so. Despite his hesitancy, Woods risks his own safety to put his political views into practice. The film shows Woods meeting with Biko on his own turf where they become friends. What are some other characters or scenes in the film that point to the challenge that to live what one "preaches" and believes in is not easy, but rather generous and courageous?

2. For the sake of truth and justice, Woods and his family give up their "comfort zone." They leave behind their home, country, extended family, friends, careers, schools, and financial security to make the truth of Steve Biko's life known to the world at large. The scenes when Mary is burned by acid and when Donald Woods reveals his intentions to his wife during a beach

outing illustrate the difficulty of the situation for the entire family. How did they manage to survive? What kept them going until they were safely on their way to England?

3. Steve Biko was not picture-perfect, as some imagine saints to be. He was a flawed human being like the rest of us. His life and death, though, leave a legacy of moral heroism, which is the substance of martyrdom and life in the Spirit. What kind of legacy will I leave at the end of my life? Will I be remembered as a person of the Spirit?

Prayer

Lord, continue to send your Spirit into our world to inspire people who are oppressed and who cry for freedom. Amen.

SEVENTH SUNDAY OF EASTER

Acts 1:12–14; John 17:1–11

A Man for All Seasons

U.K., 1966 / 120 minutes

Actors: Paul Scofield, Wendy Hiller, Susannah York,
Robert Shaw, John Hurt, Leo McKern, Orson Welles

Writer: Robert Bolt

Director: Fred Zinnemann

A Man for All Seasons

True to the End

SYNOPSIS

Thomas More becomes chancellor of England in 1529 during the reign of Henry VIII. He is immediately embroiled in the question of the annulment of King Henry's marriage to Catherine of Aragon. She has failed to produce a male heir and Henry wants to marry Anne Boleyn in order to sire a son.

The politics of England's assertion of the right to make its own ecclesiastical decisions involve Cardinal Wolsey as well as the scheming Thomas Cromwell. Other characters in this drama are Richard Rich, who seeks a position at court through his acquaintance with Thomas More, and the Duke of Norfolk, More's friend and supporter.

More confides in his eldest daughter, Meg, who senses the potential dangers to More. His second wife, Alice, seven years his senior, loves Thomas, but is much more concerned with the domestic side of their life.

Tested by the king, More declares that he must follow his conscience, which compels him to agree with the verdict of Rome declaring Henry's marriage to Catherine valid. More will not support the king's desire to divorce Catherine so he can marry Anne Boleyn. More is imprisoned in the Tower of London, tried, and executed.

Robert Bolt adapted his very successful play for the Oscar-winning 1966 screen version. In his introduction to the play, Bolt declares his admiration for More. He calls him an authentic human being, true to himself and to what he believed was right, even though it meant his death.

Paul Scofield first played More on stage and then went on to win an Oscar for his interpretation of More in the film version of *A Man for All Seasons*. Leo McKern plays the scheming Cromwell. Wendy Hiller is very good as Alice, and Orson Welles appears in a short but significant scene as Cardinal Wolsey. *A Man for All Seasons* won six Oscars and two additional nominations that year.

Robert Bolt went on to write screenplays for *Lawrence of Arabia, Doctor Zhivago, Ryan's Daughter, Lady Caroline Lamb, A Passage to India,* and *The Mission.*

Thomas More was canonized a saint in 1935. The film *A Man for All Seasons* is convincing and communicates More's integrity with quiet power and dignity.

Focus: Before he died, Jesus prayed that his self-giving death would witness to his truth and be a source of grace to his followers. Thomas More relied on Christ's grace as he witnessed to the truth, which cost him his life.

The second reading from the First Letter of Peter (cf. 4:13–16) focuses on sharing in the sufferings of Jesus and then sharing in his glory. "If you are insulted for the name of Christ, blessed are you...." This reading serves as an epitaph for Thomas More.

Today's Gospel reading is the beginning of Jesus' final prayer before his passion. In many ways, these words may be read as the final prayer of any martyr, but they suit Thomas

More particularly well. This is because, like Jesus, More was a public figure and his decisions affected others who looked to him for leadership and good example.

Jesus prays and acknowledges the reality of his coming death. He gives himself for the glory of God, and proclaims that eternal life consists in knowing the only true God. Jesus' priestly prayer parallels the moment when, after a long silence, More finally discharges his conscience before Parliament. More has finished the work that God gave him to do. He has made God's name and will known to those in government, to the king, and to his family and friends.

As he dies, More prays for the world he leaves behind. His final wish is that they know God's truth.

KEY SCENES AND THEMES

- Thomas More's integrity, the king's marriage and re-marriage; the Church's role; the role of personal integrity and conscience.

- The pressure on More from the King, Wolsey, and Cromwell; the attitudes of More's friends: Norfolk, Richard Rich, and William Roper; Meg's support; Alice's bewilderment.

- More's trial, his wisdom and grace, Cromwell's attack; More's farewell to his family; his trial; his execution.

FOR REFLECTION AND CONVERSATION

1. Thomas More believed and succeeded in living an almost seamless, integrated Christian life, one that his wife had difficulty understanding. Recall More's discussion with his friend, Norfolk. Norfolk tries to entice Thomas to come along with the others who have capitulated to the king about the divorce "for fellowship." Why wouldn't Thomas go along? What moral circumstances today (artificial birth control; premarital sex; abortion; pre-nuptial agreements; divorce and

remarriage; adultery; fetal stem cell research; human cloning; the manufacturing, selling, and use of illegal drugs; political and business ethics…) could evoke a conversation like this between "friends"? What would your answers be to such questions?

2. Few saints have influenced the modern world with such a sterling example of moral integrity and faith as Thomas More. He was consistent and true to the end. Recall his speech at the trial when he finally "discharges his conscience." How does his speech validate his position on the issue of the king's divorce from Queen Catherine? How does he address the issue of personal and public or political morals and ethics? Is Thomas More convincing to his hearers at the time? Now? Why or why not?

3. Thomas More respected the law and tried his best to use the law to his moral advantage, as he explained to his daughter Meg. Perhaps one of the most moving scenes in the film is when she and More's wife visit him in his prison cell in the Tower of London. How effectively does this dramatization of the choice More has to make between family and his beliefs portray the dilemma of the entire film? How is the viewer engaged in Thomas More's struggle?

Prayer

St. Thomas More, you were a man of integrity and conscience. Pray with us for the courage to stand by our beliefs no matter the risk. Amen.

Born on the Fourth of July

U.S., 1989 / 144 minutes

Actors: Tom Cruise, Willem Dafoe, Raymond J. Barry,
Caroline Kava, Kyra Sedgwick, Tom Berenger, Frank Whaley,
Lili Taylor, Abbie Hoffman, Tom Sizemore

Writers: Oliver Stone, Ron Kovic

Director: Oliver Stone

Born on the Fourth of July

From War to Peace

SYNOPSIS

Little boys play soldiers on Long Island in the mid-1950s. Ron Kovic, who is from a Polish-American Catholic family, is recruited during his high school years to join the Marines and go to Vietnam. He is an unquestioning enthusiast. But the experience of the war is confusing, especially when he kills Billy, a fellow-American, in "friendly fire" and is advised to cover it up.

Kovic is wounded and repatriated. He is determined to walk again and undergoes grueling rehabilitation, but must resign himself to being a paraplegic. He is feted on his return to his hometown for Independence Day celebrations (he was born on July 4). But he rages against the establishment, family, Church, Jesus, the U.S., and drops out of society on a protracted binge of drugs, alcohol, and sex. He is saved when he visits Billy's grave, confesses to Billy's family, and receives their forgiveness. This enables him to take up his life again, and he campaigns against Richard Nixon and the war.

COMMENTARY

Ron Kovic is pictured as a 1960s white, suburban, all-American man. He is a star athlete, clean-cut, idealistic, fervently religious, patriotic, filled with the American Dream: truly born on July 4. He volunteers to go to Vietnam and it becomes a journey from innocence to disillusionment. Kovic sees "action," is wounded and becomes a paraplegic. He receives a hero's welcome following an atrocious hospital and recuperation experience. The film recounts Kovic's journey from believing in the Vietnam War as a noble cause to knowing it to be an utterly destructive and immoral effort. He becomes an angry anti-war protester.

The pivotal scene in the film is when Kovic visits the family of the young soldier he mistakenly killed. The scene captures Ron's confession via flashbacks to the indiscriminate, insane killing of women and children, and the moment when he shoots Billy. The most moving and intense scene in the film occurs when Billy's mother forgives Kovic.

Kovic and director Oliver Stone *(Salvador, Wall Street, Talk Radio)* collaborated on this powerful screenplay. Stone directed the film with an almost physical intensity, making it a memorable piece of Americana. It is the second in his Vietnam "trilogy," coming between *Platoon* and *Heaven and Earth.* Though two and a half hours long, the film speeds by, propelling us through Kovic's experiences, one after the other. Tom Cruise gives such an intelligent and empathetic performance that watching him makes us feel he *is* Kovic and we can identify with him.

Focus: Ron Kovic prayed to Jesus on the cross before he went to Vietnam, then denounced Jesus on the cross when he came back maimed for life. Through successive experiences he is graced by God's Spirit, as were the disciples in the upper room. He finds new strength and a life of conviction and action.

DIALOGUE WITH THE GOSPEL

Just as the disciples were huddled in the upper room in fear and unable to comprehend what had happened to Jesus on Calvary, so Ron Kovic huddles in fear, is unable to walk, and hides himself with disillusioned friends who wallow in self-pity. He curses the Crucified Jesus saying that while Jesus can get off the cross in three days, he has to remain in his wheelchair forever.

After his war experience, Ron's spirit needs peace and strength. Ron wheels himself to Billy's gravesite, meditates, and then drives to the dead man's home. The soldier's parents, wife, and child welcome him and they tell Ron how they learned Billy was dead, and how the Army officer told them that he died quickly and heroically.

Ron confesses, and in so doing, shows his inner wounds to the family, an act that strengthens all of them. Jesus, too, showed his wounds to the disciples in today's Gospel, so they would be strengthened and would be able to believe. The father tells Kovic they don't need to hear what happened. The daughter-in-law and her son, who is playing with a gun, says that she will never be able to forgive him, but perhaps the Lord will. It is Billy's mother, her face giving way to grief at Kovic's information, who offers absolution. She breathes the peace of Christ on him so that he is forgiven and released from his guilt. Then, without a word of recrimination, and as the culmination of this spirit-filled experience, she says with heartbreaking empathy, "We know, Ron, the pain you've been going through."

KEY SCENES AND THEMES

- Ron: the idealist, John F. Kennedy's speeches; Ron's Catholic home, the religious motivations, the crucifixes, his prayer before the crucifix and his dedication; the Fourth of July parade, Ron's inability to speak, the differences at home and his attacks on the crucifix, religion, on America itself; the lies that Ron had been fed; Ron's mother ousting him from the house.

- The war pictured in brief sequences with the screen's golden hue contrasting the devastating action; the confusion and the soldier's death.

- Ron's visit to the grave, meeting the family, the sharing of memories with the mother and father, the widow and her young son; Ron's need for truth, his need to confess; the mother's care and concern about his pain.

1. Catholicism is a sacramental religion. Sacraments are visible signs that represent invisible realities. Sacramentals are religious articles or rituals (for example, the crucifix, a statue of a saint, the sign of the cross) that symbolize religious belief or devotion and point to the realities they represent. Hollywood loves Catholic symbols and imagery because they are so rich in meaning and can be used as a silent but visual kind of shorthand (such as the crucifix in the background that indicates a Catholic home), though this has the added possible disadvantage for stereotyping. *Born on the Fourth of July*, of course, is the story of a Catholic man and his journey to spiritual renewal. How does the religious imagery in the film help construct the plot? What is it meant to evoke in the audience?

FOR REFLECTION AND CONVERSATION

2. The cemetery where Billy is buried, his family home, and even the day Ron chooses to visit both places, seem bleak and lifeless. The color tone is brownish, and our emotional response to the imagery is a feeling of desolation and hopelessness. Yet today's liturgy asks the Lord to send out his Spirit and renew the face of the earth. How is Ron's spirit finally renewed? How is *Born on the Fourth of July* a Catholic film that goes beyond symbolism to action?

3. The entire sequence when Ron goes into Billy's home to meet his family is made up of close-ups so that we can identify with the characters. The expressive and intense look on the face of Billy's mother when she realizes how her son died and that Ron was responsible is one of the most poignant scenes in recent movie history. Billy's mother seems quiet and slow of speech, but she processes what is happening almost instantaneously. Through her empathy for the pain Ron is going through, we know he is forgiven. His journey from war to peace is close at hand. With our personal need for forgiveness, what are some ways that we can identify with Ron? with Billy's mother by our willingness to forgive?

Prayer

As your disciples huddled in fear, Lord, you sent your Spirit with the gift of peace. Whatever our fears, our disbelief, whatever our sufferings, send your Spirit to heal us. Amen.

Les Miserables

U.S., 1998 / 131 minutes

Actors: Liam Neeson, Geoffrey Rush, Uma Thurman,
Claire Danes, Paris Vaughan

Writer: Rafael Yglesias

Director: Bille August

Les Miserables

The Face of God

SYNOPSIS

The setting is France at the beginning of the nineteenth century. After Jean Valjean has served a sentence of almost twenty years of hard labor for stealing a loaf of bread, he is released on the condition that he report regularly to the police. On his journey he is given hospitality by a bishop, but then steals candlesticks and silverware from his house. When the bishop tells the police that the items were his gift to Valjean, Valjean decides to devote his life to helping the needy. He does not disclose his past and is so successful in developing a new town factory that, in his newfound respectability, he is elected mayor.

However, his nemesis, the unrelenting Inspector Javert who wants to arrest Valjean, is assigned to the town as Prefect of Police. This leads to the undoing of all that Valjean has achieved. When he assists an ailing factory worker named Fantine, he promises to care for Cosette, her young daughter. Fantine dies, and Valjean eludes Javert and takes refuge in Paris with Cosette. They live quietly in a convent for many years where Valjean is the caretaker.

There are political uprisings in Paris and young Republican enthusiasts join the fight against the royal forces at the barricades. Cosette falls in love with Marius, one of the Republicans. Javert arrives in Paris where he ultimately comes face to face with Valjean. Javert is captured by Marius and his companions and placed in Valjean's custody. Valjean refuses to take revenge on Javert and frees him. Marius is then captured by the royalists and Javert captures Valjean as Valjean rescues Marius. Javert cannot live with Valjean's mercy; he frees Valjean and then kills himself. Finally, Valjean walks along the river, a free man.

COMMENTARY

Nowadays, everyone has their own memories of *Les Miserables*. Besides the five previous film versions (Richard Boleslawski's in 1937; an Italian version and U.S. version in 1952, directed by Lewis Milestone; a French adaptation in 1957; another U.S. remake in 1978, directed by Glen Jordan; and numerous TV mini-series), the stage musical has become a significant part of people's experience of Victor Hugo's classic that condemns the social inequalities and injustice of nineteenth-century France.

Bille August's present dramatization is a fairly solemn interpretation and may seem somewhat flat without the now familiar musical score to accompany it. Liam Neeson is a worthy presence as Jean Valjean. Academy Award winner and nominee Geoffrey Rush (Best Actor 1997, *Shine;* Best Actor 2001, *Quills*) gives an understated performance and successfully becomes a menacing Javert, the ultimate policeman with an all-pervading sense of duty.

The first half of the movie concentrates on Valjean as mayor, while telling the tragic story of his youthful petty "crime" and extreme punishment. We see Valjean's compassion and care for Fantine, skillfully played by Uma Thurman. This part of the film also places Javert and his relentless pursuit of Valjean in context. Valjean's move to Paris, Cosette's romance, and the barricades make the movie more spectacular and melodramatic, while it remains efficient rather than emotional. This 1998 version of *Les Miserables* was filmed at beautiful sites in Prague and Paris, thus capturing the realistic atmosphere of the period.

> *Focus: God so loved the world that he sent his Son to share our lives with us. In Jesus we are able to see what God, our Father, is like. The love of the Father and the Son brings forth the Spirit. In admirable characters like Jean Valjean we see all the dimensions of the love of the Holy Trinity—Father, Son, and Spirit— for the world.*

DIALOGUE WITH THE GOSPEL

On this celebration of the Holy Trinity, the Church is invited once again to contemplate the central doctrine of the Creed and the wonder of the Incarnation, of what it means for the Divine to be found in human form. In the first reading from the Book of Exodus, we see that in the past the mystery of God was revealed in signs like the cloud at Sinai. The Gospel tells us that the Father so loved us that he sent his Son to share our human experience. Through Jesus, human and Divine, the mystery of God's love has been revealed in our world. God is truly a God of tenderness and compassion, slow to anger, rich in mercy. In Jesus, we see the Incarnation of this love.

One of the most admirable figures in literature (akin to Marcel Pagnol's less well-known Jean de Florette) is Victor Hugo's Jean Valjcan. He is one of the great heroes of fiction, along with Hugo's Quasimodo in *The Hunchback of Notre Dame*.

Jean Valjean is a Christ-figure of a high order because he embodies the great qualities of Jesus. Through the choices he makes in his life, he manifests something of the Incarnation's reality, a glimpse of the Divine in the human. Valjean is a victim of a cruel system of injustice, suffering harsh punishment for the crime of being hungry, and condemned as a criminal for the rest of his life. His conversion experience from bitterness to love, which is aided by his encounter with the generous bishop, is profound.

From that moment on, Jean Valjean sacrifices himself unselfishly for the town, for Fantine, for her daughter Cosette, for Marius, and ultimately for Javert himself. Valjean becomes an instrument of grace, a sign of the love of God. The musical captures this, especially in Valjean's lyrics and in the despairing lyrics of Javert. How can we experience the triune God? "To love another person is to see the face of God."

KEY SCENES AND THEMES

- Jean Valjean dines with the bishop, then robs him; the bishop responds with forgiveness and generosity, giving him the silver objects; Valjean's experience of "grace."

- Fantine, her reputation and desperation to find work to support her daughter; her illness; Valjean's kindness, his "tenderness and compassion;" his goodness to her and his promise to take care of Cosette; Valjean's fatherly love for Cosette; his going to the barricades and saving Marius.

- Javert as the face of vindictive justice; the confrontations with Javert at the barricades and in the sewers; Valjean does not condemn, but shows the forgiveness of God; he lets Javert go free; Javert's inability to receive this grace and his subsequent suicide.

FOR REFLECTION AND CONVERSATION

1. From novel to film, *Les Miserables* is a tale that reflects the historical context of its writing (1862) and is firmly rooted in the literary and philosophical Romanticism of its time. Romanticism as a movement (1750–1870) has many dimensions. Because the novel (and film) celebrates the triumph of freedom over tyranny and

emphasizes the rights of the individual, *Les Miserables* is one of Romanticism's notable achievements. Also, the particular "romantic" elements echo the main tenets of Christian teaching about the human person. How is human dignity celebrated in *Les Miserables*? How do the convergence of lighting, camera angles, and editing in the film draw our attention to the humanity of Valjean?

2. The reading from Paul's Second Letter to the Corinthians (cf. 13:11–13) mentions the Three Persons of the Trinity explicitly and teaches us to "live in harmony and peace so that the God of love and peace" will be with us. How do the words and actions of the bishop in the film parallel Paul's teaching? How does Jean Valjean incarnate these teachings throughout his life? How does he show the face of God? In what ways is *Les Miserables* a story that is both human and divine?

3. At the end of the film, Javert testifies that he has always tried to uphold laws and rules in his life and as a policeman...until he frees Valjean. Why does Javert take his own life? What is the source of his despair? What role did civil law play in his life? What do you think Victor Hugo was trying to say about obedience to civil law and God's law of love?

Prayer

Jesus, Word made flesh, you are the pattern for our living, the face of God on earth. Send us your Spirit so that we can share in your grace every day of our life. Amen.

Deuteronomy 8:2–3, 14–16; John 6:51–58

Places in the Heart

U.S., 1984 / 113 minutes

Actors: Sally Field, John Malkovich, Lindsay Crouse,
Danny Glover, Ed Harris, Amy Madigan

Writer: Robert Benton

Director: Robert Benton

Places in the Heart

United in Eucharist

SYNOPSIS

Edna Spalding lives with her family outside of Waxahachie, Texas in 1935. Her husband, a sheriff, is unintentionally shot by a black man who is then lynched without a trial. Because she is almost destitute, the bank manager recommends that she sell her farm. Edna decides not to, preferring to try to make it work. Moze, an itinerant black man whom she once befriended, offers to handle the work if she sows a crop of cotton.

Edna's sister Margaret lives in town and is having trouble with her husband who seems to be planning to leave her for the local schoolteacher, but he decides to stay with his wife. The bank manager insists that Edna take in a boarder in order to keep up the mortgage payments. The boarder is a young blind man named Mr. Will who is embarrassed and depressed at first, but who eventually becomes involved with life on the farm.

Moze and Mr. Will are a great help to Edna. Things are going ahead rather well when a tornado strikes and cotton prices fall. To get the best price, Edna has to get her crop in before everyone else. Moze hires black workers, and Edna persuades her family, including Margaret and her husband, to help harvest the crop

The Ku Klux Klan tries to lynch Moze, but are thwarted by Mr. Will.

The whole town gathers for a worship service. The sharing of communion symbolizes equality and the breaking down of all barriers.

COMMENTARY

Places in the Heart, nominated for seven Academy Awards in 1984 and the winner of two, is a moving piece of Americana. It is the story of a mother who tries to support her children by making her farm productive during the Great Depression.

The movie's detailed re-creation of the period gives the audience a feeling of authenticity. Robert Benton, who wrote and directed the film, based it on his own memories of the era and his family. *Places in the Heart* won Benton his second Oscar. His first was for the 1979 *Kramer vs. Kramer.* Sally Field also won her second Oscar for her portrayal of Edna, the struggling mother.

The early 1980s saw a number of movies that looked at people on the land as they tried to preserve their families, confront the hazards of weather and the pressure of banks that threatened foreclosure. Two of these films are worthy of mention: *Country,* starring Jessica Lange, and *The River,* with Mel Gibson and Sissy Spacek.

Places in the Heart's sub-plots include racism, poverty, sexism, treatment of the handicapped, and family. Danny Glover, a sharp, hard-working black man, is attacked by the KKK. John Malkovich is a blind man no one wants. Sally Field is the protected wife until she decides to live her own life; then, she is criticized and thwarted. Ed Harris (nominated for a Best Actor Academy Award in 2001 for his performance in *Pollack*) and Amy Madigan play the adulterous couple that finally decides to end their affair.

Benton's screenplay brings the themes and the characters together in a final communion celebration with a reading from St. Paul to the Corinthians on love (cf. 1 Cor 13).

DIALOGUE WITH THE GOSPEL

Focus: The characters in Places in the Heart *are ordinary people who must struggle, but are ultimately united in reconciliation and communion in the body and blood of Christ.*

The reading from Deuteronomy recalls the chosen people's years of wandering the desert which parallels the setting of *Places in the Heart*. In both situations, the people experienced hunger and thirst, were humbled and tested.

The residents of the Texas town depicted in the film are God-fearing Christians who try to live their lives well. Sometimes they fall. Often, injustice and racism bear down on them. But the bottom line, the movie tells us, is that these townsfolk are good people.

The story ends with all the main characters joined in communion in their church. The preacher reads about love from chapter 13 of Paul's First Letter to the Corinthians. Today's brief second reading from 1 Corinthians (cf. 10:16–17) sums up this final scene completely, because it shows the town as "one body," a community of love.

This cinematic sequence draws meaning from the Gospel passage in which Jesus tells his followers that they must eat his body and drink his blood to have life. In the movie, we see each character pass the bread and wine from one to the other. The bread is the real food and the wine is the real drink, symbolizing the body and blood of Christ which unites families and friends, husbands and wives, neighbors and enemies, the handicapped and the healthy, blacks and whites... Christ has found a place in the heart of each one.

KEY SCENES AND THEMES

• The hard-put Texas family; the mother's backbreaking work for her family; the children's needs; the stranger and the blind man who are taken into the family.

- The people's faults and failings, their hurts and prejudices; the blind man's struggles; the husband who betrays his wife; the Ku Klux Klan; the mother's survival in a man's world.

- The final sequence in the church: the hymns and prayers, the recitation of the Last Supper story, St. Paul's words on love, everyone sharing in communion.

FOR REFLECTION AND CONVERSATION

1. Racism, sexism, poverty, prejudices and temptations of every kind are part of the history and culture in all of human history, including the Bible. How is the story of *Places in the Heart* a perennial human story? What makes it a Christian story?

2. One key incident in the film is very reminiscent of a pivotal scene in *Les Miserables*: when Moze steals Edna's silverware and she forgives and hires him. In many ways, Moze is similar to Jean Valjean. How do the social, political, and religious elements of both stories compare? What is the moral of these stories for us today?

3. The eucharist/communion scene in the movie is a feast of love that unites the townspeople and strengthens them to emerge from their private worlds to become Christ's love for others. Why are the dead shown as part of the community at worship? How is this closing scene a vision of how things will be for those who do as Christ did and partake of his body and blood in love?

Prayer

Jesus, on the night before you died you gave us your body as the Bread of Life and your blood as Life-Giving Drink. Draw all people together in communion with you, no matter what our differences may be or the sins we have committed. Amen.

The Horse Whisperer

U.S., 1998 / 170 minutes

Actors: Robert Redford, Kristin Scott Thomas,
Scarlet Johansson, Sam Neill, Diane Wiest, Chris Cooper

Writers: Richard LaGravenese, Eric Roth

Director: Robert Redford

The Horse Whisperer

Gentle Healer

SYNOPSIS

Annie MacLean is a New York magazine editor with a thirteen-year-old daughter, Grace. Grace has a horse named Pilgrim. Grace and Pilgrim are badly injured when they collide with a truck on an icy road. It becomes evident that Grace's recovery hinges on Pilgrim's.

Tom Booker is a Montana "horse whisperer," someone who has an almost mystical way with horses. Annie asks Tom to help with Pilgrim's recovery, but he declines. Annie and Grace drive with the horse to Montana anyway, and Tom agrees to work with Pilgrim.

Frank Booker, Tom's brother, suggests that mother and daughter stay at the ranch while the horse heals. They agree and Grace gradually improves. Annie is fired from her job and her husband Robert arrives. He sees Grace riding confidently, although she lost a leg in the accident. She and Pilgrim are both healed, although it becomes evident that Annie also needs healing.

Tom, whose wife left him to go to the city, is attracted to Annie despite her sharp edges and big city persona, and she to him. Robert tells her that she can have time to decide

151

about her future. She appreciates all that Tom has done for her and, though tempted, she makes her choice: she drives back to New York and to her family.

COMMENTARY

Robert Redford obviously liked Nicholas Evans' very popular novel because he produced a visually beautiful film featuring the Rockies, the plains, and the horses of Montana. He also warms to the role of Tom Booker, the laconic horse expert who shares his work with his brother (Chris Cooper) and his wife (Dianne Wiest) and their children. The life on a Montana ranch is picturesque and ideal.

In New York, however, Annie (Kristin Scott Thomas) is a tough, workaholic editor with a husband (Sam Neill) and a teenage daughter (Scarlet Johansson) who is involved in a horrific accident with her horse. It is clear that the film is not only about the recovery of the girl and the rehabilitation of the severely injured and traumatized horse, but also a story about the freedom of open spaces and rediscovering one's true self. The film is long and sometimes languid.

Even when situations are difficult, Redford tells stories with a delicate touch, such as he demonstrated with *Ordinary People* and *A River Runs Through It. The Horse Whisperer* is a film about moral choices, about the attractions of the moment, but more importantly, about the long-term consequences of these choices and doing the right thing.

The Horse Whisperer opens with gentle visions of early morning and fresh snow. We are then treated to lavish views and impressive riding sequences. By contrast, the initial accident is almost too powerful. The film ends somewhat differently than the book, and perhaps more satisfactorily.

DIALOGUE WITH THE GOSPEL

Focus: The Gospel singles out John the Baptist as the one who announced the coming of Jesus as the fullness of life; and now, having led people to Jesus, it is time for him to take a lesser place. The horse whisperer is a healer who recedes into the background as those who are healed go on to live their lives.

The first reading from Isaiah is one of the four descriptions of the mysterious Servant of the Lord. The messianic Servant is described as one who gives light to the nations. The Gospel gives us an appealing picture of Jesus, John the Baptist, and the coming of the Spirit.

Like Isaiah's Servant Songs that described the Messiah, John the Baptist was a herald who foretold the eminent coming of the Messiah. As Jesus became more visible and important, the Baptist was able to withdraw into the background. John the Baptist was a healer of souls and a precursor of the fullness of life, the kind of fullness of life that Paul alludes to in the second reading (cf. 1 Cor 1:1–3).

By considering *The Horse Whisperer* in the context of the readings, we can see young Grace MacLean as a person who needs healing in both body and soul. The body-soul connection is symbolized by her mysterious connection to her horse Pilgrim, also needing to return to health. We know that Grace's healing is only beginning (Grace's name seems to have special meaning here) because she is young; the time in Montana will sustain her for the rest of her life. There is enough healing to go around, because when Annie chooses to follow her daughter and husband back to New York, she chooses wellbeing over selfishness.

Tom Booker can be seen as an echo of John the Baptist. As a horse whisperer, he soothes and gradually leads horses back to health. He becomes a soul healer as well. He is gentle, understanding, and patient. Like John the Baptist, at the end of the movie he has to withdraw and let something greater— the challenge of life and fidelity—take over. He must grow less and less in the lives of Annie and Grace, even as he has enabled and empowered them to live.

KEY SCENES AND THEMES

- The MacLeans' family relationships; Annie and her work, Robert and his work, their love for Grace; Grace's love for Pilgrim, the impact of the horrific accident.

- The Montana setting: Tom Booker away from the city, his special ability; Booker's family, the lifestyle at the ranch; Booker's care for horses, his skill in healing Pilgrim and Grace.

- Grace's triumphant ride, the triumph of healing; Robert and Annie watching, Annie's relationship with Tom; Annie's final choices and her own healing.

FOR REFLECTION AND CONVERSATION

1. The Gospel today focuses on humility and gentleness of spirit. How does *The Horse Whisperer* ask us to pay attention to humility, to carry out a role when needed and then to step aside? How is humility and grace at the center of the conflict in this film? Why is gentleness so important to living creatures and human relationships?

2. Thousands of people are injured in accidents every year around the world, but few have the financial means to go to a place like Tom Booker's ranch in Montana and demand healing from a reluctant healer. What social message is there in the film for those of us who may need healing, but are without the material means to do as Annie did? How do we claim our rights in truth and humility as human beings if we do not have the advantages of those who are well off? And if we have the means, what can we do to help bring healing to others with generosity, grace, and gentleness?

3. How does the cinematography of *The Horse Whisperer* reinforce the message that humility and grace are essential elements for healing? Recall the opening sequence of the film when Grace awakes, sees the statue of the horse and is happy, knowing she will soon be out riding with her friend in the snow. How does Grace, both her name and as a character, epitomize the message of *The Horse Whisperer*? What other scenes in the movie show the kind of grace that is needed for healing and living?

Prayer

Jesus, John the Baptist heralded your coming by calling people to repentance and healing. May we help to prepare your way today, and then step aside to make room for the fullness of your grace. Amen.

Saving Private Ryan
U.S., 1998 / 170 minutes
Actors: Tom Hanks, Tom Sizemore, Edward Burns,
Jeremy Davies, Matt Damon, Giovanni Ribisi
Writers: Robert Rodat, Frank Darabont
Director: Steven Spielberg

Saving Private Ryan

Embracing Your Mission in Life

SYNOPSIS

It is June 6, 1944, D-Day. The Allied troops land on Omaha Beach in Normandy. Captain Miller is a squadron leader. After the deadly and horror-filled landing, he is asked to lead his men on a special mission of dubious merit to find a Private James Ryan. Ryan is one of four sons in the U.S. military and when the other three are killed, top military officials in Washington want the surviving son to return home to his mother.

Miller and six men take on the mission. In an American-occupied town they find the wrong Private Ryan. They continue on and encounter a German guard-post where a sniper kills one of the men. The translator, Corporal Upham, persuades Miller not to kill the sniper, and they let him go. They eventually find the right Ryan in a squad defending a bridge, but he refuses to leave.

During an attack, Upham cowers in fear while the sniper they had released shoots one of the team. Miller is also killed, but U.S. planes save the troops and the bridge is held. Upham confronts the sniper and kills him. Private Ryan is saved.

Decades later, Ryan and his family visit Miller's grave in France.

156

Steven Spielberg recreates the 1944 Normandy invasion, a grizzly, compelling, visual commentary on the experience of war. The movie opens with the D-Day landing itself. The handheld camera, skillful editing, and special effects make audiences feel like they, too, are experiencing that heroic but dreadful landing.

The rest of the film is characterized by a more familiar style. It is a story of a search mission, led by Tom Hanks as Miller, to find an obscure soldier. The soldiers encounter Germans several times. The sequences do not shirk the reality of the violence or the aggressive behavior that war and the death of friends can create. Once Private Ryan is found, the film immerses the audience again in the throes of battle.

Saving Private Ryan is often very sad and quite moving because the characters and the moral dilemmas are portrayed so convincingly. This is especially true of Tom Hanks, whose presence gives the film its strength. He is a man who strives for integrity, even decency, in situations that seem impossible and are indeed horrible. This type of role suits Hanks well, as he went on to prove in his performance in *Cast Away*, for which he won a Best Actor Golden Globe in 2001.

Spielberg provides us with a cinematic experience that involves us emotionally from the first moment so that we may reflect afterward on the meaning of war, the morality of its causes, and the destruction and loss of human life that necessarily follow the decision to engage in war.

Focus: At the beginning of his ministry, Jesus is presented as a leader who chooses apostles and sends them on mission. In some way, Saving Private Ryan *mirrors this episode in Matthew's narrative.*

In the first reading from Isaiah, the people have been in darkness, but now the light shines. The yoke of their oppressors has been broken. *Saving Private Ryan's* cinematic re-enactment of the deadly D-Day invasion can be seen as breaking the Nazi's oppressive yoke, and at the same time as a commitment to life and freedom.

The quotation from Isaiah is repeated in the Gospel reading which recounts the call of the apostles. They too were ordinary men who were given an extraordinary mission: to proclaim good news, peace, and healing.

The film's action revolves around the character of Captain Miller, played by Tom Hanks. Miller is the squad leader who calls his men into action. He knows them and trusts them to do what they have been asked to do.

When Miller's squad receives the mission to save Private Ryan, the men grumble at first, but then answer their call. And despite the horrors of battle, Miller and his followers, with great personal sacrifice, fulfill their task of "salvation" for the Ryan family. Captain Miller is remembered with veneration at the opening and closing of the film because he not only saved Private Ryan, but he laid down his life for the men who answered the call to a special mission.

KEY SCENES AND THEMES

- The Normandy landing: the fear, seasickness; the barge fronts opening, the immediate mowing down of the troops, the constant barrage of bullets, deaths, and injuries; the men's courage to go on, their drive to survive, their impressive military skills.

- The soldiers as ordinary men: their backgrounds and personalities, their experience of being thrown together to fight, their personal strengths and weaknesses; Captain Miller's teaching background and leadership qualities.

- The deaths of Private Ryan's brothers, his mother's grief, the military's decision to send a search squad; war: its justice and its futility; the symbolism of the attempt to save the little French girl; Ryan's visit to Miller's grave.

1. One definition of leadership says it consists in leading others where they would not go by themselves. How does Captain Miller's leadership fit this ideal? Whose leadership did he follow? How does the film show him to be both a courageous yet hesitant leader at the same time? What is the source of his integrity?

FOR REFLECTION AND CONVERSATION

2. The opening and closing scenes of the film show wide shots of the military cemetery in Normandy covered with crosses. One Star of David is visible. Why do you think Spielberg chose to emphasize religious symbolism (crucifixes are also evident in several scenes) as part of the parallel structure of the movie? Could he have been asking how far our religion has brought us? How does our faith influence the governance of nations and the upholding of the dignity of every human being? Is peace in our day truly possible, and if it is, what is the role of religion in bringing it about?

3. On the bridge in the village, Captain Miller tells Private Ryan to do the best he can in life and that will be enough. In the final scene, Ryan approaches Miller's grave to tell him that this advice has guided him each day since the war, and that he hopes his efforts have been enough. What is required for this seemingly

simple advice to be integrated into a person's life and choices? What do you think is the overall message of *Saving Private Ryan?*

Prayer

Lord, you were the greatest leader who showed the way to life by example. You were prepared to lay down your life for us. Help those in leadership, especially when they must face life-and-death challenges. Amen.

Snow Falling on Cedars

U.S., 1999 / 126 minutes

Actors: Ethan Hawke, James Cromwell, Richard Jenkins,
James Rebhorn, Max von Sydow, Sam Shepard,
Youki Kudoh, Rick Yune, Eric Thal

Writers: Ron Bass, Scott Hicks

Director: Scott Hicks

Snow Falling on Cedars

The Poor in Spirit

The setting is Washington State in 1950. When fisherman Carl Heine is found dead on his boat, his friend Kazuo Miyamoto is charged with his murder. The trial brings back memories of racial prejudice and the internment of American-born Japanese during World War II.

SYNOPSIS

Through flashbacks we learn that Carl's father was in the process of selling some land to Kazuo's father. The negotiations were interrupted by the internment. After the war, Carl's mother refuses to honor the agreement because, at the time of his death, Carl's father was reconsidering the arrangement.

Journalist Ishmael Chambers covers the murder case and is distracted by his lifelong love for Hatsue, a Japanese woman who was also interned and is now Kazuo's wife. There were happy times for the Japanese before the war when they were able to preserve the traditions of their homeland and be Americans at the same time. Hatsue and Ishmael grow up together, first as friends and then lovers. Hatsue's mother strongly warns her not to marry an American and insists she marry a Japanese man. Though they exchanged some letters during the war, Hatsue follows her mother's demands and severs her relationship with Ishmael. He receives her letter with this news as he recovers from losing an arm in battle.

Ishmael remembers his father, the local newspaper editor, as a man who stood for values and opposed prejudice at great cost to his livelihood. Kazuo's trial is marked by the racial bias and contempt of the prosecutor, although the wise, elderly Nels Gudmundsson ably defends Kazuo. Ishmael struggles with his feelings of love and antipathy towards Hatsue, who rejected his love. He decides to put his hurt feelings aside to follow the clues that lead to the declaration of Kazuo's innocence. Hatsue embraces Ishmael for the last time and the Japanese bow in respectful thanks to him for doing the right thing. All can now resume their lives and lay the past to rest.

COMMENTARY

Snow Falling on Cedars is Ron Bass' adaptation of David Guterson's very popular novel of the same title. Both tell about life in the U.S. Northwest and its heritage of antagonism to the local Japanese during and after World War II. Australian director Scott Hicks co-wrote the screenplay. This was Hicks' first movie following his international success with *Shine*. The writers turn the feel of the novel's prose into visions of the land, seascapes, climate, and seasons of the region. The movie looks and feels authentic. The music is hauntingly beautiful, almost religious in tone.

Ethan Hawke is credible as the conflicted young journalist who loves and respects his father, but who feels he is always expected to live up to his father's reputation. A strong cast of character actors is led by Max von Sydow, who makes a significant speech about prejudice during the trial. Because of its measured pace, the film's substantial drama requires the undivided attention of its audience.

DIALOGUE WITH THE GOSPEL

Focus: The film's plot and the characters' reactions and responses illustrate various aspects of the Beatitudes.

The first reading from the prophet Zephaniah sets a tone for thinking about the community and individuals in *Snow Falling on Cedars*. Those who suffer and remain faithful, no matter the trials they undergo, can be seen as God's poor, God's humble people of the land. After their troubles, they will be at peace. By the end of the film this does indeed happen for the Japanese community, the townspeople, and Ishmael.

The words of Paul to the Corinthians (cf. 1 Cor 1:26–31) tell us who is wise and who is foolish. We see this mirrored in the movie by the cross-examinations and summations of the prosecutor, the defense counsel and the final remarks of the presiding judge.

Today's Gospel is the beginning of the Sermon on the Mount: the Beatitudes. The characters of the film illustrate aspects of the Beatitudes. The Japanese have been forced by the war and suspicion to become "the poor in spirit." They accept their plight with gentleness as they mourn the loss of their dignity and identity. They have hungered and thirsted for justice during the war and now, a few short years after their internment, they experience injustice again, this time in their own town. They have been and are persecuted.

Ishmael ultimately proves himself a man of beatitude when he decides to put his personal feelings aside and pursue leads on the case that eventually reveal the truth. He becomes a peacemaker.

KEY SCENES AND THEMES

- Island life: the fishermen, the strawberry picking, the festival, the farmers and the newspaper editor; the disruption of the war, American Japanese deportation after police harassment; the stark hardship of life in California's Manzanar camp.

- Carl and Kazuo on the boat; the various reactions to finding Carl's body, the sheriff's uprightness; the hostility of Carl's mother in court, the prosecutor's venom, the defense's calm, the grief of the Japanese.

• Ishmael's warm childhood memories of Hatsue, their separation and her silence; Ishmael's honorable father; his bitter war experience and injury, Hatsue's letter; Ishmael's decision to investigate events; the courtroom honor given by the Japanese.

FOR REFLECTION AND CONVERSATION

1. In 1944, the U.S. Supreme Court ruled 6–3 that the internment of Japanese Americans in World War II was not a racially motivated action. However, one of the justices wrote a dissenting opinion stating that military leaders had described Japanese Americans as belonging to "an enemy race." How can ordinary speech and actions reflect racial biases? How can we become more aware of the racial attitudes which create the unintentional biases underpinning our conversations and behavior? How does the film show the way racial bias seeped into all the events portrayed?

2. From childhood Ishmael and Hatsue love one another, yet Hatsue bends to her mother's insistence that she marry within her own culture, not unlike the pressure that Rose's mother exerts on her in James Cameron's 1997 blockbuster, *Titanic.* Compare the social, cultural, and racial elements of the stories of Hatsue and Rose. How free was each of them to pursue their own happiness? What kind of freedom characterizes Hatsue and Ishmael by the end of the film? What is the meaning of true human freedom?

3. At first glance the Beatitudes may seem to condone or glorify human suffering because the burden of justice seems placed on ordinary people and not on those

in power. The Beatitudes, however, do not discrimi-
nate. How can we be people of the Beatitudes and
bring justice, holiness, peace, and the reign of God
into the lives of others?

Prayer

*Lord, you care for those who have suffered unjustly, who are the poor
of the earth, who mourn and long for justice and peace. Bless all of
us with your grace and saving presence. Amen.*

Pleasantville

U.S., 1998 / 125 minutes

Actors: Tobey Maguire, Jeff Daniels, Joan Allen,
William H. Macy, Reese Witherspoon, J.T. Walsh, Don Knotts

Writer: Gary Ross

Director: Gary Ross

Pleasantville

Bland and White to Color

SYNOPSIS

When David and Jennifer break the TV set, a television repairman with a mysterious ability transports the brother and sister into the actual world of a 1950s black-and-white sitcom. The television program is called "Pleasantville," and David's favorite pastime has been watching reruns of the show. In this black-and-white world, David and Jennifer turn into the children of the sitcom's central couple, Betty and George Parker. The teenagers are now Bud and Mary Sue.

The world of the sitcom is limited to what is seen on screen (books have blank pages and bathroom stalls have no toilets). The values and morals are those portrayed on family television of the 1950s. David (Bud) decides to go along with it all so he can get back home. Instead, Jennifer (Mary Sue) brings her '90s outlook and behavior to the television program and ends up seducing the captain of the basketball team.

The brother and sister begin to affect Pleasantville with their culture, sexual awareness, and behavior. Pleasantville gradually begins to have color, as do the characters. When Betty begins to change from black and white to color, she actually leaves home. Bill Johnson, the owner of the town diner, departs from the usual "program" of making cheese-burgers and fries and doing everything according to the norm, and he starts painting.

The monochrome citizens attack the characters in color and burn the diner. The mayor makes laws to prevent people from changing into colors and doing things differently.

Bud and Bill paint a color mural that leads to a trial. Bud pleads for leniency so that everyone can experience life more fully. Pleasantville, and television itself, changes from black and white to color when the people all become "colored," including the mayor. Jennifer is transformed as well, and makes a conscious decision to abandon her promiscuous behavior. Because she wants to become serious and study, she stays in the world of Pleasantville while David returns to the present.

In 1998 and 1999, at least three U.S. movies were released that used the world of television as their means to interpret the world of the 1990s. These films examined how television's treatment of moral behavior and choices, issues of authority, control, sexuality, voyeurism, and manipulation contribute to present cultural realities.

COMMENTARY

The first of these films was *The Truman Show*. Truman Burbank has unknowingly been the subject of a continuous 24-hour-a-day television show since his adoption by a corporation shortly after birth. In *EdTV*, Ed agrees to have his whole life televised. *The Man on the Moon*, a biopic on the life of Andy Kaufman, showed how it is possible for both performer and audience to confuse reality and show business.

Pleasantville takes up the theme of the sitcom, but looks back at the blandness of the black-and-white external morality and values of the 1950s. The film illustrates how things have changed in the last four decades, both on television and in the real world. It revisits the 1950s and early 1960s and contrasts these years with the late 1990s. *Pleasantville* offers a critique of the simplistic black-and-white television world by skillfully using social and historical events as its framework: the emergence of the "teenager," suburbia, and feminism after World War II, along with McCarthy-era panic and book banning. The courtroom sequence is especially telling (everyone in the balcony becomes "colored" before the people below do), because racial segregation in public places was still in effect until 1964.

Pleasantville offered the emerging actor, Tobey Maguire, a lead role. Reese Witherspoon is a more than competent young actress who continues to show her versatility in such movies as *Election* and *American Psycho.* Academy Award nominee Joan Allen and William H. Macy are two of the best character actors in the U.S.

DIALOGUE WITH THE GOSPEL

Focus: The Gospel tells us that light transforms and gives new vision to those who can see by it. Black-and-white Pleasantville comes to life and color when people begin to see things differently, as two contemporary teenagers bring it new light.

The readings have many references to light and, therefore, to color. Light is the first medium and without it we can see nothing. The text from Isaiah could be a reference to the transformed *Pleasantville:* "Light shall rise for you in the darkness, and the gloom shall become for you like midday."

St. Paul reminds the Corinthians (cf. 1 Cor 2:1–5) that the power of the Spirit transforms, and that philosophical arguments cannot necessarily be depended on. This reading intertwines well with the color change going on in Pleasantville. Color symbolizes the reality required, as opposed to the scripted or constructed proper behavior that black-and-white television programming has come to represent.

When watching *Pleasantville* it could be a temptation to stop at the fact that the citizens only begin to see color when their sexuality is awakened. This is simply the filmmakers' way of contrasting the reality of present-day television's "unpleasantness" with that of the 1950s "pleasantness," which avoided any reference to sexuality or emotional expression. But to focus solely on this point would be to miss the "saltiness" of the movie. It can be seen as advocating the integration of all forms of sense experience along with knowledge, critical thinking, and emotional development which enable human beings to make free choices concerning life and television.

In the Gospel, we read about Jesus' images of salt and light and what happens when the salt goes flat. Yesterday's television sitcoms are vastly different from today's, but they function in the same way, simultaneously mirroring and creating culture and "normalizing" morals and beliefs. Of the many questions we can ask ourselves through this dialogue with the Gospel and the film *Pleasantville*, these two stand out: Is it television or Jesus who will make us the light of the world and the salt of the earth? And how can we be salt and light for the television industry in order to help create a Christian culture of communication?

KEY SCENES AND THEMES

- The repairman who transports David and Jennifer to Pleasantville; their discovery of a black-and-white world.

- Pleasantville's people, the one-dimensional world designed for 1950s audiences; Bud and Mary Sue's effect on Betty and on her choices; George's confusion when faced with change; Bill's painting.

- The hostile black and white characters, the rioting, the mayor's position; the court hearing during which the whole town blossoms; David, the "savior" of Pleasantville, returns home; Mary Sue's transformation.

1. Jennifer (Mary Sue) sets off the chain of events that adds "color" to Pleasantville, because she is sexually alive and aware, a product of the '90s culture. Talk about how she changes and grows beyond what culture has determined a teenage girl must be to gain acceptance and popularity.

2. Contrast the family life and relationships of David, Jennifer, and their parents with those of Bud, Mary Sue, and the Parkers. How do David and Jennifer relate to their parents compared to the way Bud and Mary Sue relate to Betty and George? Trace the role of television in their lives.

3. *Pleasantville* shows the 1950s as a golden age, an Eden of the American way of life, and at the same time asks if it really was so. In the same way, the film challenges viewers to look at their relationship with television today with its consistent power to "normalize" culture, behavior, morality, and social mores. What is the role of television and popular culture in my life? Why?

Prayer

Lord, you are the Light of the world and you turned our world into light. Grace us so that we shed light wherever we are. Amen.

Marvin's Room

U.S., 1996 / 98 minutes

Actors: Meryl Streep, Diane Keaton, Leonardo DiCaprio, Robert De Niro, Hume Cronyn, Gwen Verdon, Dan Hedaya, Hal Scardino

Writer: Scott McPherson

Director: Jerry Zaks

Marvin's Room

Reaching Out to Others

Sisters Bessie and Lee have not been in touch for twenty years. Bessie has remained at home caring for their father Marvin and their childlike aunt Ruth. When Bessie is diagnosed with leukemia, she is told that a bone marrow transplant from a healthy relative may save her.

SYNOPSIS

Lee is divorced with two sons, Hank and Charlie, and is attending a college of cosmetology. Hank is a disturbed teen who tried to burn down their home and has been in an institution. Charlie is a quiet boy, several years younger than Hank. Lee decides that it will be something of a relief to visit Bessie in Florida.

The reunion is amicable and Lee goes for a blood test hoping for a match with Bessie. At first Hank refuses to be tested, then he agrees. Difficulties soon arise between the family members, but Bessie and Hank get along very well; when Hank runs away, he leaves a note for Bessie rather than his mother.

When all the tests prove negative, Bessie resigns herself to her illness and to looking after the family. Lee wants to return home, but Hank confronts her and they decide to stay.

COMMENTARY

Marvin's Room is set in Florida, but, on another level, it is also *Secrets and Lies* territory. The family conflict here is not as intense as the British film about an adopted biracial daughter seeking her birth mother. But like *Secrets and Lies, Marvin's Room* touches on pain and regrets, especially between two sisters who have not seen each other for almost twenty years.

Diane Keaton, in an Oscar-nominated performance, plays Bessie, the sister who never marries and stays at home to look after her bedridden father (Hume Cronyn). Meryl Streep is the callow Lee who has tried to make a life of her own, but cannot communicate with her emotionally disturbed son (Leonardo DiCaprio). Robert De Niro has something of a cameo role as the sympathetic doctor.

Scott McPherson, who died of AIDS at the age of 33, wrote the play and screenplay. Because of his personal experience with illness, he was able to create convincing characters and situations from the inside out.

The film shows how opportunities for reconciliation come to us if only we can recognize them and have the courage and love to act on them.

DIALOGUE WITH THE GOSPEL

Focus: In the Sermon on the Mount, Jesus urges us to forego anger, especially toward those close to us. We have to be reconciled before we can offer other gifts to the Lord. Marvin's Room *is about family anger and reconciliation.*

The readings start with a reminder from Sirach that we are free to choose to keep the commandments and to behave faithfully. We can choose between spiritual life and spiritual death.

Paul's words about spiritual maturity and wisdom are reflected in Bessie's loving serenity (cf. 1 Cor 2:6–10).

The Gospel is a generous slice of the Sermon on the Mount. Jesus exhorts us, his listeners, to fulfill the whole law, to go deeper into our moral selves and be fully reconciled with our enemies, real or perceived. Jesus asks us to be perfect; to put no bounds to our love just as God puts no bounds to his.

Bessie's life mirrors this teaching about love. Reconciliation is a challenge for the two sisters who have grown apart and find it so difficult to forgive and forget. Bessie's illness gives her the opportunity to reach out to Lee. The illness becomes Lee's opportunity for self-sacrifice in favor of her sister. The two sisters struggle to reach the point of reconciliation.

Hank, who is emotionally disturbed and angry, has the opportunity to reconcile with his mother. Through the experience of meeting his relatives, he grows as a person. Though unaware, Hank becomes the mediator for reconciliation between the sisters.

KEY SCENES AND THEMES

- Bessie's life, her self-sacrifice in caring for her father, her childlike aunt; the contrast between Bessie and Lee; Lee's profession, her way of life, her children, her inability to cope with Hank after he burns down the house.

- The sisters meeting after twenty years, their attempt at reconciliation, their aged and ill father, past quarrels that surface; Bessie's medical tests, Lee's opportunity to help Bessie; Hank's unwillingness and then change of heart.

- Hank running away and leaving the note for Bessie rather than Lee; Bessie and Hank driving on the beach; Lee's decision to depart, her willingness to leave her family, even if Bessie is dying; Hank's intervention; his confrontation with his mother; the final imagery of light and mirrors.

1. Right after Bessie learns that there will be no bone marrow transplant, she tells Lee that her life has been filled with much love. Lee says, "Sure everyone loves you." But Bessie responds that it's not that everyone loves her, it's that she has had such wonderful opportunities to love others. What message is there in this film for people seeking to integrate film viewing and spirituality?

2. Family rifts are often so difficult to heal, and years only add to the challenge of being reconciled in Christ. How does Bessie reach out to others to try and bring her family together? Is she successful? What happens in *Marvin's Room* to bridge the three generations in the film?

3. The drama in the film revolves around Marvin, yet he hardly seems to notice. What is his role in the film? As a movie, *Marvin's Room* comments on many social realities, among them the way America treats its older citizens, whether within the family unit or as recipients of care via government programs. How do entertainment media depict older people? How much primetime television, for example, is provided for senior citizens? Why is this so and what does this have to do with justice?

Prayer

Jesus, your message is that we are to love one another. When our family members fail to love, grant them and us the grace of forgiveness and reconciliation. Amen.

The Crossing Guard

U.S., 1995 / 114 minutes

Actors: Jack Nicholson, Anjelica Huston, David Morse,
Robin Wright Penn, Piper Laurie, John Savage

Writer: Sean Penn

Director: Sean Penn

The Crossing Guard

An Eye for an Eye

SYNOPSIS

Five years after the death of their daughter Emily, who was killed by a hit-and-run drunk driver, her parents still grieve. The mother, Mary, gets help from a therapy group, but the father, Freddy, avoids the issue by drinking and womanizing. The couple splits. Freddy is obsessed with the convicted driver of the car, John Booth, and crosses off the days of Booth's sentence on a calendar.

Booth is released from prison and returns home to his parents. He does not know about Freddy's vindictiveness. Freddy visits Mary, who is living with her second husband, to tell her he intends to kill Booth. Mary rages at him for never visiting their daughter's grave.

Booth becomes attached to a young artist, Jojo, but remains depressed over Emily's death. Freddy finds Booth and tries to shoot him, but forgets to put in the ammunition clip. He then promises to return in three days to finish the job.

Freddy's behavior deteriorates. In his desperation he calls Mary. She fears he might harm himself so she meets him in a café. They quarrel and he storms out, heading for Booth's trailer, where Booth is waiting for him with a rifle. Freddy goes after Booth and wounds him. The chase ends at the cemetery where Emily is buried. Finally, at her grave, the two men reconcile.

The Crossing Guard is a striking film. Writer and director Sean Penn established his reputation as an actor in such movies as *Carlito's Way, Dead Man Walking,* and *Sweet and Lowdown.* Penn is less known as a director, although his first film, *The Indian Runner,* was a powerful study of the clash between two brothers. *Indian Runner* also starred David Morse (*The Green Mile*).

In *The Crossing Guard,* Morse portrays a young man coming out of prison for the manslaughter of a young girl whom he has killed while driving drunk. He feels guilt and the need to atone. He wants to try to build a new life. Jack Nicholson, as Emily's father, cannot come to terms with his grief. His marriage fails, he spends nights with friends at strip joints, and he is consumed by rage.

Nicholson's portrayal of the intense father is matched by Anjelica Huston's restrained and grief-stricken mother. Audiences can identify with the situation and the emotional crises. With such a cast, the story seems all the more real.

DIALOGUE WITH THE GOSPEL

Focus: Jesus says no longer is there to be an eye for an eye. He tells us simply that we must love our enemies. This is the hatred-forgiveness challenge at the heart of The Crossing Guard.

The commandment in Leviticus not to hold hatred for your brother in your heart is based on the holiness of God. It is a commandment that Freddy cannot obey. His obsessive grief numbs him. He drowns his sorrow in drink and promiscuity, which do nothing to help him. He cannot grieve or grow as a person. He literally counts the days for his chance at revenge. He is self-destructing.

The movie takes Freddy on a journey through vengeance to reconciliation, and John Booth through fear and guilt to hope.

In the Gospel's section of the Sermon on the Mount, Jesus asks for heroism from his disciples in their treatment of their enemies. Jesus says to love our enemies and pray for our persecutors.

The film's plot could have developed into an outright tale of vengeance, but it potently, believably, and almost ironically (if it weren't so tragic), shows how revenge wastes away human dignity. Freddy fails to load the gun, he gets stopped for drunk driving, pursues and wounds Booth, and then unknowingly allows Booth to lead him to Emily's grave.

The dramatic conclusion of the movie shows the futility of revenge and how easily one can turn into the equivalent of the offender—except that here, the offender truly repents. Freddy and Booth finally put into practice what Jesus teaches.

KEY SCENES AND THEMES

- Freddy's depressing life in bars, with women, crossing off the days on his calendar, waiting for the day of revenge; Freddy's contrast with Mary and her new life; Mary's acceptance of Emily's death.

- John Booth's release from jail; his love for his own parents; his relationship with Jojo, which contrasts with Freddy's inability to have meaningful relationships; Booth's guilt and sorrow about Emily's death; the meaning of the crossing guard image.

- Freddy's vengeful chase, the gun and the rifle, the wounded Booth gaining the upper hand; the final confrontation in the cemetery, their decision not to shoot, the possibility for forgiveness, healing, and reconciliation.

FOR REFLECTION AND CONVERSATION

1. What starts off looking like a sleazy movie quickly builds a context that contrasts how despair and vengeance are acted out in a human life without hope, and the possibilities for freedom offered by forgiveness. Why is Freddie so tormented? Who is he unable to forgive? How does his seeming inability to forgive almost destroy him? Will exacting "an eye for an eye" satisfy his need for vengeance? What is Mary's role in all this?

2. One person Freddy cannot forgive is John Booth. We sense that Freddy can't forgive himself either, that he somehow holds himself responsible for Emily's death, even though Booth was driving the car that killed her. How do the visuals in the film, especially at the cemetery, promise hope and ultimately forgiveness? Who is the crossing guard and what is his role in the film?

3. The final scene at Emily's grave is believable and moving. The two men extend their hands to one another and wordlessly, through tears and sorrow, reconcile. What message can we take away by paralleling *The Crossing Guard* and Jesus' words today?

Prayer

Jesus, by your own life and death, you showed us how to love and forgive those who sin against us. Teach us to love and to forgive. Drive all hatred from our hearts. Amen.

Forrest Gump

U.S., 1994 / 142 minutes

Actors: Tom Hanks, Sally Field, Robin Wright Penn, Gary Sinise, Mykelti Williamson

Writer: Eric Roth

Director: Robert Zemeckis

Forrest Gump

A Simple Life

As Forrest Gump sits at the bus stop, he recounts his amazing life.

Forrest lives with his mother who teaches him worldly-wise truths in homespun ways, "Life is like a box of chocolates; you never know what you're gonna get." Young Forrest Gump has very limited intellectual abilities, but he is a good boy, and especially generous to his friend Jenny. Though slow witted, he discovers he is able to outrun the boys who taunt him.

This knowledge stands him in good stead as he goes to college and becomes a champion football player, even meeting President Kennedy. He serves in Vietnam with his friend Bubba Blue, and heroically rescues Lieutenant Dan with whom he goes into the fishing business after the war.

Forrest experiences one remarkable historical moment after another as he runs long distance across America several times. Over the years he occasionally encounters Jenny, whom he discovers he still loves. She and Forrest spend a night together and Jenny becomes pregnant. Forrest invests in a fruit company ("Apple"), and the profits enable him to

SYNOPSIS

look after Jenny (who has become ill) and her son, whom Forrest discovers is his.

Forrest Gump, an enormously popular film, was nominated for thirteen Academy Awards and won seven, including Oscars for Best Film, Best Adapted Screenplay, Best Director, and Best Actor for Tom Hanks. The film touches an American nerve and the American heart. To those familiar with U.S. history and popular culture, the film is funny and often quite touching as it looks back and tries to assess forty years. This is done through the eyes of a rather simpleminded, but very nice, Forrest Gump. We go back to the simplicities of the '50s, spend quite a deal of time in the '60s (from Kennedy to Vietnam and its aftermath), some time in the '70s (Nixon and post-Vietnam), finishing in the early '80s. For those who lived through the period, it is a moving overview.

Jenny, played by Robin Wright Penn, shows the shadow side of those decades. Sally Field appears as Forrest's mother, Mrs. Gump. The film highlights the versatility of its director, Robert Zemeckis, whose films include the *Back to the Future* series, *Romancing the Stone, Who's Afraid of Roger Rabbit?, Contact,* and *What Lies Beneath.*

Focus: Forrest Gump sits at the bus stop with a box of chocolates in his lap, telling his story. His simple philosophy of life is a reminder of Jesus' words to not worry about food, clothing, or money.

If ever there was a screen character who exemplified this Sunday's passage from the Sermon on the Mount, it is Forrest Gump. From the outside, it might seem that Forrest has a very hard life, that God has not been good to him. He is a wise child with a low I.Q. who must wear a brace on both legs because of polio. He is ridiculed at school, becomes famous for a time, is rejected in love by Jenny, and becomes a soldier in Vietnam. He experiences racial prejudice, financial disaster, and success. When everything finally seems to come together for him, Jenny dies.

Forrest Gump is not attached to money. His innate goodness and uncomplicated belief in people (and, therefore, in God) free him from worry about what will happen to him. He is looked after most providentially, even in dire circumstances, like the birds of the air and the lilies of the field.

Jesus teaches that we are to first of all seek God's way of holiness. *Forrest Gump* is a cinematic example of Gospel-inspired goodness for our times.

KEY SCENES AND THEMES

- Forrest at the bus stop throughout the film; Forrest telling his story, his wisdom; the flashbacks; the feather's symbolism.

- Forrest's experience of childhood: school, the bus and bus driver; the other children's cruelty, Jenny's kindness, her advice to outrun the other children; Forrest running and breaking free, the braces falling off.

- Vietnam; Forrest's candid comments; the troops, drugs, his admiration for Lieutenant Dan and his advice; Forrest the hero, Dan's resistance, the pathos of Bubba's death; Forrest and his son.

FOR REFLECTION AND CONVERSATION

1. Today's Gospel has a saying that could easily have come from Forrest Gump himself: "Tomorrow will take care of itself. Today has troubles enough of its own." How does this Gospel maxim compare with the folksy one Forrest's mom always told him: "Life is like a box of chocolates; you never know what you're going to get"?

2. Just when things seem to come together for Forrest, after all his adventures and incredible encounters with

important or famous people in American history, the woman he loves dies. Forrest is resigned and turns his love and attention toward his son. Though we may not be challenged in the same way as Forrest, we can ask how we might have reacted in similar circumstances. Would we have chosen to be generous or to default to cynicism? Do we usually view our glass as half empty or half full? Why?

3.   Forrest never made distinctions between people, and his being named after Nathan Bedford Forrest (1821–1877), first head of the Ku Klux Klan, is not without irony. Though not intelligent by I.Q. standards, Forrest Gump had a great capacity for love and for seeing goodness in others, no matter who they were or what they looked like. He believed in people, especially Jenny, Bubba Blue, and Lieutenant Dan. Why does this make the discovery that he has a son so touching? Why does Forrest want to know if his son is like him or not? What does this say about Forrest's depth of insight?

Prayer

Jesus, we cling to our lives, our possessions, and worry about our future. Help us to develop simplicity of life and to trust in your providential care. Amen.

John Lithgow and Aidan Quinn in *At Play in the Fields of the Lord*.

At Play in the Fields of the Lord

U.S., 1992 / 180 minutes

Actors: Aidan Quinn, Tom Berenger, Daryl Hannah,
John Lithgow, Kathy Bates, Tom Waites, Stenio Garcia

Writers: Jean-Claude Carriere, Hector Babenco

Director: Hector Babenco

At Play in the Fields of the Lord

Like a Rock

Commandante Guzman, who wants to annex the territory of the Niaruna Indians for its gold, rules the Amazonian town of Mae de Deus. He confiscates the passports of Wolf and Moon, two stranded mercenaries, and urges them to bomb the Indians as a way to get out of the area. Two fundamentalist missionary couples from America, the Hubens and Quarriers, live in the area and try to convert the Indians. The previous Catholic mission had failed and the missionaries were killed by the Niaruna.

Moon, a half-Cheyenne Indian, refuses to bomb the Niaruna. He gets high on local liquor and drugs and parachutes into the territory where he is received as Kisu, the god of evil. He becomes a member of the tribe. He tries to get the Indians to drive the missionaries out of the country.

Complications arise when Billy Quarrier, the son of one of the missionary couples, dies from blackwater fever. This causes the mother, Hazel, to begin a downward spiral into a nervous breakdown. The Niaruna want to avenge the innocent Billy's death and choose Leslie Hubens, one of the ministers, as their victim. He flees, but is persuaded by Guzman to return to "tame" the Indians and make the mis-

SYNOPSIS

sion a barbed wire fortress. Hubens justifies Guzman's plan to exterminate the Indians, and this causes strife between Hubens and Martin Quarrier.

When Moon comes upon Leslie's wife Andy resting after a swim, they kiss and she passes on a flu virus that starts an epidemic among the Indians. Martin Quarrier goes to warn the Indians about Guzman, but the village is bombed and he is killed. Between the flu, the Indians fighting each other, and the bombing, the Niaruna are destroyed.

COMMENTARY

At Play in the Fields of the Lord is based on the 1965 novel about the Amazon region, Indian culture, religion, and the environment, by Peter Matthiessen. Director Hector Babenco made *Pixote*, the celebrated film of the Latin-American slums, and directed *Ironweed* and the Academy Award-nominated film, *Kiss of the Spider Woman*.

The film has a strong cast. Tom Berenger gives a noteworthy performance as the half-Cheyenne mercenary who immerses himself in the life of the Amazon Indians. Aidan Quinn is admirable as a sincere missionary willing to ask difficult questions and accept his humanity. John Lithgow's role as the fundamentalist missionary leader is best described as manic. Daryl Hannah, though attractive, seems rather unlikely as his missionary wife. Kathy Bates is intense and convincing.

At Play in the Fields of the Lord is a kind of morality play, a story with a purpose. The film supports the rights of indigenous peoples and their religious beliefs. Through the characters who move across the screen, we see what happens when sincere people tread unaware in unknown places, and the consequences of economic, political, and religious colonialism.

The film was shot entirely in the Amazon's extraordinarily beautiful locations. While it may be slow moving and not always dramatically persuasive, it is an interesting look at the influence of North American religious culture in the South American mission fields of the 1980s and '90s.

> *Focus: Jesus warns that simply using his name in not enough to justify or sanctify what we do. This admonition goes for everyone, including preachers and missionaries who figure prominently in this movie. A faith commitment that is solid as rock is the foundation for doing good to others, rather than faith built on shifting beds of sand.*

DIALOGUE WITH THE GOSPEL

One of the major themes of *At Play in the Fields of the Lord* is colonialism, specifically religious colonialism. The film depicts American fundamentalist missionaries in Brazil getting caught up in their own problems while trying to convert the Indians. Leslie Hubens, the more experienced missionary, wants domination, whatever the cost.

The parable in today's Gospel offers some criteria for discerning whether missionaries are true or false prophets, whether what they construct is founded on sand or rock. The missionaries in the movie build on sand made up of their own personal dilemmas and unrealistic religious ambitions. Leslie Hubens seems to construct a rock-like fortress, but it is ultimately for the destruction rather than the good of the native peoples.

The irony for the missionaries is that the Indians accept the mercenary, Moon, among them. He is the one who is willing to understand their culture and change his mind about oppressing them. The further irony is that through his selfishness and carelessness in kissing Andy Hubens, he brings back the flu virus that decimates the tribe. The message of today's Gospel and movie merge by showing us that any preaching of the Good News is for the benefit of those who hear it, not those who preach it.

KEY SCENES AND THEMES

- National colonialism, Spanish and Portuguese heritage, twentieth-century Americans and their culture; religious colonialism; traditional Catholicism, domineering fundamentalists; the culture of the Indians, their primitive lifestyle, the question of land ownership.

- Moon's flight over the village, the archer's threat; Moon's decision not to bomb the Indians; the threat to crash the plane, the hallucinatory drink, Moon parachuting into the village; his reception by the tribe, the religious interpretation of his arrival.

- The Quarriers and the Hubans: their convictions, attitudes, prayer, and supervision of the missions; Leslie's dominance and bigotry; the disaster and Huban's final letter to the missionary superiors.

FOR REFLECTION AND CONVERSATION

1. *At Play in the Fields of the Lord* is about how people's religious beliefs motivate them. How are the two Protestant missionary families and the Catholic missionaries to the Indians portrayed? Of all the characters, Martin Quarrier is the strongest seeker of truth, sincerely intrigued by his new surroundings. He openly questions his own beliefs and also the attitudes and approaches of the missionaries. During one conversation about how much the Indians have to teach the missionaries, Quarrier says that if this is so, why do the missionaries keep talking to the Indians without listening to them? What does Martin's question mean for inter-religious (between Christian and non-Christian faiths) and ecumenical (between Christian faiths) dialogue today?

2. The film makes us pay attention to the real meaning of the destruction of the rain forest. When the trees are gone, the ecosystem is destroyed. So are the means of sustenance and the very religion of the people who believe that God dwells in their natural habitat. How are the human rights of people guaranteed when they are no longer able to live and worship according to their culture and tradition? What does a film like this say to multinational corporations and governments that exploit the natural resources of countries under the guise of progress?

3. This movie takes place in the latter part of the twentieth century, but it calls to mind the 1986 film, *The Mission,* about eighteenth-century Brazil and the greed and foreign imperialism that threatened the jungles and indigenous peoples. How can the two films be contrasted?

Prayer

Lord Jesus, when we do anything in your name may it be with a sincere heart and built on the solid foundation of faith in you. Amen.

TENTH SUNDAY OF THE YEAR

Hosea 6:3–6; Matthew 9:9–13

The Doctor

U.S., 1991 / 123 minutes

Actors: William Hurt, Christine Lahti, Elizabeth Perkins,
Mandy Patinkin, Adam Arkin

Writer: Robert Caswell

Director: Randa Haines

 *The Doctor*

Learning Compassion

SYNOPSIS

Jack McKee is a top surgeon and proud of it, a man absorbed by his work who keeps an emotional distance from his patients. He affects a very cavalier attitude by singing and holding discussions during operations.

When Jack is troubled by a persistent cough, Dr. Abbott finds a malignant tumor in Jack's larynx. Suddenly, the tables are turned and Jack is the patient. He has more tests and begins to notice how some patients are treated impersonally, even badly. While waiting for his radiation treatment, he befriends June, who is dying from a brain tumor that could have been diagnosed earlier if medical insurance would have paid for the test. When June's radiation treatments fail, Jack takes her on a trip to the desert.

Instead of allowing Dr. Abbott to operate on him, Jack asks Eli to do the surgery. This surprises Eli, since neither Jack nor his partners had ever shown him any respect. But Jack trusts Eli because he is known as a compassionate man, something Jack has never allowed himself to be. June dies. Jack refuses to testify on behalf of his partner, Murray, who is involved in a malpractice suit.

After Jack's operation, he is far more caring. He tries to make up the distance he has put between himself and his wife and sons. He urges medical students to spend three days in the hospital as patients so that they will learn empathy.

The Doctor is one of several films of the early 1990s that examined the lives of professional people. Almost all the plot lines of these films revolved around a central character (usually a male) who finds that he has lived an empty life and wants to begin anew *(Regarding Henry, The Fisher King, City of Joy)*.

Randa Haines previously directed William Hurt in *Children of a Lesser God*. The screenplay for *The Doctor* was written by Australian Robert Caswell *(A Cry in the Dark)* and based on the book, *A Taste of My Own Medicine*, by Dr. Edward Rosenbaum.

The film has a solid supporting cast, led by Christine Lahti as Hurt's wife and Elizabeth Perkins as a terminally ill patient. Mandy Patinkin is the colleague being sued for medical malpractice.

The film predates the popular television series about doctors like *ER* and *Chicago Hope*, which followed *The Doctor* beginning in the mid-1990s. The strength of the direction and the acting makes *The Doctor* more memorable than many other productions of its kind. The movie indicates a trend for professional people in human services to reassess their ambitions and to reawaken the humane element in their lives and work.

Focus: Jesus quotes Hosea from the first reading, saying that love is more important than sacrifice, and he uses a medical analogy to support it. The Doctor *provides a meaningful parallel to this theme.*

It is interesting to note that the verses prior to this section of Hosea refer to God as someone who, with wine and oil, soothes the wounds that the chosen people suffer. In *The Doctor*, Jack is a professional healer who needs to discover love and compassion rather than add to the professional excellence and success he has already achieved.

This lesson is reinforced by the Gospel text where Jesus quotes Hosea and uses the analogy of the doctor and healing to teach humility and compassion for sinners, that is, the spiritually or religiously unwell. The religious leaders, the religious "professionals" of Jesus' day, criticize him for eating with the tax collector Matthew and other "sinners." These professionals are the target of Jesus' remarks when he reminds them that healthy people don't need a doctor, sick people do. Religious leaders, like doctors, ought to be persons of compassion. Jack discovers through the experience of his illness that compassion is more important than anything else.

Jesus then draws the parallel that just like the sick, sinners—and all of us are sinners of some kind—need compassion.

KEY SCENES AND THEMES

- The operating room's environment: the songs, the jokes and wisecracks, the surgeons' attitudes, smug and impersonal professionals at work, the surgery's buddy system; Jack McKee's skill and treatment of patients, his rounds with the interns, his remarks on cutting straighter and caring less.

- Jack's diagnosis: opinions, radiation therapy; Jack meets June, their connecting and talking; her condition, the lies regarding her chances of recovery, money needed for operations; June's fighting spirit, the roof as her special place; June urging Jack to fight the system, his going to the roof to read her letter.

• Jack changing his attitude toward patients: the personal touch, people's names; his new requirement for the interns to dress as patients and undergo tests to develop empathy for their patients.

1. Health care is a major social and political issue today. Lack of universal accessibility, the impersonal face of health management organizations, and the economic criteria used to determine who gets needed tests and surgery have alienated many people. How does the film reflect this reality? How do the majority of doctors in the film show what it means to be professional? How humble and compassionate are they? Who stands out as an example of the kind of doctor we would want to have caring for us? Who does June represent in the film?

2. Dr. Jack is on the fast track to becoming a super doctor. He is ambitious and cocky, but then he is stopped cold by his own mortality. How do his values and priorities as a professional change? Who and what events finally teach him humility? How does the story structure and characters engage us in the experience of a man brought low by his own vulnerability?

3. Jack's wife wants to reach him, but he doesn't let her. At one point, he confesses, "I've spent so much time pushing her away, I don't know how to let her come close." Yet he becomes very close to June. What does June teach him about how precious life and loved ones are? Finally, how does Jack learn that mercy and compassion are what will make him happy, rather than ambition and power?

Prayer

Jesus, help us to understand your teaching that love is more important than sacrifice, and that caring for those in need is more important than a ritual offering. Amen.

Men with Guns

U.S., 1997 / 128 minutes

Actors: Federico Lupi, Damian Alcazar, Tania Cruz,
Dan Rivera Gonzalez, Mandy Patinkin, Kathryn Grody

Writer: John Sayles

Director: John Sayles

Men with Guns

To Love Is to Serve

SYNOPSIS

In a Latin American city, the well-respected Dr. Fuentes teaches a group of medical students with the hope that they will be of service to the poor. As he nears retirement, he decides to visit seven of his past students, six men and one woman, who have gone into the countryside to serve the needs of the people.

As he starts his journey he is warned that there are armed guerillas and the military in the area. He discovers that men with guns burned one of his students. He continues his journey with an orphan boy, Conejo, and learns that more of his students are dead. He hears stories about torture and destroyed villages.

An army medic named Domingo who deserted his troop and a former priest who has lost his faith, join in the journey. A mute girl who has been raped also joins the group. They each have a story.

Finally, dismayed by the brutality of the military and guerillas—all men with guns—the doctor wants to visit the furthest village. Hidden high in the mountains, the village is his last hope for finding that at least one of his students has survived. On the journey, however, Dr. Fuentes dies. A young girl coming for help meets the group, and Domingo takes the doctor's bag and accompanies her.

COMMENTARY

This masterful film was written and directed by John Sayles, a filmmaker with a social conscience. Sayles has written clever, popular scripts for other directors, but his own movies are far more serious and thoughtful, for example, *City of Hope, Passion Fish, Lone Star,* and *Limbo.* Here his approach is almost documentary-like. The film was shot on location in Mexico, but the country in the story is unnamed because the situation played out could happen anywhere. The cast is almost entirely Latino and the dialogue is in Spanish.

Sayles is obviously moved by the political troubles that have tormented Latin Americans for decades. He is disturbed by the warfare and the victimization of villagers by men with guns, whether they are military or rebel guerillas. In power struggles, it is always the ordinary people who suffer. The issue of a gun culture, violence, and pacifism, seen first almost in microcosm in Sayles' *Matewan,* has moved to a macro level in *Men with Guns.*

Because the story is about a doctor who taught medicine in a city all his life and never had any firsthand experience in the field, Sayles does two things. First, he highlights the heroism of those who work in poor, rural, dangerous areas and give their lives for a noble cause. Second, we learn, along with Dr. Fuentes, that we cannot presume to really know what we have not experienced. Fuentes learns much more on his journey than his life as a teacher of medicine could ever have taught him.

Sayles uses the cinematic road trip convention to tell the story, collecting a variety of co-travelers as Dr. Fuentes goes along: an orphan, a mute rape victim, a deserter, and an anguished priest. They each learn or teach something to the others. At the end, the doctor dies, leaving his legacy to the deserted soldier who continues Fuentes' medical mission.

Focus: The Gospel tells about the compassion of Jesus and the importance of choosing and sending disciples to help and heal the needy. Dr. Fuentes practices this teaching on his journey through the villages that have been destroyed by the men with guns.

DIALOGUE WITH THE GOSPEL

In the first reading from Exodus, God's people are on a journey that will purify them and bring them closer to God in a covenantal relationship.

In the Gospel, Jesus is moved with compassion for people who are harassed and dejected. He urges his disciples to pray for more and more laborers to help with the harvest. Jesus chooses special disciples to go out on mission with authority to cast out evil and to heal. His advice is to go to search out those in need and give them hope that God will cure them. The disciples are to give their services freely.

This Gospel passage is something of a blueprint for John Sayles' movie. Dr. Fuentes chose and trained his young doctor-"disciples" and then sent them out to the countryside to serve and heal those most in need. Like Jesus' disciples, these young doctors served without charge and laid down their lives for others.

Dr. Fuentes' journey shows that the doctors have given everything, including their lives. This has a profound effect on the doctor as he realizes he is dying. He has learned more about real life than he ever imagined and the journey has had an empowering effect on those who have accompanied him. His legacy and mission can continue.

- Dr. Fuentes' life: training students; sending them as doctors to help the poor; his desire to see them again and to hear what they have achieved.

KEY SCENES AND THEMES

- Fuentes' journey, his discovery of the barbaric handling of his students, the cruelty of the "men with guns"; the small group of Fuentes' followers: Conejo, Domingo, the rape victim, the priest.

- Each member of the group transformed; the last village and the end of Dr. Fuentes' quest; his death and Domingo continuing his mission.

FOR REFLECTION AND CONVERSATION

1. Dr. Fuentes is a good but somewhat naïve man. He is only able to find one of his former medical students on his odyssey, and the young man tells him, "You are the most learned man I have ever met, but also the most ignorant." Why did he say this to Dr. Fuentes? What does this say about the need for teaching to be based on experience? for the teacher to go first, before his students and disciples?

2. *Men with Guns* is a socially conscious film that could have taken place in any country in the world. This is why John Sayles did not identify the location, though we know the people speak Spanish and we imagine Central or South America. The men with guns are the ones in power, whether they are government (the oppressors) or revolutionary forces (the oppressed), and the people caught in the middle are the ones who end up dead. Paulo Friere, the great Brazilian educator, once said that if the oppressed become the oppressors, then what progress has humanity made? How is this scenario played out in the film? What social and political message is Sayles trying to convey?

3. *Men with Guns* uses the conventional road movie structure to tell its story. The main protagonist, Dr. Fuentes, sets off on a journey, acquires companions, has ad-

ventures, and learns lessons along the way. What do Dr. Fuentes, the boy, the ex-medic, the former priest, and the young woman learn? How do they demonstrate love and service in their lives?

Prayer

Lord, you were moved when you saw so many people in need. Just as you chose disciples for your mission, continue to send generous laborers to the harvest. Amen.

A Cry in the Dark (Evil Angels)

Living with Calumny

SYNOPSIS

In 1980, the Chamberlains, a devout Seventh Day Adventist family are camping at Uluru (Ayer's Rock) in Central Australia. While the family is eating supper, Azaria, the baby daughter, disappears from the tent. Lindy, the mother, hears a cry and rushes to check on the baby. Lindy sees a dingo (wild dog) running away and no trace of the child is ever found.

Although experts, dingo trackers, and forensic scientists disagree on the evidence, Lindy Chamberlain is charged with the murder of her child, and the father, Michael, as an accessory to the murder. The case becomes the most celebrated and notorious in Australian legal history. Everybody in Australia has an opinion about the disappearance and rumor and gossip are rife, with the media playing a lurid role in the court of public opinion.

In Australia the Seventh Day Adventists are considered a religious sect. Australians, wary of non-mainstream religions and strange religious interpretations, begin to circulate rumors about the events. But Michael Chamberlain is a pastor and the couple professes their faith in God.

The trial is complex and experts continue to disagree. Lindy Chamberlain is found guilty and sentenced to life in prison at hard labor. She gives birth to another daughter soon after she is incarcerated. The Chamberlains, supported by friends, lose appeal after appeal. Finally when new evidence is discovered, the Chamberlains win the fight to prove their innocence. A panel of three judges exonerates Lindy and Michael in 1988.

COMMENTARY

A Cry in the Dark is based on the book *Evil Angels* by John Bryson. The book details the actual events at Uluru and the subsequent hearings and trial. It also examines the effect of the trial on the Australian public, especially the role of the media in shaping public opinion, influencing the trial, and creating a negative persona for Lindy Chamberlain.

For Australian release, the film was titled *Evil Angels*, but in the U.S. it was released as *A Cry in the Dark*.

Fred Schepisi is one of Australia's leading international directors, best known for his Australian films, *The Devil's Playground* and *The Chant of Jimmie Blacksmith*, and for international films such as *Plenty, Roxanne, The Russia House,* and *Six Degrees of Separation*.

In *A Cry in the Dark*, Schepisi recreates the events with accuracy, drama, and power. Meryl Streep gives a fine, telling performance as Lindy Chamberlain. Sam Neill is convincing as Michael, a man both weak and strong. A Who's Who of Australian cinema appear in supporting roles.

This is a film that asks the audience to reflect on many realities of contemporary life, especially the influence and role of the media and how we as audience interact with them.

DIALOGUE WITH THE GOSPEL

Focus: Lindy and Michael Chamberlain are people of faith who were forced to go through public trial and punishment, and who suffered hostility and calumny. They were finally partially exonerated. In today's Gospel, Jesus instructs the Twelve, telling them how to deal with injustice, false accusations, and calumny. He assures his followers that their faith in God will be justified.

The promise of final exoneration is what kept the Chamberlains, especially Lindy, going during their trials. Jesus tells the apostles to trust in Providence because God even takes care of the sparrows, and they are more precious than an entire flock of sparrows. Lindy Chamberlain held on to her faith and believed that God would ultimately declare himself in her favor.

It was tragic enough when Lindy lost her child and Azaria's body was never recovered. But this was followed by the indignity of a mother going to trial, shamed both in court and in public opinion, and serving a prison sentence. Through all this, Lindy Chamberlain showed that she did not fear those who turned against her.

Today's first reading reinforces the dialogue between *A Cry in the Dark* and the Gospel message. The sufferings of the prophet Jeremiah echo the Chamberlains' sufferings. Like them, Jeremiah is publicly denounced and his downfall is enjoyed by those around him. The screenplay dramatizes the Chamberlains' faith-struggle, and yet highlights the support they receive from the solidarity of their faith community.

(The ordeal had sad consequences for the Chamberlains. Even though the couple was finally declared innocent, the court appeals took years and their marriage eventually ended in divorce.)

KEY SCENES AND THEMES

- The Adventist congregation in Mt. Isa, the truck driver's judgment about them; the consequences of this throughout the film.

- The disappearance of Azaria Chamberlain, the dingo, Lindy's reaction, the search; Lindy and Michael in the hotel trying to grapple with what has happened and why; their faith in God.

- The gossiping Australian public; the authoritative statements based on hearsay; the media's role: their questions, attitudes, sensationalizing, interviewing the Chamberlains, victimizing them.

FOR REFLECTION AND CONVERSATION

1. As often happens in the U.S. and other countries, the Chamberlains were tried in the court of public opinion, via the media. The film tells a true story. Because people spread rumors based on ignorance, bias, and prejudice, the Chamberlains were demonized. Given the nature of the mass audience created by mass communications such as radio, television, the press (and now the Internet), how might people have responded in a more responsible way to the events that unfolded at Ayer's Rock that fateful night?

2. The Chamberlains were Seventh Day Adventists. Why did this make a difference in how people perceived them? Why did their membership in this particular faith community contribute to the moral panic with the Australian media and among the people? How could supposedly religious people who believed the rumors and who spread "popular opinion" about the Chamberlains, justify their talk and actions?

3. What happened to the Chamberlains was a tragedy beyond all telling; regardless of the outcome, a cloud of suspicion will always hang over them. Does the film make us want to empathize or identify with the Chamberlains? Why or why not? How can movies like

this help us question what we see and hear in the media, and reflect on our own media practices and responses?

Prayer

Jesus, you know what it is like to have those you loved turn against you and deny you. May all those who suffer such treatment be strengthened in hope and believe that you will one day vindicate them. Amen.

Charlton Heston cast as Ben-Hur.

Ben-Hur

U.S., 1959 / 210 minutes

Actors: Charlton Heston, Stephen Boyd, Jack Hawkins,
Haya Harareet, Martha Scott, Cathy O'Donnell,
Sam Jaffe, Hugh Griffith, Finlay Currie

Writer: Karl Tunberg

Director: William Wyler

Ben-Hur

Unconditional Kindness

SYNOPSIS

It is about the year 30. The family of Hur is wealthy and well-respected in Jerusalem. The Roman occupation has both the conquerors and citizens on edge. Messala, a childhood friend of Judah Ben-Hur, returns to Jerusalem with the Roman legions. Messala wants Judah to help him subdue the Jews, but Ben-Hur refuses and argues with Messala, insisting on the Jews' need for independence. When a loose tile from the rooftop of Ben-Hur's home upsets the governor's entry procession, the family is imprisoned.

Judah is sent to the galleys. On the way, a stranger gives him water to drink. Judah attracts the attention of Quintus Arrius, who unlocked his chains during an ocean battle, thus saving his life. Judah rescues Arrius and stops him from killing himself when it seems the battle is lost. Instead, the battle is a victory and they go to Rome, where Arrius adopts Judah as his son and he is trained as a charioteer.

Judah longs for news of his family and returns to Jerusalem. On the way he encounters a sheikh and becomes the driver of his chariot team. In a spectacular chariot race in Jerusalem, Messala wagers that he will beat Judah, but instead is injured and dies after losing the race.

Judah finds his love, Esther, and discovers that his mother and sister are lepers. He listens to Jesus preach. On Jesus' way to Calvary, Judah offers him water only to discover that this was the stranger who had given Judah water as he passed through Nazareth to the galleys so long ago. As Jesus dies, Judah Ben-Hur's mother and sister are healed and the family begins their life again.

COMMENTARY Fred Niblo filmed the second version of *Ben-Hur: A Tale of the Christ,* at the end of the silent era in 1926. This film is worth seeing and stands up well beside its lavish remake, especially the chariot race sequence. Cinema techniques and the changes in acting style brought about by the move from silent to sound movies demonstrate the new level of sophistication in this 1959 version. *Ben-Hur* was nominated for twelve Oscars and won eleven, including Best Picture, Best Actor, and Best Supporting Actor.

In many ways, Hollywood filmmaking reached its 1950s pinnacle with *Ben-Hur,* when television began to compete with movies as a main form of popular entertainment. *Ben-Hur* is a long and lavish big screen production that offered a much more thrilling experience than could be seen at home. Most of the Oscars *Ben-Hur* won were for its advanced techniques and special effects.

General Lew Wallace wrote the original novel on which the film versions were based in 1880. The novel skillfully interweaves themes and details relevant to Biblical history, the culture of the Roman Empire, the occupation of Palestine by the Romans, and the oppression of Judea. The narrative makes it abundantly clear that the author intended the Gospel story and teachings to be the rationale for the novel. The film accomplishes the same goal and is perhaps one of the greatest moving pictures of all time.

Along with films like *The Robe* (1953) and *The Ten Commandments* (1956), *Ben-Hur* brought biblical epics back into public favor after a gap of a quarter of a century. A reverent, devotional tone characterizes some of *Ben-Hur*, especially the opening Nativity sequence that is holy card-like and relies on a literal reading of the Infancy narratives. This tendency in filmmaking would disappear in the 1960s, even though biblical films continued to be made.

The movie is rightly famous for the spectacular chariot race, though it overshadows the well-dramatized Gospel scenes that follow.

Focus: The teaching of Christ in today's Gospel is dramatized in Ben-Hur: *Jesus gives a cup of water to Judah when he is desperately thirsty, and the young man gives water to Jesus a few years later under similar dire circumstances.*

DIALOGUE WITH THE GOSPEL

The first reading from the Second Book of Kings introduces the theme of unconditional generosity and kindness with the story of a childless woman who offers hospitality to the prophet Elisha. Though she expects nothing in return, Elisha promises that she will be rewarded and have a child, and a new life, within a year.

Paul's Letter to the Romans (cf. 6:3–4, 8–11) contributes the theme of baptism, and thus water, to today's Scripture teaching. Paul speaks of dying with Christ in baptism so that we may live with him and rise to new life.

The Gospel unites the themes of kindness and water when Jesus says that whoever gives a cup of cold water to lowly ones for his sake will be rewarded. This strong connection literally flows between today's Gospel and the film in the scene where the centurion refuses to give water to the thirsty Judah when the prisoners stop to rest at Nazareth on their torturous trek to the sea. Judah says, "God, help me," and the shadow of Jesus falls on him. Jesus soothes Judah, washes his face, and gives him water to drink, silently defying the Roman to take action.

Years later when Judah sees Jesus carrying his cross, he risks the anger of the soldiers to offer Jesus the relief of a cup of water. Ben-Hur receives his reward when his life and family are restored to him.

In the Scriptures, water is the symbol of life, grace, cleansing, and healing. In the film, the simple act of giving a drink of water for love of Jesus to someone who is thirsty is raised to the level of the sacred. The film echoes the teaching and promises of Christ that kindness will be rewarded.

KEY SCENES AND THEMES

- Judah and the other prisoners chained together, going through the desert and arriving in Nazareth; the previous scenes of Jesus' presence in the carpenter's shop and out in the hills; Jesus soothing Judah with water.

- Ben-Hur's mother and sister abandoned in a cell, getting their food, discovered as lepers and hiding in the caves; Judah discovering their whereabouts and his grief at their state.

- Ben-Hur giving Jesus the water on the way to Calvary and recognizing him; Jesus dies on the cross, his blood flows out from the cross; the healing of Ben-Hur's mother and sister from leprosy.

FOR REFLECTION AND CONVERSATION

1. Today's Gospel and the film focus on one of the corporal works of mercy: to give drink to the thirsty and the reward for doing so. The two incidents in the film create a parallel structure for the story and enhance its overall ability to inspire. What other works of mercy are evident in the story of *Ben-Hur*? How easy is it to practice works of mercy in today's society?

2. Along with the symbol of water, there is also a thematic thread running through the film: that of injus-

tice, injury, anger, vengeance and, finally, forgiveness and peace. How does the film show the spiritual cleansing of Judah and the physical cleansing of his mother and sister? How are both "washed clean"?

3. The film immerses us in the moment when Ben-Hur realizes how the past, the present, and the future are tied together in Christ. What is the story of my life in Christ? Do I recognize his presence in the people, relationships, and events of my life, family, community and society?

Prayer

Jesus, you call the person who gives a cup of water in your name a disciple. Help us to recognize those in our daily lives who need the small but necessary care that we can offer. Amen.

Simon Birch

U.S., 1998 / 114 minutes

Actors: Ian Michael Smith, Joseph Mazzello, Ashley Judd, Oliver Platt, David Strathairn, Jim Carrey, Dana Ivey

Writer: Mark Stephen Johnson

Director: Mark Stephen Johnson

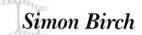

Simon Birch

A Friend Is a Sturdy Shelter

SYNOPSIS

Twelve-year-old Simon Birch and Joe Wentworth are friends. It is 1964 and they live in Gravestown. Simon is the smallest baby ever born in the town's hospital and remains very small in size and stature. Despite his dwarfism, he is very popular with the children at school, but neglected, even resented, at home.

Joe, on the other hand, has a loving mother, Rebecca, who also acts as a mother to Simon. She has never revealed the identity of Joe's father. Drama teacher Ben Goodrich dates Rebecca and meets with Joe's approval.

At the Sunday school run by Reverend Russell, Simon causes some mayhem by announcing that he is an "instrument of God," even though he is not sure what this means. However, grief and disaster follow when he hits his first baseball and it strikes Rebecca on the head and she dies. Someone steals the baseball and Joe thinks that it was taken by his unknown father. Joe and Simon try to find the ball. They break into the school to search the files because they suspect that the swimming coach is Joe's father. When caught, they are sentenced to community service. Then Simon causes chaos

212

as Baby Jesus during the Nativity play and is barred from the school retreat.

Simon finds the baseball and Reverend Russell tells Joe that he is his father. Simon is finally permitted to join the retreat. On the way back, the bus crashes into a river. Simon saves the other children, realizing that this is how he is God's instrument. He cannot escape from the bus himself, however, and dies.

In many ways, *Simon Birch* is like a movie about a junior odd couple because of the unlikely match of Joe and Simon as friends. The movie is suggested by a John Irving *(World According to Garp, Hotel New Hampshire, Cider House Rules)* novel, *A Prayer for Owen Meany.* Irving approved the adaptation.

COMMENTARY

The strength of the movie is provided by the screen presence of Ian Michael Smith as Simon. He might be physically diminutive, but he makes a powerful impression. Joseph Mazzello *(Radio Flyers, Shadowlands, Jurassic Park, River Wild)* plays the straight man to Smith's comedian. There is a strong supporting adult cast, with a quiet Jim Carrey introducing the movie as the adult Joe reminiscing on the events of his childhood.

The movie has to be interpreted in religious tones because of the religious atmosphere created by the story's dramatic elements: the Sunday school, the Nativity play, the ambiguous role of Reverend Russell, and Simon believing himself to be an "instrument of God." Other major details are linked to the religious theme, such as the "orphan" experiences of the two boys, the harsh reality of Rebecca's death, and Reverend Russell's guilt. The film is manifestly theological when Simon gives his own life to rescue the children.

A great deal of American storytelling wears its heart on its sleeve, and audiences from more reserved cultures can find this lack of realism difficult to deal with. *Simon Birch* falls into this category and plays on the heartstrings of its audience, but gets away with it in a faith context.

DIALOGUE WITH THE GOSPEL

Focus: Jesus blesses the Father who reveals to children that God helps those who are overburdened in carrying their load. Simon Birch is such a child.

Jesus' words to the Father are a prayer about Simon Birch. Simon is not learned or clever, although he is smart and able, even distressingly shrewd at times. Simon possesses the wisdom of children and according to Jesus, it is to children that everything holy is revealed.

In the reading from Zechariah, we find the scriptural tradition that heroes are healers as well, but they are often "wounded healers." Zechariah says the Savior is a humble hero riding on a donkey. Further on in Zechariah (12:10) the Savior is described as being "thrust through," wounded, a reference that foreshadows Jesus being pierced on the cross. It is revealed to the malformed diminutive Simon that he is an instrument of God, a hero, and he dies acknowledged as one.

Simon carries a heavy physical burden, and his own family does not seem to love him. At the same time he supports others who have cares and worries. He is a friend to Joe and another son for Rebecca. He is the life of the class and the Nativity play for the other children.

Ultimately, he literally bears other's burdens on his own fragile shoulders when he saves the children from drowning. Joe, for one, learns from Simon what it means to be the kind of living spirit that St. Paul refers to in the second reading (cf. Rom 8:9, 11–13).

KEY SCENES AND THEMES

* Simon at home: fragile and small, yet full of life; his family's hostile attitude; Rebecca's care for Simon.

- Joe and Simon's friendship: outings, walks, conversations; their scheme to find Joe's father; the baseball game and Rebecca's shocking death; the consequences for Simon and for Joe.

- Reverend Russell's exasperation, the way he deals with Simon, his care for Joe; the bus crash and Simon's heroism; Simon as an instrument of God; his death as a hero.

1. Rebecca has a child out of wedlock, and is the film's runner-up to Simon for generosity and kindness. Others in the film live socially acceptable and seemingly moral lives, but their charity is limited. Contrasting Rebecca and Simon with everyone else is a common storytelling device that draws our attention, in this case, to the fact that everyone is capable of goodness, even the "public sinners" we may thoughtlessly toss away as unredeemable. Which characters in this film show goodness? Which ones are less than generous in their attitudes toward others? Who is isolated and lonely? Why? How do the characters grow, especially Simon, Joe, and Joe's father?

2. A well-told story, even if sentimental, will only work if we can identify with the characters and take meaning from what we are experiencing in front of the silver screen (or television). What is there about the child Simon that draws us to him? What are his burdens? What is so special about Simon and Joe's friendship and what makes it endure?

3. When Simon Birch gives his life to save the other children, he seems to take on the role of Christ-figure. He lays down his life for others freely. His friendship

FOR REFLECTION AND CONVERSATION

toward the children is unconditional and it seems as if dying to save them is something he must do, something he has been called to do. How does Simon Birch measure up to Christ-figures in other films, from *Superman* to *Terminator 2: Judgment Day* to *Jesus' Son, E.T.: The Extra-Terrestrial, Babette's Feast, Erin Brockovich,* and any others that come to mind? What makes them similar or different kinds of Christ-figures?

Prayer

Jesus, help us carry our burdens when they are too heavy for us. Help us be like you and make us gentle and humble in heart so that we can help others carry their burdens in times of need. Amen.

Oscar and Lucinda

Australia, 1997 / 132 minutes

Actors: Ralph Fiennes, Cate Blanchett, Tom Wilkinson,
Ciaran Hinds, Richard Roxburgh, Clive Russell, Linda Bassett

Writer: Laura Jones

Director: Gillian Armstrong

Oscar and Lucinda

Through a Glass Clearly

Oscar Hopkins grows up in a strict religious sect in England in the early 1800s. He fights with his beloved father, becomes disillusioned, and while still an adolescent, tosses a marker in a game to decide which church he should join. He runs away to the home of an Anglican priest and his wife. Oscar joins the Church of England and during his training to become a priest, discovers gambling and becomes addicted. Attempting to overcome it, he migrates to New South Wales, Australia.

SYNOPSIS

Lucinda Leplastrier has grown up poor in New South Wales, but becomes wealthy when she inherits a glass factory in Sydney. She too is a gambler. Lucinda befriends the Reverend Hassett until he is sent to the country because of his relationship with her. She sails to England on business.

On the return voyage, Lucinda meets Oscar on his way to Australia. He hears her confession and is enthralled to meet another gambler. Together, they begin to gamble on ship and continue to in Sydney. This has such a devastating effect on Oscar that the two pledge never to gamble again.

But Oscar and Lucinda make a wager that he can transport Lucinda's glass church, packed in numerous crates, overland to Hassett's parish. The journey is arduous and Oscar fights with Jeffris, a bigoted member of the transport team who murdered some Aborigines in cold blood. During the fight, Oscar kills Jeffris. The expedition arrives at the river and assembles the church. They float the church down river to Bellingen and dock the barge at the landing. Oscar is not well and a widow seduces him when she tends to him. Distraught at the depths to which his choices have led him, he goes to the glass church, still moored at the dock, to pray and confess his sins to God. He drowns when the church, too heavy for the barge, sinks.

COMMENTARY

Oscar and Lucinda is a beautifully filmed period piece and a pleasure to watch. The film was shot on location in England and Sydney, as well as the bush and rivers around Grafton. *Oscar and Lucinda* is a faithfully adapted version of Australian Peter Carey's 1988 novel of the same title.

The burden of the characterization and plot fall to the two stars who play opposites in all things except their love for gambling. Cate Blanchett's Lucinda—like the strong, individual women of Gillian Armstrong's other period films (*My Brilliant Career, Little Women*)—is a determined woman who succeeds in business and discovers she has a flair and love for gambling. She encounters Oscar, the idiosyncratic priest, whose gambling obsession is even stronger than hers. However, what might seem to be a set-up for a romantic and passionate love story moves in other directions. Ralph Fiennes' eccentrically scruffy-looking Oscar is a bundle of nerves, desires, and idealism.

The religious dimension of both the film and its characters make both the book and film fascinating. Oscar comes from the severe Plymouth Brethren community, but converts to the Church of England. Lucinda is also a believer. The gambling theme and its obsessions that are woven through the story culminate in the wager to move a glass church from

Sydney to Bellingen, and a confession scene that captures an experience of repentance. The brutal treatment of Aborigines is another thematic element in the film.

Focus: Jesus teaches in parables. Today's is about the farmer whose seed grew up among weeds. Oscar and Lucinda might be considered fields on which the seeds of grace are sown, seeds that sprang up for a while and then died.

DIALOGUE WITH THE GOSPEL

Oscar and Lucinda is a parable about two protagonists who are unable to accept an orderly and religious world because they are both gamblers who are disappointed in their lives and relationships.

Oscar and Lucinda illustrate the parable of the sower in that grace has different effects in their lives. Lucinda is more straightforward. She has staked her fortune on a combination of management and risk, and succumbs to Oscar's charm and "theology of gambling." She lets opportunities fall to the side of the path, squanders them, and lets her gambling addiction choke other opportunities. Her main investment is her reticently expressed love for Oscar and the bet on whether or not he can transport the glass church to Bellingen.

Oscar is the more obviously passionate of the two, but shy. At first it seems that his youthful gamble about his religious affiliation might lead to spiritual fulfillment. But when his teacher, the Reverend Stratton, commits suicide because of Oscar's gambling addiction, his moral structure is no longer stable.

Oscar finds many opportunities. Seeds are continually sown for him, but he continues to gamble them away. He hears Lucinda's confession and finds a soulmate, but when they begin to gamble in Sydney, he is once again choked, so to speak, by his addiction. Oscar has two final opportunities for growth: his pact with Lucinda and the expedition to transport the glass church. Ironically, yet providentially, Oscar resolves to change his life just as the glass church in which he is trapped begins to sink.

Oscar is a good man in spite of the fact that he wastes so much of the good seed of grace sown in his life. He is like someone praying Paul's prayer in the reading from Romans (cf. 8:18–23), groaning with creation for the freedom of the children of God.

KEY SCENES AND THEMES

- Oscar and his father; the strictness of the Brethren, the Christmas cake incident; Oscar's choice of church by gamble.

- Lucinda's upbringing; her glass factory inheritance; Lucinda's confession and Oscar's happiness in finding a fellow-gambler; Oscar's theological justification of his habit, his destructive path in Sydney.

- The church: its design, its construction, its material; the trek to Bellingen and its achievement; Oscar's sin, confession, his death by drowning within the church.

FOR REFLECTION AND CONVERSATION

1. The events in the film seem tied together by coincidence, like winning a bet: "a dream, a lie, a wager, and love," says the voice-over at the end. As Oscar and Lucinda's lives begin to entwine, is it really coincidence that governs what happens? Are they responsible for their choices? Why or why not? What is the role of Providence in this tale?

2. Oscar and Lucinda are both addicted to gambling and both are Christians who struggle with that addiction. As we watch their struggles, compressed into a little more than two hours, the story seems almost like a parable, a place where we, as viewers, can go with our moral imagination to play out the scenario as if it were us instead of Oscar and Lucinda. How is film a safe

place to exercise our moral imaginations and the application of our beliefs so that we can test possible choices and their consequences? What might we have done differently than Oscar or Lucinda?

3. Leon Garfield, a British writer, once wrote, "Mirrors are the windows of the devil, overlooking nothing but a landscape of lies!" But the church that Lucinda builds and that Oscar transports and ultimately drowns in, is made of transparent glass; it becomes a means of grace, of transformation from lies to truth, from a gamble to a solid choice. However, it can also be said that the glass church ultimately acts like a mirror, not because it tells lies, but because it finally reflects the truth to both Oscar and Lucinda. It becomes a visual metaphor or symbol for them and us to see through to their very souls. How deeply do I allow the truth that is reflected back to me by others or by situations I encounter to be a source of transformation in my life?

Prayer

Jesus, you continue to teach us in parables. Open our hearts to hear your stories and apply them to our lives. Today, may your grace not fall by the wayside, but produce good fruit in us. Amen.

Wisdom 12:13, 16–19; Matthew 13:24–43

Secrets and Lies

U.K., 1996 / 141 minutes

Actors: Brenda Blethyn, Marianne Jean-Baptiste,
Timothy Spall, Phyllis Logan, Claire Rushbrook

Writer: Mike Leigh

Director: Mike Leigh

Secrets and Lies

Revelations and Reconciliation

SYNOPSIS

Hortense, a British optometrist who is black, wants to find her birth mother after the death of her adoptive mother. She obtains the file from social services and finds that her mother is Cynthia, a troubled white woman.

Cynthia lives with her daughter, Roxanne, who is a sanitation worker. Cynthia's brother, Maurice, is a successful photographer who lives with his wife, Monica, in a beautiful home. Monica dislikes her mother-in-law, because she thinks she is a depressed loser.

When Hortense calls, Cynthia is wary but agrees to meet her for coffee. As they talk, Cynthia tells the story of her pregnancy and the adoption. They establish a rapport and become friends. Cynthia enjoys going out with Hortense and begins to come alive again. Cynthia invites Hortense to Roxanne's birthday party, but when she lets it slip that Hortense is her daughter, Roxanne gets angry and storms out. Maurice persuades her to come back. This is the catalyst for everyone to speak openly and to reveal the secrets that have hurt their lives. Forgiveness and reconciliation come with truth, tears, and the clasping of hands.

Secrets and Lies won the Ecumenical Jury Award and Golden Palm at Cannes in 1996. Mike Leigh has a reputation for making films that sensitively portray life among England's ordinary people. He demonstrates a master's skill by developing characters of substance quickly and often humorously, with great insight into the good and evil sides of the human spirit.

Brenda Blethyn won the Best Actress Award at the Cannes festival for her work in *Secrets and Lies.* She plays Cynthia, an unmarried mother with a 20-year-old daughter who cleans streets. Cynthia works in a box factory. Her brother (Timothy Spall) is a professional photographer (and Leigh has some wonderfully telling moments with clients posing for portraits). Meanwhile Hortense, a black Englishwoman, buries her adoptive mother and then sets out to find her birth mother. Secrets and lies are revealed.

The film was crafted using an innovative method. Leigh gave the cast ideas for their roles, which they then created themselves, making up the dialogue for their scenes as they went along. After much improvisation and rehearsing, the script was tightly written and filmed. The result is a captivating movie with an energetic assortment of original characters. The picture of injured relationships, pain, and the discovery of the secrets of a dysfunctional family is not easily forgotten.

COMMENTARY

Focus: Weeds and wheat, sin and goodness, secrets and lies grow in the fields that are families. There is a time for revelation so that the fields can be weeded without harming the wheat. Secrets and Lies *illustrates this parable because it shows family frailty and ends with discovery and reconciliation.*

DIALOGUE WITH THE GOSPEL

The first reading from the Book of Wisdom speaks of a just God who grants the gift of repentance to those who have sinned. It is also the theme of the response: Lord, you are good and forgiving (cf. Ps 86:5–16). This is the prayer that underpins the human dilemmas in *Secrets and Lies*.

The Gospel begins with a secret: the enemy sows weeds among the wheat. Jesus gives an allegorical interpretation of the parable, explaining what the field is and identifying the seeds and the weeds. The moral of the parable is that in human experience, both good and bad exist together; there is a right time to discover truth.

Secrets and Lies embodies a complex family world. Each person has sown a secret that has harmed them and, by extension, others. These include Cynthia's unintentional pregnancy which is followed by giving her baby up without seeing her; Maurice, who allows himself to be victimized by his childless wife Monica; Roxanne's bitterness; and Hortense, who wonders persistently about her birth mother.

Cynthia and Hortense find their "right time," and friendship grows. For the others, the revelation is at first devastating. Then Maurice, like a good angel, enables the family to begin the process of reconciliation, however fragile.

KEY SCENES AND THEMES

- Cynthia's poverty in her life and relationships; her love for Maurice and Roxanne; Roxanne's hard attitude; the culmination of Roxanne's anger, her rude departure.

- Maurice's work and photography; Maurice as a good man despite Monica's attitude; his care for Cynthia; Maurice arranging the party and persuading Roxanne to return.

- Hortense's character and her life; Hortense's contact with Cynthia, their pleasant meeting over coffee, their outings, the final revelation of the truth; the family's many angers, their own revelations; the family's tears, hand holding, forgiveness.

1. Hortense began to search among the wheat and the weeds to find the truth about her identity. The story ends well, but just barely—which often happens in real life. How is this film a Gospel parallel? Who represents the wheat and the weeds in this touching human drama? Are the secrets wheat and the lies weeds? Why or why not?

2. This is a carefully constructed story about seeing truth through the debris of life. Hortense is an optometrist, someone who can examine people's eyes and prescribe glasses so they can see better. Maurice, her half-brother, is a photographer who sees things professionally. Roxanne, her half-sister, is a sanitation worker who cleans up garbage for a living. How does the film *Secrets and Lies* suggest that it's worth looking through the messiness of life to see the people around us clearly and in the best light possible, especially when it comes to family? and conversely, to give others a chance to see us? How did this work for Hortense and her family?

3. *Secrets and Lies* also makes a social statement about being bi-racial in a white family. How is Hortense a revelation to her family and vice versa? How are the characters in the story able to reconcile despite socially and culturally ingrained biases?

Prayer

O Lord, you are good and forgiving. Give us the wisdom to know when to speak the truth and when to be silent and always to foster forgiveness and healing. Amen.

SEVENTEENTH SUNDAY OF THE YEAR

1 Kings 3:5, 7–12; Matthew 13:44–52

Bagdad Cafe

Germany, 1988 / 91 minutes

Actors: Marianne Saegebrecht, Jack Palance, CCH Pounder

Writers: Percy Adlon, Eleonore Adlon, Christopher Doherty

Director: Percy Adlon

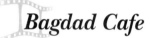 *Bagdad Cafe*

Where Your Treasure Is

SYNOPSIS

Jasmin, a German tourist, quarrels with her husband during their trip through the Mojave Desert and he abandons her. She makes her way to the Bagdad Cafe, a motel that has fallen on hard times.

Brenda, the manager of the cafe, is angry with her husband Sal, who has moved out and who watches the action at the cafe from his car across the highway. Brenda's children, Sal Jr., who wants to study music, and Phyllis, who just wants a good time, irritate her. Bagdad Cafe has two permanent residents, Rudi Cox, a painter who used to work as a set designer in Hollywood, and Debby, a tattoo artist. Sal Jr.'s baby is also a member of this unique cafe community.

Brenda is suspicious of Jasmin, who arrives with no luggage except her husband's suitcase, which she accidentally took from the car. Brenda becomes downright hostile when she returns from a shopping trip to find that Jasmin has systematically cleaned the whole place. Jasmin does not respond in kind but emanates a gentle and jovial presence that begins to transform everyone.

Rudi feels creative again and wants to paint Jasmin. Sal Jr. and Jasmin bond over Bach and the baby, and Phyllis enjoys Jasmin's company. In her spare time, Jasmin learns magic and starts doing magic tricks as she waits on tables. The Bagdad Cafe turns into a popular tourist and truck stop.

When Jasmin is told that her visa has expired, she organizes a song and dance performance with Phyllis before leaving. Sal Jr. provides the music. Jasmin goes back to Germany for a short while. When she returns to the cafe, Rudi proposes to her.

COMMENTARY

Bagdad Cafe is a small but delightfully offbeat comedy written by German director Percy Adlon and his wife Eleonore. Adlon's previous films were made in Germany and included *Celeste* (about Proust's maid) and *Sugar Baby,* also starring Marianne Saegebrecht.

Marianne Saegebrecht uses her ample physical presence to project a strong and vibrant on-screen personality. She makes the abandoned German housewife stuck in the American desert quite credible. In *Bagdad Cafe,* she is an intelligent and genteel person who generously shows how people's lives can be transformed. (Saegebrecht also appeared in several American movies, including her role as a maid in *The War of the Roses.*)

CCH Pounder plays the role of Brenda, the owner of the Bagdad Cafe, with just the right amount of edgy humor. The supporting cast includes Jack Palance as Rudi, the former Hollywood set painter who is attracted to Jasmin and wants to marry her. The cafe collects an odd assortment of characters, from Jasmin to the under-worked Native American sheriff, to a hiker with boomerangs, to Brenda herself. They all come under Jasmin's spell. The song, "Calling You," was nominated for an Oscar. The movie led to a short-lived television series starring Whoopi Goldberg.

DIALOGUE WITH THE GOSPEL

Focus: In the Parables of the Kingdom, Jesus speaks of giving up everything we possess to gain our pearl of great price, our treasure. Jasmin discovers her treasure at the Bagdad Cafe and enables others to find theirs.

The first reading from the First Book of Kings contains Solomon's famous dream of God offering him any gift he wants. Solomon chooses wisdom, "a heart to understand how to discern between good and evil," and he is given "a heart wise and shrewd." This is his treasure. The Gospel parables are also about treasures, and Jesus' final words allow us to understand them in the context of wisdom of the heart.

When Jasmin walks away from her thoughtless husband and is subsequently abandoned in a foreign country, she is left with virtually nothing. She walks down the highway to an isolated desert truck stop with an unusual cafe. Jasmin has a good heart and in her simple way, she is wise. She has the ability to transform each person she meets (except her cantankerous husband).

KEY SCENES AND THEMES

- In the desert, by allowing herself to know and to love others, Jasmin discovers her true heart. It is her pearl of great price, her hidden treasure which she does not keep for herself, but shares with everyone. Jesus says that this is what the kingdom of heaven is like.

- Our introduction to Jasmin, her quarrel with her husband, his curious indifference; Jasmin's quaint appearance in the desert; the transformation of the Bagdad Cafe and the people.

- The cafe atmosphere: Brenda's anger and critical attitude; Sal's irresponsibility, his distant observation and lack of involvement; Brenda's son, his music and the baby; the daughter and the truck drivers; Rudi, his art, his desire to paint Jasmin.

○ Jasmin's decision to stay, her magic, the joyful celebration; Rudi's proposal, Jasmin's hesitation, wanting to talk to Brenda first.

1. This slightly off-center story is a look at how very different people can let down their defenses and become friends. How does this happen in the film? How do Brenda and Jasmin change and grow? How do these two people discover the treasure in the other and in the people who make up their truck-stop community? How does the film's construction, in its offbeat way, show how opposites can complete one another in friendship?

2. The parable *Bagdad Cafe* shows that goodness is a treasure present within everyone and can change anyone who is open to growth. Jasmin's relationship with her husband disintegrates and he drives off. Brenda's husband has already departed, but he furtively watches the action at Brenda's motel from across the highway. How do the women's relationships with their husbands figure into the story? What is the film saying about family and the family that results from friendship and trust at the Bagdad Cafe? Do these and the other characters in the movie change for the better? Why and how?

3. Any "normal" person in Jasmin's place would take a hint and leave the motel because no one appreciates her or wants her there. She's too "different." Jasmin perseveres and wins people over with her generous spirit and because she is willing to work at relationships. How does she eventually find "where her treasure is"?

Prayer

When you offer us gifts, Lord, help us to ask first for wisdom and a kind and discerning heart. Amen.

Isaiah 55:1–3; Matthew 14:13–21

City of Joy

U.K. / France, 1992 / 135 minutes

Actors: Patrick Swayze, Om Puri, Pauline Collins, Art Malik

Writer: Mark Medoff

Director: Roland Joffe

City of Joy

God Provides

SYNOPSIS

The place is Calcutta, India. Hasari and his poor family leave Bihar to go to the city to make money to send back home. Bewildered by the crowds, they are taken in by a crook and lose what money they have. Hasari sees an American, Max, being beaten and robbed and takes him to the City of Joy Self-Help Clinic and School and Dispensary, run by Joan Bethel.

A local godfather and his callous son, Ashoka, control who gets work in the area. Hasari becomes indebted to them because they permit him to run a rickshaw. As his small business grows, things improve for his family.

Dr. Max Lowe comes to India searching for enlightenment because he feels responsible for a patient's death. He is disillusioned, but Joan wants to help him. However, despite her best efforts at raising his social consciousness, Max refuses to assist in her work. He gives in when faced with lepers in need and then he assists at a difficult birth. He finally agrees to stay for three months. He helps better organize the clinic and improves the area for the lepers. Max asks Hasari's wife to work at the clinic.

Hasari is loyal to the godfather even when Max urges him and others to take a stand. Ashoka organizes violence against the people and leads a riot against the lepers. Then the godfather dies and Ashoka asserts his power. He attacks Hasari's children and threatens Max. Hasari fights Ashoka and the new godfather is shamed before his associates.

The leper colony is threatened by a monsoon and Hasari saves Max from the flood. Hasari realizes he cannot remain socially passive. Max finds that he is more alive than he has ever been. He decides to stay.

COMMENTARY

City of Joy is based on the 1985 international bestseller of the same title by Dominique Lapierre. Lapierre's previous works included books about Indian partition and Mother Teresa. (The movie is dedicated to several people, among them the rickshaw drivers of Calcutta, Mother Teresa, and the Missionaries of Charity). Roland Joffe directed *City of Joy*, joining his other socially-minded sagas that include *The Killing Fields, The Mission,* and *Fat Man and Little Boy.*

City of Joy was filmed in Calcutta, capturing the city's vistas as well as providing detailed glimpses into both poor and rich areas. The filming was troubled by protests that questioned whether such a movie was exploiting or helping the social situation of Calcutta. Much of the screenplay by Mark Medoff concerns the issue of the West's (particularly the United States) self-righteous positions and interference in other troubled countries. At the same time, it centers on the interaction between Max and Hasari, thus showing that collaboration and mutual understanding are possible.

City of Joy, in microcosm, opens a window into the overwhelming world of India and its poverty. This close-up enables the audience to identify emotionally with characters and situations. The moral of the story is that even though most people will not be able to do great, memorable things on a grand scale, their efforts to improve the world around them, no matter how small, will benefit all people.

Focus: Today's Gospel is an example of how Jesus used some fish and a few loaves of bread to feed at least five thousand people. In the City of Joy there are only few resources, but they, too, can be blessed and multiplied just the same.

DIALOGUE WITH THE GOSPEL

The first reading expresses an ideal society where God feeds those who come and place their trust in him. The second reading from Paul to the Romans (cf. 8:35, 37–39) presents the actual world of need and suffering, realities that will not separate us from the love of God. These are the social polarities that we find in our world, from extreme want to great wealth. The story of the feeding of the five thousand shows how Jesus answers the dilemma of those in need of the barest essentials and those who have the means to share.

Jesus is compassionate, moved by the crowds and their needs. He asks what resources the apostles and the people have and they respond: five loaves and two fish. Jesus blesses and miraculously multiplies these few provisions so they will feed the crowd in abundance.

Faced with the masses of needy people in a country like India, what can be done? *City of Joy* dramatizes the problem and the answer. The resources are small and seemingly inadequate, but if they are used with trust and hope, the effect multiplies and more people are able to benefit. Joan Bethel had few resources in the City of Joy Self-Help Clinic, but she gave what she could. Through her hard work and others' generosity, the supplies and rations "multiplied." Max agrees to stay, work, and organize; Hasari's wife agrees to help in the clinic; a man offers a space for the lepers; the lepers help one another; the godfather is challenged and his son defied. The few, limited resources were indeed multiplied.

KEY SCENES AND THEMES

- The Hasari family's arrival in the city, their situation: tricked and robbed, poor and needy, yet generous; Hasari finding employment, his wife assisting in the clinic; Hasari learning to assert his rights.

- Joan's background, her desire to do what she can with few resources; her ability to motivate people.

- Max's American "attitudes," the crisis and robbery; Max's decision to deliver the baby, the consequences; Max's commitment; his freedom to stay in Calcutta.

FOR REFLECTION AND CONVERSATION

1. Like two of Roland Joffe's other films, *The Mission* (1986) and *The Killing Fields* (1984), *City of Joy* places white Westerners among social and cultural realities completely different from their own. All three films involve social injustice. How can these three films be contrasted, not only in their ability to tell their stories, but in the way they communicate messages that raise social awareness, responsibility, and respect for human dignity?

2. One principle of the spiritual life maintains that we will only have peace when we can give of ourselves to others. Max's experience of failure has made him apathetic and weary. He goes to India in search of enlightenment and peace. How does he find these things? What lesson is there in this for people who search for greater meaning in their spiritual lives? Talk about how Christian charity is not necessarily a special effort, but the ordinary way for us to collaborate with a loving God who will provide for his people.

3. The Gospel says that Jesus fed at least 5,000 people, not counting women and children. From the evangelist's cultural perspective, women and children clearly

did not count as much as men. This same situation is mirrored in the society featured in *City of Joy*. What can contribute to reconciling these inequalities with the teachings of Jesus?

Prayer

Lord, you took the meager provisions of the people and blessed them so that they multiplied and nourished thousands. Bless us and the resources we have so that these may be multiplied for the service of others. Amen.

NINETEENTH SUNDAY OF THE YEAR

1 Kings 19:9, 11–13; Matthew 14:22–33

Touch

U.S., 1997 / 96 minutes

Actors: Skeet Ulrich, Bridget Fonda, Christopher Walken,
Tom Arnold, Gina Gershon, Lolita Davidovich,
Paul Mazursky, Janeane Garofalo

Writer: Paul Schrader

Director: Paul Schrader

 Touch

Walking on Water

SYNOPSIS

Juvenal is a former Franciscan missionary to South America. While there, he receives the stigmata, like St. Francis, and the power to heal. When the demands and the gift itself overwhelm him, he leaves the Order and returns to Los Angeles where he is employed as a social worker at a Catholic rehab center.

An evangelical preacher-turned-car-salesman, Bill Hill, discovers Juvenal. Hill tries to enlist his former assistant Lyn, a beautiful young woman, to help exploit Juvenal financially through promotions and news interviews. At first, Juvenal is unwilling to cooperate, wanting to avoid the limelight. But Bill is cunningly persuasive, and things become more confusing as Juvenal openly indulges his infatuation with the young married assistant.

Juvenal agrees to an appearance arranged by Hill on a daytime talk-show. Meanwhile, a fanatical Catholic named August attacks Juvenal and in the fight that follows, August is severely injured. August is then persuaded by the talk-show host to come to the studio to debunk the gentle Juvenal on live television. Instead, Juvenal heals him. In the commotion

236

that follows, Juvenal and Lyn drive away from Los Angeles to seek a quiet life elsewhere. The film ends with the question, "What would God think...?"

Touch raises a number of religious issues, especially about the nature of faith, miracles, and the moral standing of the miracle worker. It is an adaptation of a novel by Elmore Leonard, better known for his offbeat tough thrillers. *Touch*, a different kind of novel for Leonard, shows through its subject and tone his familiarity with various contemporary expressions of Catholicism.

Paul Schrader, who comes from an austere religious background, wrote the screen adaptation for *Touch*. He also wrote the screenplay for *Taxi Driver*, *The Last Temptation of Christ*, and *Bringing Out the Dead* for director Martin Scorsese. Among Schrader's own films are *American Gigolo*, *Mishima*, and *Affliction*.

The tenor of the film is comic, sometimes farcical, though Schrader invests this bizarre tale with some depth. Double standards in church professionals are criticized in the same way the personal holiness of the miracle worker, Juvenal, is questioned due to his sexual indulgences. The screenplay has Juvenal quoting Jesus' challenges to the religious leaders of his time, while at the same time the film supports religion and the following of Jesus. When God sees a story like this, what does he think...?

Focus: Juvenal was a missionary who discovered he had healing power. People now want to exploit it and he doubts his own faith. He is invited to perform miracles, to "walk on water," but he sinks when he questions his faith.

Elijah tells us in the first reading of this Sunday from the First Book of Kings, that God is not found in the wind, the earthquake, or the fire, but in a gentle breeze. In the film we see the contrast between fundamentalist fervor and the gentle approach to ministry.

In the Gospel, Jesus retires from his busy ministry to take some personal time to pray. The pressures of his preaching and healing ministry require this. He sends the disciples off to the other side of the lake ahead of him. When they are caught in a storm, they are full of fear. Jesus comes to them walking on the water, but they think he is something extraordinary, a ghost. Peter puts his own faith to the test when he responds to Jesus' invitation to walk on the water. When Peter doubts, he begins to sink.

Touch is about ministry and its burdens, about the need for ministers to get away from the public gaze and find new life for their spirit. The film is also about people's superstitions and the manipulative pressure they can bring to bear on those who seek to serve them. According to the film, would-be disciples create their own storms, look for saviors everywhere, and then set them up. Ministers are tempted to walk on water, but when they try, they experience doubt and sink.

Juvenal is presented as a Christ-figure, a healer and a stigmatist, but one who needs to get away from center stage. Like Peter, he has seen the Lord, but is now alone in his boat. When a false prophet lures him out of the boat, he, like Peter, begins to sink. The media and the people want him to heal, show his wounds, and walk on water if he can. After temptations and failure, Juvenal gathers what faith he has left and seeks a less public place for his faith and himself.

KEY SCENES AND THEMES

- Juvenal's arrival: helping, healing Virginia, the blood from the stigmata; Juvenal as the young Franciscan who left his Order, his clothing and appearance, his manner of speaking; Juvenal's mundane work at the rehab center; his encounter with Lyn; Lyn seeing the stigmata at the washbasin; the stigmata itself (and the tradition of St. Francis); Juvenal's side and hands.

- Juvenal's love for God, the discussions about God acting through him, his critique of the church he attends; Juvenal's continued references to the Gospel's scribes and Pharisees and to Jesus as a sincere healer.

- Bill Hill: his cross and his shady past, his record deals; Bill setting up Juvenal; Juvenal's decision, his experience of the limelight, his awareness of both his faith and lack of faith.

1. The opening prayer for today's liturgy asks God to touch our hearts so that we will grow toward the promise of eternal life, and to touch our lives to make us signs of love for everyone. How has God touched Juvenal? Juvenal is a kind of Christ-figure, but one who is flawed and struggles with the burden of his power to touch others. Ultimately, he disappoints because he cannot walk on water. By the end of the film, however, how does Juvenal's integrity show forth? Can we identify with Juvenal in the story, or are there other characters who are perhaps easier to understand and sympathize with? Why?

FOR REFLECTION AND CONVERSATION

2. Sometimes the authenticity of a message that asks people to believe or to sacrifice is judged by the virtue of the messenger. This works very well if the messenger is Jesus, and not so well if the religious (or political) leader is less than perfect. People, often with the help of the media, are left with visions of humanity's limits that can sometimes diminish hope. Despite Juvenal's limitations, how is *Touch* a hopeful

story? What lessons does it teach about supporting leaders so they can find the strength to be more authentic?

3. *Touch* shows how some Catholics advocate a traditional form of life and liturgy, others a more progressive approach, while still others do not seem to have an opinion. They just want to love God, carry out God's will, and believe. Does this film make a statement about unity in the Church, or is it more of an examination of the polarization that exists? What does Juvenal's story say to the other characters that represent various approaches to Catholicism and Evangelicalism?

Prayer

Jesus, you ask us to step out in faith into the unknown. We hesitate, we sink, afraid we will drown. Reach out to hold on to us, steady us, and lead us to touch the lives of others with faith and love. Amen.

Nick Nolte and Susan Sarandon star in *Lorenzo's Oil.*

Lorenzo's Oil

U.S., 1992 / 154 minutes

Actors: Nick Nolte, Susan Sarandon, Peter Ustinov,
Zach O'Malley-Greenberg

Writers: Nick Enright, George Miller

Director: George Miller

Lorenzo's Oil

Blessed Are the Persistent

SYNOPSIS

Lorenzo Odone, born in 1978, is a young boy suffering from adrenoleukodystrophy (ALD), a rare degenerative neurological disease that occurs only in males and is transmitted through the mother. The disease leads to seizures, paralysis and death. Struggling to discover a diagnosis and treatment along with the medical profession in the mid-'80s, Lorenzo's parents begin to study the disease and become experts in understanding how it affects the body. They discover a way to halt the progress of the disease, a remedy they call "Lorenzo's Oil."

The Odones are an ordinary couple living in Washington, D.C., who decide they will fight for their son's recovery, no matter what the cost is. As Lorenzo's health deteriorates, his mother spends all her time with him and voraciously learns more and more about his condition. She finds out that despite the disease and his difficulties in communicating, her son is maturing intellectually. She stops reading children's books to him and chooses more age appropriate material. She almost wills him to learn how to blink and move his finger to communicate. She is a relentless, formidable adversary to the doctors she believes do not do enough for her son.

243

Michaela Odone died in 2000 of lung cancer, exhausted by her devotion to her son. Lorenzo is still living.

Lorenzo's Oil is a fine, although grueling, movie. It is not a so-called disease-of-the-week film. It is a human drama, a portrait of a family as well as a medical case study. The screenplay by Australians Nick Enright and George Miller was written as if it were a file report on Lorenzo's progress from 1983 to 1992. The screenplay received an Oscar nomination, as did Susan Sarandon for Best Actress in her role as Michaela Odone.

Director George Miller (*Mad Max* trilogy, *Witches of Eastwick, Babe: Pig in the City*) was a doctor before he became a filmmaker. He was in a unique position to employ his expertise to communicate the medical dilemmas of the situation on screen, such as the complexities of the illness, the criteria for testing of treatments, and the reaction of the medical profession and the drug companies.

The movie is mentally and emotionally demanding and is indeed a tribute to the extremes to which the human spirit will go for the sake of love. Susan Sarandon gives a fierce, intense, almost harrowing performance. Nick Nolte, with a more or less realistic Italian accent, is persevering, balanced, and solid. Peter Ustinov is believable as Dr. Nickolais, the only doctor who is sympathetic to the Odones' cause.

Focus: If anyone in movies reminds us of the Canaanite woman and her plea for a healing of her daughter, it is Michaela Odone. Her quest for healing for her son, Lorenzo, was incessant.

The Canaanite woman who lived in the region of Tyre and Sidon has to be one of the most persevering characters in the Gospels. This woman reminds us of the widow in Luke 18:1–8 who kept pestering the judge until he became so irritated at her persistence that he granted what she asked. In

Gospel passages such as these, Jesus urges us to develop a spirituality of perseverance in prayer.

The apostles are annoyed by the woman who follows Jesus with her cries and pleas that he heal her daughter. At first Jesus ignores her. When she does not go away, Jesus continues the drama with some witty dialogue and bargaining in a style characteristic of his culture. He says it's not right to throw the children's food to the dogs, meaning that he has been sent to the house of Israel, not to foreigners. The woman is up to the challenge and retorts that even the dogs eat the scraps from the table. Jesus admires her faith and grants her prayer.

Michaela Odone is an outsider to the medical profession. The doctors seem to have given up on her son. Michaela has the gift of perseverance, however, and she pesters. She does her best to learn about her son's disease, perhaps because she blames herself for transmitting it to him. She challenges the doctors and, much to their irritation, does not go away.

Michaela shows incredible determination, and her Catholic background is the source of her faith that Lorenzo will make some kind of recovery. The Odones' persistence is finally rewarded when the combination of olive and rapeseed oil they develop seems to halt the disease's progress. Though ALD has a lasting effect on Lorenzo, he begins to communicate and move in small ways. The example of how his parents fought for him can inspire parents in similar situations and encourage people to follow medical careers. "Woman, you have great faith."

- The African prologue; Lorenzo: at play, his knowledge of languages, behavior at home in the Comoro Islands; Lorenzo's family: his parents and their work in Africa; Lorenzo at school, his angry outbursts, the teachers' puzzlement.

KEY SCENES AND THEMES

• Lorenzo's doctor visits, the diagnosis, the hospital, the treatment and tests, the nurses; the medical explanations, theories, treatments, diet; prognosis; Lorenzo's physical decline, in the hospital and at home, increasingly disabled; Michaela's continual care and tenderness, her ability to understand his signals, her perseverance in getting him to will to move his finger.

• Michaela's strength and sense of family, her reaction to the doctors; the friendship and struggles with Dr. Nikolais, the meetings, the awkward questions, Michaela's frustration; Michaela's research, the Odones' intense study, the international seminar, the experts and discussions, their mutual help and collaboration; the oil.

FOR REFLECTION AND CONVERSATION

1. Michaela Odone's persistence and seeming lack of social skills did not win her a popularity contest with the medical community. But no force on earth could stop this mother. What was the source of her perseverance?

2. For those inspired by love, there is no obstacle too great to try, work, and struggle to find a solution to a problem. How can a movie like *Lorenzo's Oil* inspire others to dedicate themselves to research and helping people? What are some other true stories told through movies that can inspire people to dedicate their energies to advance the cause of human knowledge and life through science and technology? (For more information about *Lorenzo's Oil* you can go to www.myelin.org.)

3. What about Lorenzo? We have little indication about what he is thinking all day long or what his hopes and dreams might be. So many people's dreams are limited by physical problems. In what ways can each of us help another person to fulfill his or her dreams and live in dignity?

Prayer

Lord, you told us to ask and we will receive. The Canaanite woman asked again and again, and you finally answered her prayer. Help us to be constant and persevering in our petitions to you. Amen.

Anthony Quinn stars in *Shoes of the Fisherman*

The Shoes of the Fisherman

U.S., 1968 / 157 minutes

Actors: Anthony Quinn, Laurence Olivier, Oskar Werner,
David Janssen, Vittorio De Sica, Leo McKern, John Gielgud

Writers: John Patrick, James Kennaway

Director: Michael Anderson

The Shoes of the Fisherman

Authority for Service

When the Italian pope dies in the latter part of the twentieth century, the cardinals of the Catholic Church debate over who will succeed him. There are those who want to maintain traditions and, therefore, want a like-minded Italian pope. Others feel that modern times call for a different approach so the Church can speak to the real needs of the people.

SYNOPSIS

The world outside the Vatican is wrought with Cold-War hostilities; China is on the brink of famine and wants to invade the Soviet Union to obtain food and resources. A nuclear world war is possible.

Journalists covering the Vatican have personal and marital problems. A noted theologian is under suspicion from the Holy Office for expounding evolutionary views about creation, the world, and spirituality.

The conclave elects a Slavic cardinal who was imprisoned for twenty years by the Communists. He becomes Pope Kiril I. He feels constricted by Vatican protocol, so he ventures out one night to meet the real people of Rome. He also relates to the theologian in difficulties with pastoral kindness and understanding.

At his papal coronation, he gives away his tiara, under the eye of a Cardinal with whom he has clashed. Kiril tries to negotiate an accord between China and Russia and says he is willing to sell the treasures of the Vatican to alleviate starvation in China. The premiers of Russia and China watch on television and the crowds in St. Peter's Square applaud.

COMMENTARY

When Morris West's novel first appeared in 1963, it was regarded as prophetic. Changes in how the Catholic Church viewed itself and the world had just begun with the opening of the Second Vatican Council in October 1962 under Pope John XXIII. He died the following June. Paul VI was then elected. He completed the Vatican Council and worked for deténte with Soviet block countries. When John Paul I died in 1978 after barely a month in office, the Slavic Pope, Karol Wojtyla, was elected. John Paul II is considered to have been one of the chief influences in the collapse of the Soviet Union. Morris West was even more prophetic than people realized.

The film was a big-budget, spectacular epic with a star-studded cast. Anthony Quinn gives a credible performance as the pope, while Laurence Olivier looks severe as the Soviet premier. The journalist sub-plot seems somewhat trite. Oskar Werner's character is based on Teilhard de Chardin. Leo McKern and others enjoy themselves as Vatican cardinals.

The film raises often-discussed issues, especially concerning the wealth of the Church and the plight of the poor. Selling off the Vatican treasury is a temporary solution that seems simplistic, but Pope John Paul II has said that if it were ever necessary, he would do it.

DIALOGUE WITH THE GOSPEL

Focus: In today's Gospel and The Shoes of the Fisherman, *we reflect on Jesus' promises to Peter, and their meaning in our contemporary world. Peter is the rock and center of unity in the Church.*

Jesus' promise to entrust the keys of the kingdom to Peter is considered the fundamental text or scriptural basis for the primacy of the pope. If interpreted only literally, the historical development of the Office of Peter is sometimes overlooked. Our understanding of the Gospel may be enriched by the first reading from Isaiah, which uses the keys as a symbol of stewardship in authority and empowerment rather than power.

Peter's authority is based on his acknowledgment of who Jesus is and his confession of faith. This is the core of this Gospel reading. Peter's faith and his confession are not his own work, but a gift from the Father; authority in the Gospel is a service.

The Shoes of the Fisherman takes past perceptions of the papacy and papal authority and looks at them in new ways. The theology of the film and the perspectives of the Second Vatican Council converged in remarkable ways, seen all the more clearly from the distance of almost forty years. Add to this the fact that a Slavic Pope has been in office for more than two decades. He, like Pope Kiril in the film, has traveled the world and entered into dialogue with everyone. He has exercised spiritual authority and tried to show that the role of the papacy is for service, especially in the political and economic arenas. The film shows us the end of one era and the beginning of a new one. *The Shoes of the Fisherman* continues to challenge audiences to understand the papacy more deeply.

KEY SCENES AND THEMES

- The pope's death rituals; the cardinals' response; the conclave discussions, the possibility of a pope from a Communist country.

- The Pope's personal style: venturing out at night to meet people; his negotiations with the Chinese and the Russians.

- Theologian Fr. Oskar's encouragement and affirmation to Kiril that "you are Peter"; the papal mass and coronation, the cardinals, the premiers watching; the new pope laying aside his tiara and his promise to sell the Vatican treasures if needed.

FOR REFLECTION AND CONVERSATION

1. St. Matthew's Gospel is the only one to use the word "church." What is the relationship between various models of the Church and the papacy? How does the story in *The Shoes of the Fisherman* express the different yet converging definitions of what "Church" means? How do these models and expressions reflect the teaching of the Second Vatican Council?

2. *The Shoes of the Fisherman* is almost a blueprint for the papacy of John Paul II. What are some of the social, political, and religious similarities between the film and John Paul II's pontificate? What influence has his style of authority and service, and his teaching on the dignity of the human person, had in the world?

3. The responsorial psalm (cf. Ps 138:1–8) acknowledges that God's love is eternal and prays that God not forsake the works of his hands. How can the Church and the role of the pope be seen as ongoing works of God's love? How important is service and stewardship in our own lives as well as in the lives and teachings of those who carry out roles of authority in the Church?

Prayer

Jesus, you promised to be with your Church until the end of time and that the gates of hell would not prevail against it. We pray for the Church in our times, that its leaders may always act as you would act and serve as you would serve. Amen.

The Devil's Advocate

U.S., 1997 / 140 minutes

Actors: Al Pacino, Keanu Reeves, Charlize Theron, Judith Ivey, Craig T. Nelson, Heather Matarazzo, Peter Vaughn

Writers: Jonathan Lemkin, Tony Gilroy

Director: Taylor Hackford

The Devil's Advocate

Gaining the World

SYNOPSIS

When a very talented small town Southern lawyer, Kevin Lomax, discovers his client is guilty, he goes to the restroom to compose himself. He returns to the courtroom, humiliates the prosecution's young witness and emerges victorious. Soon after, he is offered an opportunity to join a prestigious law firm in New York. His wife is uncertain about the move and his very religious mother is against it. Nevertheless, they move and discover an affluent lifestyle and a clientele of the rich and famous. The company's head is the intense and persuasive John Milton.

Strange things begin happening in New York. Kevin's wife is lonely and begins to hallucinate. Kevin's confidence in his work begins to falter. He becomes attracted to a female lawyer and his relationship with his wife suffers. He gets a wealthy, but guilty, businessman acquitted of murder charges.

Kevin's wife claims that Milton has assaulted her. She takes refuge in a church but is committed to an institution where she kills herself. When Kevin confronts Milton, he discovers that Milton is the devil incarnate who then offers Kevin the world and the opportunity to sire an Antichrist. Milton reveals that Kevin is actually his son, and Kevin puts a gun to his head and pulls the trigger.

Suddenly, Kevin is back in the restroom where he had gone to plan his next move for his guilty client. He decides to do the right and noble thing—to discontinue defending the client, knowing that he will be disbarred. But as he leaves the courtroom, a journalist asks Kevin for an interview that will make him a celebrity.... .

COMMENTARY

The movie is very stylishly produced, corresponding well to the melodramatic, apocalyptic plot, writing, and direction. It deals explicitly with sin, and there are some disturbing sequences. However, the screenplay raises themes of God, the devil, salvation, damnation, and free will. It is rather clever that the name of the devil, John Milton, is also the name of the famous English poet who wrote the epics *Paradise Lost* and *Paradise Regained* (1667–1671), similar in theme to *The Devil's Advocate*.

The film opens in a courtroom with Keanu Reeves playing a hotshot Florida attorney who has never lost a case, even though some of his clients disgust him. When he is sought after for a top New York firm, he willingly starts on a journey to the top. The odyssey takes him deep inside his inner self and becomes a struggle for his conscience and soul.

The head of the firm, John Milton, is played with panache by Al Pacino. He excels at controlling, testing, and tempting others with genial and reasonable advice. His multinational legal firm is corrupt, and soon the young lawyer discovers more about himself than he wanted to. He is vain and ambitious, neglects his wife and is prepared to double-deal, like others before him.

The situation brings Kevin face to face with the devil and a debate about his own responsibility in his moral downfall. Even though the devil scoffs at God, he adheres to a theology of free will, where human beings can't blame others for the selfish choices they make. The movie is a grim variation on *It's a Wonderful Life*, where the hero sees what might have been.

Focus: Peter wants Jesus to avoid suffering and thus to "save" his life. Kevin Lomax learns that in order to gain his life back, he has to lose the one gained through his association with the devil, because Kevin is tempted to literally become the devil's advocate.

DIALOGUE WITH THE GOSPEL

The Gospel begins with Jesus announcing that he must suffer and Peter's very understandable, if overprotective, declaration that this must not happen. Jesus speaks severely to Peter, calling him a Satan, similar to the devil's advocate in the Book of Job, where it is the role of Satan to test the faith of humans and to make them suffer.

Jesus chastises Peter for his protectiveness. Peter falls into the "rescuing syndrome" that can lead to a denial of reality, for Jesus has to suffer so that he can rise on the third day. But Peter doesn't understand, and after fervently protesting that he will support Jesus to the end, he denies Jesus three times.

Jesus says that we must face reality and its hardships. Reality is a daily cross. If daily life with all its ups and downs is not accepted, then the comfortable life, even gaining the whole world, will mean nothing but ultimate ruin. Jesus reminds us that we are responsible for our own behavior. These are the themes of *The Devil's Advocate*.

Kevin Lomax is living a comfortable life and has a successful career. He is promised even more luxury so that he and his wife will never need anything again because the multinational corporation and its ethos will protect them.

The way of the devil is attractive. He offers every worldly advantage that appeals to human vanity, such as comfort, success, and fame, sounding much like the devil's earlier temptations of Jesus (cf. Mt 4). But Kevin discovers that the reality and crosses of daily life cannot be completely avoided, even though his new life leads him to evade his responsibilities and to neglect his wife. The consequences for his sins of omission are far worse than the daily grind of reality because Kevin loses his wife, his career, his comfort and, finally, his life.

This movie is a "what if..." fantasy that ends with a twist: another temptation to fame and vanity. The film ends where it began and the film's message comes full circle. Despite his "experience," Kevin is challenged to choose between good and evil once again.

KEY SCENES AND THEMES

- Kevin's choice to defend the pedophile, the distraught child, Kevin going into the restroom to examine his conscience; Kevin's temptation to the easy and comfortable life, his move to New York with the world at his feet.

- The fears of Kevin's mother, Mary Ann's suffering, Milton's assault, Mary Ann going to the church, her illness and death.

- John Milton as the devil: his intense speeches, his board and its evil decisions; Kevin caught up in defending the wealthy murderer; Kevin's final confrontation with Milton and Christabella; Kevin's decision to opt out; his opportunity to begin again.

FOR REFLECTION AND CONVERSATION

1. Jesus taught us by example and words that there is no easy way to live life. We can gain the whole world and lose much happiness by doing so. The tabloids and celebrity magazines are full of stories of the rich and famous who are unhappy, despite computer-enhanced smiles and perfect bodies. Perhaps few of us will reach celebrity status, but if we did, how would we handle

it? How would we prioritize our lives so that our values would transcend the choices we would have to make?

2. Life can be very messy. The parts of *The Devil's Advocate* that can make some viewers uncomfortable show harsh realities. Although in today's Gospel Jesus says we cannot avoid all sufferings, he consistently teaches that we are to work to alleviate the sufferings of others. How does Kevin Lomax eventually do this with regard to the victim of the pedophile and his own wife?

3. Popular culture, particularly advertising, insists that the more things we acquire the happier we will be. Advertising teaches consumers one basic skill: to buy. Do we question the commercial practices of mass media that try to convince us that our lives are incomplete without the comfort of more and more things? When is enough truly enough? Though certainly exaggerated, how can we identify with Kevin's struggle with temptation? How are the temptations Milton taunts Kevin with like those the devil tried with Jesus?

Prayer

Jesus, be with us when we are tempted to avoid pain and suffering, when we are tempted to want the whole world. Teach us the wisdom of losing our lives for your sake. Amen.

TWENTY-THIRD SUNDAY OF THE YEAR

Ezekiel 33:7–9; Matthew 18:15–20

The Crucible

U.S., 1996 / 123 minutes

Actors: Daniel Day-Lewis, Winona Ryder, Paul Scofield, Joan Allen, Jeffrey Jones, Bruce Davison, George Gaines

Writer: Arthur Miller

Director: Nicholas Hytner

 *The Crucible*

Authentic Community

SYNOPSIS

One night in Salem, Massachusetts, in 1692, Reverend Paris discovers some girls, including his daughter and his niece, Abigail Williams, dancing in the woods and indulging in strange rituals. There are rumors about witchcraft in the town.

The Reverend John Hale comes to examine the girls who blame a servant, Tituba, for casting spells over them. Paris beats Tituba and she "confesses." Then she and the girls begin to accuse other people of being involved with the devil.

Abigail is the leader and protects herself from prosecution by inciting the other girls to provide names and fall into trances. She is also motivated by her anger with John Proctor, a married man with whom she previously had an affair, who has rejected her. Hearing the wild accusations against innocent people, John suspects that Abigail is at the root of it. With his wife Elizabeth's support, he goes to the authorities to denounce her.

Abigail resents Elizabeth and plots against her. A doll with a needle stuck in it is found in the Proctor house. Before Judge Danforth, Abigail claims that Elizabeth has wounded her by witchcraft, but John reveals his adultery to prove

Abigail's motive of vengeance. When called to testify, Elizabeth denies John's affair, in the hope of protecting his reputation. Instead, the judge believes Abigail and arrests John for dealing with the devil.

Hysteria continues to reign in the village. Many innocent people are accused of witchcraft and hanged. Their property is confiscated and given to upright citizens. After failing to persuade John to escape and leave with her, Abigail flees. Hale tries to persuade Elizabeth to save John by having him "confess" to witchcraft. He does. But then, out of self-respect, he recants and is hanged.

COMMENTARY

Arthur Miller's 1953 classic touched a nerve with its Salem witch trials that reflected the witch hunt atmosphere of the McCarthy/Hollywood Blacklist era. The screenplay for the film is given a 1990s treatment by Miller himself, and is directed by Nicholas Hytner, whose movie directing debut was *The Madness of King George*.

The Salem witch trials made an indelible mark on the American psyche. Salem was a very religious Puritan community, faced with the fact that some of its young girls danced in the woods and played at casting spells. The discovery unleashes a movement of fanaticism, superstition, persecution, mock trials, and executions that become a warning to those who would engage in unfounded moral panics. The events revealed that a righteous community could have a destructive and dark side at the same time. Winona Ryder is more than convincing as Abigail, whose malevolence grows as she controls the justice in Salem.

The character of John Proctor allows us to explore the inner turmoil of an ordinary man who sins, repents, and chooses integrity over his life. The final sequence, with its religious imagery and prayer, is jolting. Daniel Day-Lewis gives yet another solid performance as Proctor, matched by Joan Allen as his wife Elizabeth, who plays a loving, wronged wife, rather than the mere shrew that some interpretations give this role in other productions.

DIALOGUE WITH THE GOSPEL

Focus: In the early Christian communities, divisions arose due to jealousy, envy, and greed—all in the name of God. Salem, Massachusetts of the 1690s became one of the most notorious religious communities ever to be tested by a spirit of evil.

The community of Salem, 1692, might have read each of the readings for today and thought they were putting them fully into practice. The Puritan community centered on the Word. However, their interpretation of Scripture was distinguished by a Calvinist emphasis, first on predestination, and then on prosperity as the main indicator of God's grace. The more they prospered, the more graced they thought they were. The accusers believed they were blessed when they obtained the property of the condemned, even though the trials were manifestly unjust and based on the testimony of a group of hysterical girls. This was especially true of Judge Danforth's character.

The reading from the prophet Ezekiel is about personal, individual responsibility for one's good and one's evil. But discernment is needed. Perhaps the inhabitants of Salem thought they were doing precisely what the last sentence of Ezekiel says: that the unrepentant person shall die because of guilt. Perhaps they thought their trials, condemnations, and burnings were fulfilling the last line of the reading from Romans (cf. 13:8–10), that love never does any wrong to one's neighbor, therefore love fulfills the law and the community was right to put the guilty to death.

Today's Gospel challenges the behavior of Salem's religious community that believed the hysteria of the immature Abigail and the other girls, persecuted the older citizens, and condoned the havoc wreaked on the lives of John and Elizabeth Proctor, all in the name of righteousness. Today, Jesus reminds us of the nature of the Christian community: how disputes and unchristian behavior are to be dealt with, the character of appropriate confrontation, and God's presence when people pray together—this is authentic community.

- The scene in the woods: the girls, Tituba, the incantations and dancing, the hysteria; the girls' ages, their rebellion against authority, peer pressure, sexuality, the potion; Reverend Paris' disgust, his interrogating and beating Tituba.

- John Proctor's affair with Abigail, his pseudo-reconciliation with Elizabeth; Elizabeth's honesty, her severe manner and beliefs, her desire to protect her husband, the court's decision.

- Judge Danforth: his authority, religious beliefs, theological background, his administration of justice; the executions, the viciousness of the crowd; John's integrity, his condemnation, his reciting the Lord's Prayer, his execution.

1. Even in our own time, with so much information and the many hi-tech ways to obtain it, innocent people are still condemned. As of this writing, eighty-five people in the U.S. have been released from prison and ten from death row because DNA testing on evidence which initially convicted them of criminal acts has now proved them innocent. Public opinion and gossip, stirred up by media coverage can influence the judicial processes. Why are moral panics dangerous? How is wisdom and objectivity possible amid hysteria such as that perpetrated by Abigail and her companions? How does it come about that innocent people are demonized by false accusations? What so-

cial dynamic causes this to happen, whether in families, groups, places of business, faith communities, or societies?

2. Compare this film with what happened to the Chamberlain family in the true story told in the film *A Cry in the Dark*. What role did public opinion and religion play in both of these films? What would the responsibility of a citizen and Christian be if faced with the dilemmas depicted in these movies? How can authentic communities offer an alternative to this phenomenon? What marks would characterize an authentic community?

3. One of the most heart-wrenching scenes in *The Crucible* is at the end when John Proctor signs his name on a false document asserting that he is guilty of witchcraft. He then recants because, after everything that has happened, all he has left is his good name. Why is he willing to die for his good name and the memory of his integrity?

Prayer

Lord, the spirit of evil is one of deception and destruction, and it can blind a community that believes in you. Help us to be faithful and to truly discern your presence in our midst. Amen.

Unforgiven

U.S., 1992 / 127 minutes

Actors: Clint Eastwood, Gene Hackman, Morgan Freeman, Richard Harris, Frances Fisher, Saul Rubinek, Jaimz Woolvett

Writer: David Webb Peoples

Director: Clint Eastwood

 *Unforgiven*

Anger and Revenge Bring Death

A group of prostitutes in the town of Big Whiskey, Wyoming, band together and defy the sheriff by putting up reward money for anyone who will kill the cowboys who brutally slashed the face of one of their girls. The sheriff, Little Bill, ruthlessly rules the town as his "personal kingdom." He does not think the victim, Delilah, deserves justice. He despises assassins as cowards and does not permit anyone to carry a gun. Little Bill savagely beats the legendary gunslinger, English Bob. Mr. Beauchamp, a pulp-Western writer who was traveling with the polished gunman, attaches himself to Little Bill so he can document Bill's exploits.

William Munny is a reformed gunfighter living in Missouri. His wife is now dead and he has two young children and responsibilities. He is persuaded by a young bounty hunter to find and kill the cowboys who brutalized the prostitute, and collect the $1,000 reward. Munny enlists the help of his old partner in crime, Ned. When they arrive in Big Whiskey, Little Bill confronts Munny who has become ill and beats him almost to death.

SYNOPSIS

Munny returns to something of his old cruel and wild self when Little Bill kills his friend Ned. In the end, the women are avenged and Little Bill is killed in a climactic shoot-out. Beauchamp observes everything. Munny disappears into obscurity and the folklore of the West.

COMMENTARY

Released in 1992, *Unforgiven* was considered a climax to Clint Eastwood's acting and directing career. At various stages in his career, this American icon has given new energy to the Western genre: in the 1960s, with films he made with Sergio Leone *(A Fistful of Dollars; The Good, the Bad and the Ugly)*, in the 1970s with Don Siegel *(High Plains Drifter, The Outlaw Josey Wales)*, and again in the 1980s *(Pale Rider, which he directed)*. Eastwood was most successful, however, with *Unforgiven*, which won four Oscars (he won for Best Director), and was nominated for five more.

The movie is a grim look at the legendary West and its decline. *Unforgiven* contains a critique of the myths and the heroes who are shown as drunken killers who don't know what they are doing. We also learn that stories about these "heroes" were exaggerated and became the core of pulp novels and a long mythical tradition.

The focus of the film is split between Eastwood as William Munny and the ruthless but smiling sheriff, vigorously played by Gene Hackman who was nominated for Best Supporting Actor. The screenplay is much more realistic than the romantic Westerns of the past. Overall, *Unforgiven* is a pessimistic elegy to the myths of the American West.

DIALOGUE WITH THE GOSPEL

Focus: Jesus' parable is about the consequences of the unjust servant's actions and the necessity to forgive one another from the heart. The film Unforgiven *is about anger, revenge, injustice, and the unwillingness to forgive.*

The reading from Sirach illustrates almost the exact opposite of the themes found in *Unforgiven*. The reading tells us that anger and resentment are hateful things and that by responding to them with mercy and forgiveness we will receive healing from the Lord. Conversely, the film focuses on resentment, anger, vengeance, wrath, faultfinding, and injustice.

William Munny is a man who was converted from a life of vengeance by his now deceased wife who, as today's Gospel teaches, forgave him from the heart. But he is tempted to take up his violent life once again when he hears of the vicious attack on Delilah. Aside from his need for the reward money, he feels a righteous indignation that he uses to justify his actions. When he confronts a man who is even more ruthless and unforgiving than he ever was, Munny is thrust into the violent ways of his past.

Little Bill, well groomed and spotless on the outside, is merciless when it comes to people who cross him. Unforgiving, he ends up at the mercy of the man he tortures—William Munny. In the spirit of the American West and Clint Eastwood's Westerns where the righter of wrongs is both the instrument of God and a hellish avenger, Munny becomes the torturer—and the sheriff pays his debts with his life.

The somber story told in *Unforgiven* is a great challenge to those who heed today's Gospel message, which teaches us to be endlessly forgiving to others. *Unforgiven* is such an extreme example of the violence that results when those who have been forgiven do not in turn forgive others from the heart.

KEY SCENES AND THEMES

- Symbolic landscapes: the grim West, the farms, the town, the brothel, that contrast with the beauty of the snow-clad mountains, the valleys; starkness and beauty, the dark, the rain; the brothel, the vicious attack on

Delilah; the summons to Little Billy for justice, his threats, agreeing to let the horses pay the debt to the prostitutes instead of punishing the man, the treatment of the women as animals, their anger.

• William Munny, his work on the farm, his decision to go and his motives; the money, the children; Ned, the whipping, his death and being exposed in the town; Munny's angry reaction.

• Munny's identity as a gunfighter, his skills, doing the job, his final motivations; Munny's rationalized sense of justice, his confrontation with Little Bill, Munny's final state.

FOR REFLECTION AND CONVERSATION

1. There are only hints of mercy in *Unforgiven*. Even when the partner of the cowboy who slashed Delilah wants to apologize and make restitution, the prostitutes, themselves victims of those who abuse them, refuse to forgive. If the women had forgiven the cowboys, how might the story have changed? According to what you know about the American West (e.g., real cowboys only existed between 1865 and 1880, ending when the beef industry floundered and homesteading was completed), would the film have been realistic if the women had offered forgiveness?

2. Munny and his band went to avenge the mutilation of a prostitute so they could get a reward. They convinced themselves it was also the right thing to do. Is vigilante justice ever warranted? What is the purpose of civil law in society? What kind of moral universe is portrayed in the film as compared to the one we live in today?

3. The responsorial psalm says that the Lord is kind, merciful, slow to anger and rich in compassion. Each of us can ask how we reflect these Divine attributes in our own lives, at home, work, school, and community. What are the consequences of anger, revenge, and the refusal to forgive?

Prayer

Lord, you warned us against anger and violence, yet there is so much cruelty and injustice in our world. Guide us with wisdom so that we may work for human rights in justice and hope. Amen.

TWENTY-FIFTH SUNDAY OF THE YEAR

Isaiah 55:6–9; Matthew 20:1–16

Matewan

U.S., 1987 / 133 minutes

Actors: Chris Cooper, Mary McDonnell, William Oldham,
David Strathairn, Bob Gunton, James Earl Jones

Writer: John Sayles

Director: John Sayles

Matewan

Justice for Workers

SYNOPSIS

In the town of Matewan, West Virginia, 1920, black migrant workers and Italian scab laborers are brought in by the mining company to break a strike. A union organizer, Joe Kenehan, arrives to work with the miners and formulates an agreement that says scabs will be welcomed into the union if they do not cross the picket lines.

Joe takes a room at a boarding house run by Elma Radno, but has to move to the hotel when two arrogant company strikebreakers arrive in town. Elma's fifteen-year-old son, Danny, is a pro-union miner and a lay preacher who clashes with the men. Meanwhile, the miners hold meetings to form a union at a restaurant owned by C.E. Lively who, in fact, is a spy and an informer for the company.

The new union members are evicted from their company homes and build a tent town. Various confrontations occur between the company men and the pro-union workers and townspeople. The miners' camp is ambushed. Joe becomes a target when Lively plants a rumor that persuades people to believe that Joe is really a strikebreaker and not the union organizer he claims to be. Plans are made to kill him. However, Danny cleverly reveals the truth about the situation during a sermon, and the assassination is called off. Lively's restaurant is burned down when the miners realize who he really is.

The final confrontation begins when a young miner, Willard, is caught stealing coal and executed because he won't name names. Joe advocates non-violence, but the miners have had enough. In a final battle, the mayor, many of the miners, the new "hired guns" the company brings in to evict the miners, the company agents, and Joe are killed.

COMMENTARY

John Sayles writes scripts for popular movies as well as his own projects, which he also directs. Initially, his stories were about relationships; with *Matewan,* he moved to more social-minded themes, which he continued to address in films such as *City of Hope* and *Men with Guns.* Other Sayles' films include *Passion Fish, Lone Star,* and *Limbo.*

A number of movies have been made about workers and strike action, including *The Angry Silence, The Molly Maguires, The Ballad of Joe Hill, F*I*S*T,* and *October Sky* (also with *Matewan's* star, Chris Cooper), as well as many documentaries, including the Oscar-winning *Harlan County, U.S.A.* These films favor workers and present a grim picture of government, company owners, and management.

Sayles creates a persuasive portrait of a West Virginia mining town and the social struggles brought on by a strike. He also relies on audience appreciation of the conventions of the Western genre when he sets up a violent confrontation in the final shootout. Unlike most Westerns, however, the ending is dark, and hope for a final solution for the miners is many years away.

A number of experienced character actors bring the story to life, especially James Earl Jones, who picks the short straw and is slated to kill Joe, and Bub Gunton as Lively. Because

Sayles made the movie for a wide audience, he is rarely subtle and makes powerful, unambiguous social statements.

DIALOGUE WITH THE GOSPEL

Focus: Matewan is a twentieth-century story about workers who struggle for social justice. The Gospel parable portrays the "absurd generosity" of God, who repays according to his own terms. It also serves to remind owners that they are to be magnanimous to workers.

The parable of the laborers in the vineyard is a parable about Divine generosity that goes beyond the limits of strict justice. It is also about work.

Matewan reminds us that the history of industrial relations is often a sad and violent one. The term "industrialist" is sometimes synonymous with exploitation. The nineteenth and early twentieth centuries gave birth to labor unions to protect workers' rights, because the ever-present danger of power struggles that came with industrialization led to abuses of justice on all sides.

Most people would expect Jesus' parable to end with some extra money given to those who had worked the full day. But Jesus disappoints these expectations. The laborers hired in the morning received the pay they agreed on. The story concludes with the owner's generosity to the latecomers, treating them the same as those who worked all day.

This parable reminds owners that they must respect workers, fulfill contracts, establish safe working conditions, and reward employees generously.

The story of *Matewan* highlights the tragic consequences of the oppression of workers and what happens when dishonest and violent people manipulate just policies and procedures.

- The mining town's social situation, the company owners and their demands, workers' needs for humane conditions, the strike and the strike-breaking tactics.

- The strike's effect on people in the town, Elma's boarding house, her son Danny; the sheriff and the mayor who help evict the family; C.E. Lively's double-dealing; the relations between whites, Italians, blacks, and the hill people.

- Joe's role as mediator, his relationships with people, his interventions; James as the target of murder; Danny's sermon and the truth; the final violence and Joe's death.

KEY SCENES AND THEMES

1. Labor disputes and strikes have long been with us. According to the Church's social teaching, when is a strike just? What are the rights and duties of employers and workers? Who should speak up in the face of injustice? Is violence ever warranted? Would non-violence have changed the outcome of what happened in *Matewan,* given the social, economic and political context of the times?

2. In today's alternative opening prayer, we acknowledge that the perfection of justice is found in God's love and that all humanity is in need of the Divine law. Love, justice, and obedience to God are required for peace and right living. When the miners banded together in *Matewan,* how did they show love and justice for one another? What law guided them in their choices and actions? Was the ending of the film inevi-

FOR REFLECTION AND CONVERSATION

table in terms of how a story is told or in terms of how strikes were carried out during the historical period depicted? Why or why not?

3. The reading from Isaiah prays that the scoundrel may forsake his way and the wicked turn their thoughts to the Lord for mercy. What about workers' rights in developing countries, for example, where multinational corporations establish facilities that meet neither the physical needs of workers nor pay a just wage? How can we work for corporate change when human rights demand it?

Prayer

Lord of justice, look with compassion on workers who are exploited and have few resources to seek justice. Change the hearts of those who have power over others so that human rights may be respected everywhere. Amen.

A Civil Action

U.S., 1998 / 130 minutes

Actors: John Travolta, Robert Duvall, Kathleen Quinlan, William H. Macy, Tony Shalhoub, James Gandolfini, John Lithgow, Sydney Pollack

Writer: Steven Zaillian

Director: Steven Zaillian

A Civil Action

Righteous Lawyer

Jan Schlichtmann is a flashy, successful personal injury lawyer. On a radio talk show, he is challenged to do something for the families with children who have leukemia because of the chemical pollution of some wells that supply water to neighborhoods in Woburn, Massachusetts. To save face, he meets with some of the parents, but has no intention of taking on the case because he doesn't think it will pay. However, when the police stop him on the way out of town for speeding, he happens to see a polluted river and evidence of dumped chemicals. He decides to take the case.

Because this is a contingency case where the firm has to pay all expenses out-of-pocket in view of a final financial settlement, Schlichtmann and his partners dedicate themselves to it completely. The members of the firm become more desperate as they spend all they own on the investigation and preparation for the case. Schlichtmann tangles with one of the chemical company's crack lawyers, Facher, and a company boss. He holds out for a bigger settlement. He originally took the case for the money, but as things go downhill, his motivations change and he begins working for the sake of the children.

SYNOPSIS

Schlichtmann loses the case for lack of persuasive witnesses. The case is eventually won for the plaintiffs, but not by him. Besides losing his high-flying lifestyle, Schlichtmann loses his partners and friends. He begins to practice environmental law and simplifies his life.

COMMENTARY

Steven Zaillian is best known as a writer *(Awakenings, Hannibal)*. His dramatization of Thomas Kineally's 1982 book, *Schindler's Ark,* won an Oscar. His directing debut was *Searching for Bobby Fischer,* the moving story of a child chess prodigy. Zaillian keeps his quietly controlled, intense style in *A Civil Action,* the story of a hotshot lawyer with neither shame nor self-doubt, who gets caught up in preparing a case for families with ill or deceased children who suffer from the effects of the environmental negligence of high-powered companies.

The film is based on a true story and is fairly accurate, but it does not progress as expected. The lawyer has to discover some element of his own humanity; his partners give everything they have, but go broke; his wise and wily adversary, played by Robert Duvall, is successful; and the families who have come to depend on Schlichtmann end up disappointed. This does not sound like a formula for an upbeat film. Nevertheless, *A Civil Action* shows the necessity of social concern and how ordinary folk, when joined together, can question the law, justice, and corporations with positive results. *A Civil Action* is a healthy reminder of the David and Goliath archetypal story. John Travolta, in the role of Jan Schlichtmann, is energetic, effective, and convincing.

DIALOGUE WITH THE GOSPEL

Focus: Jan Schlichtmann's life and career serves as a kind of analogy to the story of the two brothers of Jesus' parable: the one who said "yes" but did not go to do what his father asked, and the one who said "no," but went.

Jesus' story in the Gospel is brief and pointed. It concerns discerning and doing God's will, a meditative story-reflection on Ezekiel's comments about moral responsibility in the first reading.

In his professional behavior, lawyer Jan Schlichtmann can be seen as embodying the two sons in today's Gospel. Schlichtmann's two sides, one "good" and one "bad," dialogue as he tries to find the moral strength to do the right thing.

Schlichtmann is an "ambulance chaser," and as scenes in the movie show, he makes extravagant amounts of money by bluffing and working out legal deals that are primarily self-serving. When asked if he is doing the right thing by practicing law like this, he answers without hesitation that he is.

One day a woman phones in to a radio talk show and calls his bluff. In his conceit, Schlichtmann boasts that he is a righteous lawyer. The woman challenges him to take a case against the industrial companies that are polluting the water supplies, which allegedly caused many people to develop cancer. On the radio, like the righteous son to his father, Schlichtmann says he will do what is asked, although he has no intention of following through. When he meets the townspeople, he smoothly tries to talk his way out of his predicament.

Providence intervenes when the police stop his car near a pollution site. He reflects, and despite having said no to the townspeople's pleas (like the seemingly less dutiful son), Schlichtmann takes the case. Ultimately, he loses his friends, his firm, the lawsuit, and his wealth.

Schlichtmann is a contemporary example of the tax collectors (the big moneymakers of Jesus' day) entering into the kingdom of God first. Schlichtmann is headed toward the kingdom as he begins to work more honestly in the field of environmental justice.

KEY SCENES AND THEMES

- Schlichtmann propelling his client down the corridor; his bluffing and dealing millions for court damages; the firm's subsequent celebration.

- Schlichtmann's smooth radio spiel; his glib promise to the caller; the interview with the parents and families, Schlichtmann's refusal of the case, then his stark view of the polluted water.

- Schlichtmann's discussions with Jerome Facher about the law and justice; the hard decisions regarding the case; the desperation of the firm members; Schlichtmann's choice and its consequences; the judge's last question.

FOR REFLECTION AND CONVERSATION

1. Lawyer jokes always get big laughs and attorneys like Jan Schlichtmann only make the stereotype more difficult to change. Initially, Schlichtmann's motives for taking the case were all wrong. But in the film he changes. Why? What were his motives for fighting the case through to the bitter end?

2. *A Civil Action* and *Erin Brockovich* have similar themes because they are about people who stand with the "Davids," the victims, and take on the "Goliaths," the huge corporations, and win. How do the stories, the two lead characters, the victims, and the toll on the environment compare? When a stockholder becomes aware of a company's activities, whether at home or abroad, such as those portrayed in either of these films, what elements could a responsible Christian response include?

3. Sometimes ideas and movements become so trendy and politically correct that we tire of them and cease to care, if we ever did. Stewardship for the natural environment is a moral imperative, however, because the environment is a gift from God and the future of humanity depends on how we care for it today. Are the lawyers in *A Civil Action* righteous? Do they really care about the environment or the human victims of environmental abuse, or do they just care about winning the case? What message is there in the film for us, not only as potential victims of careless business practices, but also as co-caretakers of the environment, at home and abroad?

Prayer

God our Father, you teach us to do your will by following the commandments. Give us the grace to say "yes" to you and to see our commitments through to the end. Amen.

Sam Waterston and Haing S. Ngor star in *The Killing Fields*.

TWENTY-SEVENTH SUNDAY OF THE YEAR

Isaiah 5:1–7; Matthew 21:33–43

The Killing Fields

U.K., 1984 / 141 minutes

Actors: Sam Waterston, Haing S. Ngor,
John Malkovich, Julian Sands, Bill Paterson,
Craig T. Nelson, Athol Fugard, Spalding Gray

Writer: Bruce Robinson

Director: Roland Joffe

The Killing Fields

Massacre in Our Times

In 1973, Dith Pran, a well-educated interpreter, helps U.S. journalist Sydney Schanberg to get into Phnom Penh, Cambodia. By 1975, the Khmer Rouge is advancing on the capital, and Pran's family is evacuated while Pran stays with Schanberg. While the people rejoice and welcome the Khmer Rouge, Shanberg and other journalists are interned. They watch as the Khmer Rouge carries out executions. Pran argues for the journalists' release. They take refuge in the French embassy and are then expelled from the country.

SYNOPSIS

Schanberg tries to get Pran out as well but the Khmer Rouge sends him to a re-education labor camp. Pran conceals his language abilities.

Back in New York, Schanberg wins awards, but an associate criticizes him for not finding a way to get his friend Pran out of Cambodia. Schanberg commences efforts to find Pran through the agency of the U.S. government and the Red Cross.

Pran finally escapes and endures a long trek through the killing fields. A Khmer chief asks Pran to help his son escape the country. The boy dies when he steps on a mine. Finally, Pran is reunited with Sydney Schanberg in Thailand.

COMMENTARY

The Killing Fields is based on a 1980 article entitled "The Death and Life of Dith Pran" by the *New York Times'* journalist Sydney Schanberg, portrayed here by Sam Waterston. Schanberg was a reporter who stayed in Cambodia when other Western journalists were evacuated. *The Killing Fields* tells the story of Schanberg's work, with glimpses of the other journalists covering the war, and eventually focuses on the experiences of Schanberg's assistant and translator, Dith Pran. Pran is played in the film by Haing S. Ngor, a doctor who lived in Cambodia during the era of the killing fields. This was Ngor's movie debut, and he won an Oscar for Best Supporting Actor for his efforts. He subsequently appeared in a number of movies until he was tragically murdered by thieves in Los Angeles.

The film recreates for a Western audience the horror of the Pol Pot regime and its cruel genocide. Through the film's lens, we see the sufferings of the Cambodian people and their heroic struggle for survival. The film jolted the Western conscience in the mid-80s and contributed to an understanding of the history and reality of the people of Cambodia.

The film was the directing debut of Roland Joffe who went on to make *The Mission, City of Joy* and *Vatel*. The film was nominated for seven Academy Awards and won three, for Best Supporting Actor, Best Cinematography, and Best Editing.

**DIALOGUE WITH
THE GOSPEL**

Focus: God loves each nation, each people. The savage behavior that turned Cambodia into killing fields is like today's Gospel parable about the evil tenants who refuse to give the owner his due. Those they murder, the servants and the owner's beloved son, are like the innocent victims of the despotic regime of the Khmer Rouge.

The first reading for today's liturgy is the minstrel song from Isaiah 5. It tells of the love of the vineyard owner for the vineyard and of his regret that despite the care he has given, its only produce is sour grapes.

Jesus tells a parable that echoes this canticle, but develops it into an allegory about his own persecution, suffering, and death. Jesus' contemporaries have turned the vineyard into a small killing field. They plot the torture and murder of the owner's servants and do not spare his only son because they want his inheritance. Jesus told this story to wake up the religious leaders with the message that whoever rejected Jesus would be rejected too.

In terms of justice, this part of Matthew's Gospel can be applied to contemporary killing fields such as those of Kosovo or of East Timor in the late 1990s. Prosperous lands were invaded, and their owners and heirs tortured and killed by those who wanted the inheritance for themselves. Yes, prosperity and justice are for all citizens. But the Pol Pot regime, portrayed in *The Killing Fields,* took over Cambodia and destroyed all its servants and heirs in a massive genocide. It was the classic case of the oppressed becoming the oppressor.

Ultimately, the rightful citizens and owners of the land obtained the opportunity for self-rule and independence, and were able to build again. Like Jesus and the kingdom, the survivors eventually became the cornerstones of a new society. The unjust persecutors were ousted and condemned.

The second reading from Philippians (cf. 4:6–9) encourages respect, honesty, purity, decency, and virtue among the community—noble sentiments that counterbalance the sorrow of those who suffer so grievously in the killing fields of the world.

- The political and moral crisis in Cambodia; the journalists' attitudes; Sydney Schanberg's escape, writing about the horror of the killing fields.

KEY SCENES AND THEMES

- Dith Pran as Schanberg's translator: his dilemma over escaping, the details of his journey; the violence and massacres in the countryside; the starving and the poor, the millions who suffered and died.

- The story's aftermath; the memories stirring the conscience of the world.

FOR REFLECTION AND CONVERSATION

1. *The Killing Fields* is a stark reminder of the horrors inflicted on people by other human beings. We look on the events through the eyes of a journalist and the interpreter who helped him, Dith Pran. The first reading from Isaiah and the Gospel both speak about vineyards that have been trampled and misused, a parallel for Cambodia. How does the film raise our awareness about what happened in Cambodia just as the war in Vietnam was ending? Why would our knowing about these events still be important? What kind of men are Sydney Schanberg and Dith Pran? How are they finally reunited?

2. The twentieth century inaugurated a culture of death never before chronicled in the history of the world: war, genocide, abortion, the death penalty, and euthanasia. How are these crimes against humanity rooted in a disregard for the dignity and value of each and every human person? What defines a human being?

3. Mother Teresa is supposed to have once said that Christianity is meant not to comfort the afflicted but to afflict the comfortable. Sydney's sense of comfort in the movie is upset because a colleague and his own conscience nag at him to do the right thing: to find his friend, Dith Pran. How can films like *The Killing*

Fields (and others) shake our comfort zone and spur us to take an active role as Christians in the modern world?

Prayer

God, you said that you love all people and want each person to be saved. Help us to work to rid the world of oppression and cruelty. Shield those who suffer with your love. Amen.

Big Night

U.S., 1996 / 107 minutes

Actors: Stanley Tucci, Tony Shalhoub, Ian Holm,
Isabella Rosselini, Minnie Driver, Campbell Scott,
Allison Janney, Marc Anthony

Writers: Stanley Tucci, Campbell Scott

Directors: Stanley Tucci, Campbell Scott

Big Night

Come to the Feast

SYNOPSIS

It is the late 1950s. Two Italian immigrant brothers, Primo and Secondo Pilaggi, run a restaurant called "The Paradiso" in the seaside town of Keyport, New Jersey.

Primo is the chef and Secondo perseveringly tries to hustle business and look after the accounts. He often finds Primo's single-minded integrity exasperating because Primo will only cook authentic Italian dishes.

Across the street is another restaurant, "Pascal's Italian Grotto." The proprietor runs a very showy, successful and popular venue because he cooks the kind of Italian food people expect. When Secondo approaches him for a loan, Pascal suggests that the brothers come to work for him. Secondo, meanwhile, is involved in a liaison with Pascal's mistress, Gabriella, although he already has a girlfriend named Phyllis.

Pascal offers to invite the famous singer, Louis Prima, to The Paradiso to attract more customers, and the brothers prepare a lavish meal. Everyone works hard and various people come, including Ann, a quiet flower-seller, who is attracted to Primo.

The exquisite meal is served and there is much singing and dancing. The fact that Louis Prima never arrives does not surprise Pascal, who used it as a ruse to discredit the brothers and persuade them to come and work for him. Phyllis discovers Secondo with Gabriella. Primo, who has been offered a job back in Italy, leaves the restaurant with Ann. On his return the brothers argue and wrestle on the beach. In the morning, Secondo cooks an omelet and Primo joins him. They reconcile.

COMMENTARY

Big Night is a small-budget movie that was a critical and popular success.

Like the preparations for a good meal, the film takes a lot of time to get to the main course. First we discover that the brothers are in a financial crisis and Primo, a purist, will not change either the menu or his cooking style to increase business. Then the film concentrates on the rich variety of food which will welcome the singer Louis Prima to their restaurant; the preparations, the eating, and the aftermath are shown in loving detail.

Stanley Tucci, who co-wrote and co-directed the film, is often frantic in an abrasive kind of way as the would-be contemporary restaurateur. Tony Shalhoub, the uncompromising chef unwilling to sacrifice quality, plays Tucci's opposite and gives a very human feel to the film. An assorted set of characters from the district are sketched in: rival restaurateur Ian Holm; his mistress, Isabella Rosselini; a florist; a car salesman. Each is invited to the "big night." The first half of the film meticulously sets up the satiating and entertaining second part—especially for food connoisseurs.

Stanley Tucci is an intelligent, versatile character actor who also directed *The Imposters* and *Joe Gould's Secret*.

DIALOGUE WITH THE GOSPEL

Focus: In Big Night, *a feast is prepared for a guest who does not come, a variation on the Gospel's theme of the great wedding feast and the invited guests who do not come.*

Chef Primo prepares a meal for his special guest, which is, in the words of the first reading from Isaiah: "a banquet of rich food, a banquet of fine wines, of food rich and juicy and fine strained wines." The great banquet is an image of the final times, the banquet that God offers his faithful guests. It is interesting to note that the brothers' restaurant is called "The Paradiso."

The Gospel also describes the preparation for a wonderful banquet, a wedding feast, and the difficulties with the invitation list prepared by the king. Though not a strict Gospel parallel, *Big Night* dwells in great detail on the preparation of the food—an opportunity for viewers to appreciate what it takes to prepare a banquet—and on the people who come.

In the Gospel story the invited guests refuse to come to the banquet and instead go about business as usual. The brothers think that their guest has decided not to come, but they are the victims of Pascal's malice because the guest had never even been invited. Their disappointment is palpable nonetheless.

The king in the Gospel story does not take rejection so well. He becomes vindictive and destructive. Then he invites anyone from the open roads to come to the banquet. Primo and Secondo were more congenial and opened their doors sooner. Everyone who came enjoyed the banquet, even though the guest of honor never showed.

Returning to the wedding feast, the king discovers that there is a man present without the required wedding garment, and he is ousted from the feast. In the movie, Secondo is the one who is not properly "ready" for the feast because of his fickle relationships and his wheeling and dealing.

Secondo is the one who receives his comeuppance from Phyllis and Primo. The film ends in reconciliation, unlike this week's Gospel parable.

KEY SCENES AND THEMES

- The contrast of the two brothers: their personalities, their workstyles and dedication, their relationships (Primo with Ann, Secondo with Phyllis and Gabriella).

- The banquet's preparations, the participation of their silent employee; the friends and the rich feast.

- The missing guest; Pascal's deceit and its effect on the brothers; their fight, their understated reconciliation.

FOR REFLECTION AND CONVERSATION

1. Primo is a perfectionist and Secondo is a pragmatist. Primo is an artist and Secondo is a businessman. As the brothers' relationship becomes more strained, we can see how each is right in his own way, according to how they see their business goals. How does the film try to teach viewers about family relationships? For the brothers, how do the big banquet and the small, quiet breakfast at the end compare? Which one is more meaningful to the brothers and to the audience?

2. *Big Night* can be a metaphor for life and faith. Primo represents the tried and true ways of preparing Italian cuisine that will not be changed. He'd rather go back to Italy. Secondo wants to be more contemporary and relevant in the restaurant world so they can make their way in America. How might we resolve this conflict if we were in the place of one of the brothers? How are dialogue, compromise, negotiation, anger, violence, love, and reconciliation present in this "feast" of a film?

3. Food, for the two brothers, is a sign of love, communication, and even spirituality. "To eat good food is to be close to God," Primo tells his brother. This statement has distant eucharistic overtones. How central is the Eucharistic Meal in my Christian life? What is the value and role of family meals and family worship in our lives?

Prayer

Lord, you promise us the feast of heaven. Make us ready through reconciliation and love to share with others in your heavenly banquet. Amen.

TWENTY-NINTH SUNDAY OF THE YEAR

Isaiah 45:1, 4–6; Matthew 22:15–21

True Confessions

U.S., 1981 / 108 minutes

Actors: Robert De Niro, Robert Duvall, Charles Durning,
Ed Flanders, Cyril Cusack, Burgess Meredith

Writers: John Gregory Dunne, Joan Didion

Director: Ulu Grosbard

True Confessions

God or the World

SYNOPSIS

In 1948, the Catholic Archdiocese of Los Angeles is experiencing a post-war boom, with new Catholic schools being built at a rapid rate. It is discovered that the building contractor, Jack Amsterdam, is a philanderer with financial skeletons in his closet that may cause scandal to the Church. The archdiocese decides to name him "Layman of the Year" and to disassociate itself from him as tactfully as possible.

The chancellor of the diocese, Monsignor Desmond, is a skilled administrator and an ambitious cleric. He helps smooth over the situation with the contractor and also manages to hush up a murder investigation about a priest who dies in a brothel. Desmond's brother Thomas, a chief detective, is peripherally involved because he has been accepting payoffs to keep quiet, which also has the potential of embarrassing the monsignor.

Thomas informs Desmond that the details of another murder can no longer be hidden. Jack and the archdiocesan lawyer had a relationship with a girl who has been found dead by the side of the road; Desmond had once offered her a ride. Because all three men can be linked to her, all are under suspicion. Desmond is faced with a dilemma: to begin

289

living by the values of his vocation as a priest, or to continue living the "good life," fixing situations so that the Church will look good. He decides to leave his administrative post and retire to a parish in the desert. Thomas visits his brother Desmond, who discloses that he is terminally ill.

COMMENTARY

True Confessions is a grim viewing, yet it is one of the best dramatic portrayals of a diocesan priest caught in a web of ministry who tries to cover up potential scandals out of a sense of loyalty to the Church. As a chancellor, the priest carries out an administrative role that brings with it the power to make deals and control information. The plot of *True Confessions* is a long way from the problems of Barry Fitzgerald and Bing Crosby in *Going My Way,* though both films are set in approximately the same time frame of the 1940s.

The story is based on an incident recounted in James Ellroys' *Who is the Black Dahlia.* John Gregory Nunn wrote a novel about the incident, and then he and his wife, Joan Didion, wrote the actual screenplay. Although Ulu Grosbard is mainly a stage director, his films include *The Subject Was Roses, Straight Time,* and *The Deep End of the Ocean.*

The re-creation of Los Angeles and its archdiocese of the 1940s, with Cyril Cusack as an imposing and enigmatic archbishop, is convincing. The central performances of Robert De Niro as the priest and Robert Duvall as the detective play out the story with compelling dramatic force. De Niro makes a good priest (and a controversial one, as he does in the 1994 *Sleepers*); he capably involves us in the soul-searching struggle between clerical ambition and the priestly vocation.

A companion film released at the same time, which shows the failure rather than success of a priest's vocation, is the melodramatic *Monsignor* with Christopher Reeve. *True Confessions* is not the stuff of "nice" movies, but it is real, challenging, and compelling.

Focus: The conclusion of today's Gospel responds to those who try to trap Jesus in a political web by saying that we are not to neglect our duties, but that we are to give to God what is God's. True Confessions is a spin on the same dilemma: are religious people, specifically clerics, exempt from the law, whether civil or divine?

Jesus is being tested in today's Gospel. The political supporters of Herod's family want to trap him, so they turn to the ancient "world-or-God" dilemma, presented within the context of politics and treason.

The ambitious monsignor in *True Confessions* is caught between God and things that are not of God. Jesus says in Luke 16 that we cannot be servants both of God and of money. Power and money are temptations that challenge the convictions of church ministers every day.

Jesus offers a prophetic symbolic action to demonstrate the two sides of the dilemma. He holds up a coin, the money with the imprint of the one who rules. His answer to the question involves giving whatever is due, as long as it does not take away from the gift of self to God. Loyalty to God takes place within the world, but often requires clarity and personal sacrifice.

The two brothers, the monsignor and the detective, work in two separate worlds that overlap. The world of the monsignor, while it needs its buildings and organizations, can and does at times sell out to corruption by looking the other way. It often fails to render to God what belongs to God. The film offers us a portrait of a man who is weak yet courageous enough to make a total option for God in the end, thus gaining his soul while losing what seems to be the whole world.

- The Archdiocese of Los Angeles: power and money; the banquet; the builder named "Catholic Layman of the Year;" the dinner guests' knowledge of his corruption.

• The chancellor at work, his handling of the archdiocesan finances and dealings with corrupt people, his dilemma between clerical ambition and his true vocation; the cardinal: presiding at liturgies, his enigmatic answers to his chancellor's questions.

• The two brothers' discussions, each ambitious in their chosen vocation; the non-religious detective who challenges the priest's conscience; the aging and ill monsignor, his retirement in the desert, the brother's visit, the monsignor's assessment of his life.

FOR REFLECTION AND CONVERSATION

1. Clergy today seem to have less and less time for pastoral ministry because of administrative demands. Parishes and dioceses have fewer resources to carry out ministries and to support local parishes. Even though *True Confessions* takes place in the late 1940s, how does the film speak to these challenges? What effect do these challenges or problems have on the people, represented by Thomas and Jack Amsterdam, and on the clergy, represented by Monsignor Desmond, the cardinal, and the priest who is exiled to the parish in the desert?

2. The world is full of temptations involving money, sex, and power. Jesus counters these temptations with the invitation to follow him more closely by living the virtues of poverty, chastity, and obedience in our daily lives. What do these "evangelical counsels" mean for all Christians, not just those who are religious "professionals"?

3. As members of the people of God we place high expectations on our priests, bishops, and men and women religious. When they fail, it somehow always seems worse than when others fall from grace; yet we are all human. What can we do to support the men and women in our dioceses and parishes who live lives committed to following Christ in priesthood or religious life?

Prayer

Jesus, we are often confused about possessions and our use of money for ourselves and for the good of others. Help us to discern what belongs to Caesar and what belongs to God, and to give each one their due. Amen.

Sister Act

U.S., 1992 / 100 minutes

Actors: Whoopi Goldberg, Maggie Smith, Harvey Keitel,
Kathy Najimy, Bill Nunn, Wendy Makkena,
Mary Wickes, Joseph Maher

Writer: Joseph Howard

Director: Emile Ardolino

Sister Act

I Will Follow Him

SYNOPSIS

Reno lounge singer Deloris Van Cartier inadvertently sees her gangster boyfriend commit a murder. Placed in the witness protection program, she is taken to an enclosed convent and given the name Sister Mary Clarence. She clashes with the Mother Superior and at the same time makes friends with the other nuns. She is invited to take over the choir and urges the nuns to go beyond the convent walls and get involved with people and their needs. Deloris' choir is very popular with those coming to the church because of her non-traditional rock 'n' roll-style hymns; soon the number of those attending the church grows.

When Deloris is shown on TV helping people, the gangsters recognize her. They kidnap her and take her back to Reno. All the nuns now know who Deloris really is and, with the help of the police, they go to Reno to rescue her. They manage this when they "mingle" with the casino patrons and cause chaos. Back at the church, Deloris conducts the choir for a visit of the Pope, who gives the choir a standing ovation.

Sister Act relies on a combination of elements that made it a surprise box office hit: the comic abilities and charm of Whoopi Goldberg, old-fashioned stereotyped images of nuns and convents (with hints of *Going My Way, Bells of St. Mary's, Come to the Stable),* and even the predictable storyline. Goldberg adds a touch of sentiment—in the vein of *Clara's Heart* and *Corinna, Corinna*—to her comedic performance, and it works. Emile Ardolino *(Dirty Dancing, Chances Are, Gypsy)* directed the movie.

Maggie Smith is perfect as the starchy Mother Superior, and Harvey Keitel is well cast as the small-time gangster. Most of the genuinely funny scenes are practically stolen by Kathy Najimy as the exuberant Sister Patrick.

The film is high-spirited and good-natured. The scene with Sister Mary Clarence (Whoopi Goldberg) in red high heels, directing the choir of nuns who sing the hymn "My God" instead of "My Guy," has already gone down in cinematic history.

Sister Act is a corny but entertaining film. Its message is to share our gifts of love and faith with everyone—no exceptions.

COMMENTARY

Focus: The Gospel is clear: we are to love our neighbors as ourselves. Sister Act *uses a light touch to help us visualize what it means to love God and others with our whole hearts.*

DIALOGUE WITH THE GOSPEL

There are a number of passages in the Gospels which highlight the great commandments of the law that Jesus reinforces in his teaching. In today's Gospel, the Pharisees want to confuse Jesus by asking him which law is the greatest. They want Jesus to make a mistake regarding the Law of Moses and the rabbinical traditions they believe in.

Jesus not only answers that complete love of God (as stated in Deuteronomy 6:4) is the greatest commandment, but he adds for their benefit that love of neighbor is the second. To confirm this, he tells them that all the books and teachings of the law and prophets are based on these two laws.

Deloris Van Cartier finds herself in a convent founded on love of God, but the community is in something of a rut. The sisters are going through the motions of religious life, but their energy has diminished and their lives have turned inward. There are signs of hope with the novice, Sister Mary Robert, and the exuberant Sister Patrick, who join with the new "Sister" to add joy and a human touch to the life of the nuns.

Following Sister Clarence's lead, the sisters reach out beyond the convent walls to serve their neighbors. This contact re-energizes them and further enhances their lives.

KEY SCENES AND THEMES

- The nuns: their traditional order, their ascetic style and naïve manner; the nuns' curiosity regarding the people in need across the street; Mother Superior's primness, her hold over Sister Clarence, their clashes.

- Deloris as Sister Mary Clarence, her acceptance by the community and her decision to stay; her sneaking to the bar to make a phone call, Sisters Robert and Patrick following; the bikers' bar: the patrons' reaction, the drinking and dancing; the beginning of an apostolate.

- Sister Clarence as choir director, choir practices, the polyphony and harmony, "My God"; the people outside hearing, coming in, and filling the church; the Pope's visit and his enjoying the concert.

FOR REFLECTION AND CONVERSATION

1. Despite the fact that many women religious in the United States did not appreciate the laughs induced by the stereotypes in *Sister Act,* it proved to be an ex

tremely popular film in many countries around the world, among both Catholic and non-Catholic moviegoers. What makes it an engaging and even inspirational film? What accounts for the different ways various people interpret the same film? What role does the fulfillment or disappointment of our expectations play in how we might enjoy a movie such as *Sister Act*?

2. One sequence in *Sister Act* shows the sisters raiding the freezer at midnight and sharing ice scream together after spending the day helping others. This is truly a moment of "community," when fatigue, differences of opinion, likes and dislikes are put aside and the love of God and a common purpose shared. How can we build community at home, church, and in the workplace?

3. Faith and life are brought together for the spiritual good of all when the secular love songs, "I Will Follow Him" and "My Guy" are turned into contemporary "hymns." How might there be a message in these songs for people of faith who seek to bring Jesus to our popular culture, and pop culture to Jesus? Do you think a film like *Sister Act* can be used as a place of dialogue or conversation about human and spiritual values? Why or why not?

Prayer

Jesus, you have given us the two greatest commandments, that we love God above all things and our neighbor as ourselves. Give us the grace to recognize you in our neighbor and to serve God and others with love. Amen.

THIRTY-FIRST SUNDAY OF THE YEAR
Malachi 1:14–2:2, 8–10; Matthew 23:1–12

Bob Roberts
U.S., 1992 / 101 minutes
Actors: Tim Robbins, Giancarlo Esposito, Ray Wise,
Alan Rickman, Gore Vidal, David Strathairn, Bob Balaban,
James Spader, Helen Hunt, Rebecca Jenkins, Brian Murray
Writer: Tim Robbins
Director: Tim Robbins

 *Bob Roberts*

Exalting Oneself

SYNOPSIS

Bob Roberts is a clean-cut candidate running for the Senate in Pennsylvania. He is a Wall Street wizard, divorced from his hippy parents, and a folksinger whose lyrics, music videos, and television commercials exemplify a right wing reaction against the liberalism of the 1960s. Bob Roberts despises liberals who wear their hearts on their sleeves and are caught up in allegedly trendy causes. A British television team making a documentary brings Bob Robert's campaign to us, from folk song to folk song peppered with commentary.

Millionaire Andrew Harte funds Roberts' campaign. Harte is engaged in shady financial deals and illegal activities (drugs and gun-running) carried out under the double guise of a non-profit charitable organization and his reputation as an American patriot. A disabled black journalist named Bugs Raplin stalks the campaign, trying to question Roberts about social issues. When this fails he begins doing background checks on the campaign. The mainstream media, however, are eager to follow Bob and enthusiastically applaud his every move.

Roberts' opponent is incumbent Senator Brickley Paiste, who is lampooned on TV in debates and in commercials as soft and out of touch. When doctored photos appear in the press which picture him with a young girl, his reputation suffers.

An assassination attempt on Bob is blamed on Bugs, who protests his innocence but is framed by the Roberts' team. Roberts, the hero and family man, is now a martyr, confined to a wheel chair. When some members of his campaign become disillusioned and suspicious, they "conveniently disappear."

Roberts is elected. At the post-election celebration, we see that he is tapping his foot to the music. We realize the shooting was engineered and that Roberts is faking his injuries.

COMMENTARY

Tim Robbins wrote, directed, starred in, composed and sang the repertoire of patriotic songs in *Bob Roberts*. It is a satirical look at American politics in the early 1990s from the perspective of the Left at the time of the Gulf War.

By playing Bob Roberts as "Mr. Clean," Tim Robbins is able to draw attention to the smooth and cunning shallowness of the allegedly flawless candidate. Behind the smile is a completely ruthless and ambitious man who wants only to win and gain power. Alan Rickman plays the shady financier behind the Roberts' campaign with much cunning. He too is a hypocrite who appears at Senate committee hearings protesting his innocence and praying in times of crisis.

Gore Vidal plays Senator Paiste who is ridiculed and set up by the Roberts' campaign. As the incumbent, his character represents many of the views Vidal actually supported in real life. He brings pathos to his role as a good man unjustly accused and left without recourse. Giancarlo Esposito is Bugs, the scapegoat and mouthpiece for justice.

A gallery of stars make cameo appearances as smiling TV personalities with penchants for adulation and/or inane chatter. Tim Robbins went on to direct *Dead Man Walking* and

The Cradle Will Rock, about the left-wing theater in New York of the 1930s.

Focus: Bob Roberts represents the political, social, and religious hypocrite who tries to win people with empty promises couched in charm. The Gospel leaves us in no doubt about the hypocrisy of some leaders.

This Sunday's Gospel contains the opening of Jesus' words to some religious leaders of his day regarding their religious hypocrisy, their show of authority, and exercise of power. He contrasts this with a genuine acknowledgment of God as the one Lord and Teacher, referring to the words of the prophet Malachi in the first reading. The ultimate message of Jesus is that his disciples are to be truly humble and honest without indulging in self-adulation.

Bob Roberts is a satiric tale of self-promotion in leadership, abuse of authority and power, and hypocrisy in using the name of God for self-promotion. Jesus condemns leaders who place burdens on others, who don't practice what they preach, who dress ostentatiously, and demand submission from others.

Bob Roberts is a portrait of a smiling, superficial, corrupt politician who lives by a double standard and is only interested in the power that political office brings.

KEY SCENES AND THEMES

- Bob Roberts' folk songs, his country and western style; the lyrics: "Bleeding Heart," "God," "Complain and Complain," "Alive"; the homespun music's appeal, the guitar, the choir, the religious settings; the music videos.

- The effect of the documentary format: its realism, the glimpses of Bob Roberts and his entourage behind the scenes; the controllers, the bodyguards, censor-

ship and editing, the spin-doctors and the possibility
of critique.

- Bugs as the fall guy; the truth about the palsied hand
and the assassination attempt; Bugs' death and the
rejoicing crowd; Paiste and his political, social, and
cultural background; the mockery of the '90s youth;
the advertisements, doctored photo, TV debates,
Paiste's explanation of the dangerous Bob Roberts;
the finale and Bob Roberts' tapping foot, ultimate lies.

FOR REFLECTION AND CONVERSATION

1. Today's alternative opening prayer asks God to "remove the selfishness that blurs our faith." How is this
the perfect prayer for a false political candidate and
anyone even tempted to hypocrisy and exaltation of
self? How do selfishness and self-promotion color Bob
Roberts as a candidate as well as the members of his
campaign staff? What happens to those who see
through his hypocrisy to the truth, and try to do the
right thing? Talk about what "doing the right thing"
might mean in circumstances such as these.

2. In the responsorial psalm (cf. Ps 131:1–3) the psalmist acknowledges that he has learned what it means to
be humble and to accept his limitations in peace. Does
Bob Roberts ever practice authentic humility? What
does the movie say about the political electoral process in America, some politicians, and the voters?

3. After *Bob Roberts* was released in 1992, the U.S. pro-
duced three other films that speak to contemporary
American politics: the satires *Primary Colors* and
Bulworth (both in 1998), and a more serious look in
The Contender (2000). How does the focus on candi-

dates for high political office compare in these three films? How is the message of the films the same or different? We can also ask: what is the role of a Christian in the democratic process? What does it mean to be a citizen and a Christian?

Prayer

Lord of truth, give our leaders the gift of integrity so that their words and actions are consistent and beneficial for all. Amen.

A Chorus Line

U.S., 1985 / 115 minutes

Actors: Michael Douglas, Terrence Mann, Alyson Reed,
Cameron English, Vicki Frederick

Writer: Arnold Schulman

Director: Richard Attenborough

A Chorus Line

Be Ready

It is audition day for dancers who will make up the chorus line for a Broadway musical. The initial singing and dancing routines help in the process of eliminating the less talented and isolating a group of sixteen finalists. At the end of the day, only four men and four women will be chosen for the production.

SYNOPSIS

Zach, a former dancer and now a star choreographer with a tough veneer, arrives and sits with his assistant in a dimly lit section of the theater to assess the dancers. For some reason, Zach requires each of them to step into the spotlight and talk about their lives, their hopes, ambitions, talents—anything and everything they want to tell, in order to get a role. Some are more exhibitionistic than others, and some invent stories. Gradually, the group becomes more honest. Zach's former partner, Cassie, arrives in the midst of everything and Zach gets angry when she begs for an interview. Paul cannot speak about himself in front of the others, but walks on stage during the break and reveals himself to a much more sympathetic Zach.

Finally, the cut is made. The chosen ones prepare for the show as those not chosen leave.

COMMENTARY

Michael Bennet's award-winning musical broke records in the '70s and '80s for high attendance and number of performances. *A Chorus Line* toured beyond Broadway and became popular the world over. The musical relied on the impact of its lead dancers and the teamwork of the chorus line for its impact. Its songs tended to be character revelations rather than show stoppers. "What I Did for Love" (Cassie's song) and "One" are Marvin Hamlisch's best-known compositions.

Richard Attenborough made this film version of *A Chorus Line* between *Gandhi* and *Cry Freedom*. The movie was criticized because of its static transfer to film, a common difficulty with this kind of a project. The filmmakers did their best, however, to keep the action going, and with the passing of time the strength of the dialogue and characterizations demonstrate that the film version has legitimate emotional power.

Michael Douglas was in transition from television's *Streets of San Francisco* to the big screen (winning his Oscar for *Wall Street* two years later). The seemingly ruthless choreographer role suits him, "playing God" as regards who will be eliminated and who will stay. The sequence where he listens to the timid Paul, and comes up to the stage to reassure him as a father would, is a fine moment.

DIALOGUE WITH THE GOSPEL

Focus: When the ten bridesmaids' readiness is tested in today's Gospel, it is similar to a theater audition, though the film's criteria for selection is different. In both Gospel and film, some will make it and others won't.

Jesus structures a very stylized parable with his story of the ten bridesmaids. He is drawing on the Jewish Scripture's image of Wisdom, found in the first reading. Wisdom is personified as feminine, and she searches out those who are alert, those who seek her, those who are worthy of her. The five wise bridesmaids exemplify such qualities in this reading; the five foolish ones do not.

Jesus' parable is not so much about the bridegroom, the wedding party, and whether or not they are late. Instead, Jesus sets up something like an audition parable: which of the bridesmaids are ready to assist the newlyweds, and which are not? The foolish will be eliminated after they scurry off to buy oil for their lamps and are thus not ready for their "performance on cue." The wise will go into the celebration. They will be like a chorus line, an integral part of the wedding show.

In *A Chorus Line*, the judgment on those auditioning is severe, although all the dancers have talent. For a reason we do not discover, Zach's criteria for choosing the dancers is not talent per se, but how they tell their stories. Perhaps he wants to see if they are indeed "ready" as persons to dance in the chorus line he is selecting. The aging Sheila and the married couple who stretch their résumés are not eliminated as severely as the bridesmaids in the parable, but their disappointment is just as keenly felt.

KEY SCENES AND THEMES

- The initial song and dance routines; the hopefuls voicing their ambitions, their yearnings and uncertainties; the method of elimination.

- Paul: his fear, his unhappiness with his sexuality, his mother and father attending the revue; Paul's father calling him son for the first time; Zach's attentive listening to Paul, his acceptance and reaching out to him.

- Zach asking individuals to come forward; their surprise at being dismissed; the joy and relief of the chosen; the final sequence where talents are finally revealed.

1. Each dancer's story offers insight into his or her character and talents. As we listen to the dancers, we might ask ourselves if we would eliminate them from the chorus line. What is Zach's criteria? What would our criteria be? Why should a dancer's story make any difference as to whether or not that person makes the final cut? Why does Zach care, anyway? Is he trying to play God? Why or why not?

2. Zach, a derivative of the Hebrew name "Zechariah," meaning "Yahweh remembers," is a kind of God-figure because he decides who will work and who won't, who gets a chance and who doesn't. What kind of image of God does he project? After Paul tells his story in what is certainly the emotional high point of the film, how does Zach show a different image of God and a father's remembered tenderness toward a son?

3. How does *A Chorus Line* show that the world of entertainment is more difficult than popular magazines and celebrity shows might have us believe? How can the believing community support and celebrate the writers, artists, actors, actresses, directors, and all those whose gifts light up both theater and cinema and provide audiences with heightened awareness of their human condition? How can media literacy education help young people develop critical thinking skills that will allow them to become future media professionals who will tell stories and create productions characterized by human dignity, truth, beauty, and goodness?

Prayer

God our Father, you have gifted us all with talents. Help us, in the name of Jesus your Son, to be ready to use them for the good of our brothers and sisters. Amen.

Chris Cooper and Jake Gyllenhaal star in *October Sky*.

October Sky

U.S., 1998 / 102 minutes

Actors: Jake Gyllenhaal, Chris Cooper,
Laura Dern, Chris Owen

Writer: Lewis Colick

Director: Joe Johnston

October Sky

Talents Well Used

SYNOPSIS

It is October 1957 in Coalwood, West Virginia. The Russian *Sputnik* is launched. Students and townspeople watch it streak across the night sky. High school students are concerned about football and girls, while the adults are anxious about keeping their coal mine open amid recent accidents and strikes.

Homer is an eager student who decides to study and build rockets with the help of his friends and the encouragement of a teacher. However, John, his father who manages the mine, thinks Homer should follow in his footsteps. The high school principal agrees. Unless they win sports scholarships to play football, mining is the only future occupation for the boys of Coalwood.

Homer and his friends build increasingly larger and more successful rockets, and some of the townspeople come to admire them. The students are arrested when one of their rockets is suspected of causing a fire. Homer calculates the trajectory arc and figures out that the fire was not their fault. The boys win the county science fair and Homer is selected for the national fair in Indianapolis.

When his father has an accident, Homer goes to work at the mine but soon returns to science. He wins in Indianapolis and goes home for his final launch. Homer's mother, Elise, challenges the disapproving father. The whole town gathers and Homer asks his father to press the launch button. Some years later the mine closes, but Homer has become a NASA engineer.

COMMENTARY

October Sky is a piece of Americana, based on Homer Hickam's memoirs, *Rocket Boys*. It does for science, space exploration, and engineering, what films like *Stand and Deliver* did for mathematics, calculus, and teaching.

The film contrasts two worldviews, showing the limitations of underground mining and the limitless frontiers of space.

Chris Cooper is excellent as the mine manager who disapproves of his son's dreams. Jake Gyllenhaal plays the young student, Homer, and Laura Dern has a cameo role as a teacher who inspires her students. Director Joe Johnston is better known for special effects work on the *Star Wars* movies and imaginary tales like *Honey, I Shrunk the Kids*, *The Rocketeer*, and *Jumani*, but he does a more than effective job with *October Sky*. This film is replete with positive values, and successfully inspires the audience to follow their dreams.

DIALOGUE WITH THE GOSPEL

Focus: Like the servants in today's Gospel, young Homer is gifted with many talents and must struggle to use them well.

There are many movies about people with talents. *October Sky* focuses on ordinary people in ordinary, difficult circumstances. Homer is the son of a mine manager, and his expected destiny is the mine. But Homer is a dreamer, fascinated by the advances in space exploration, and he sees a future for himself in science.

The king in the Gospel parable gives opportunities and talents to his servants according to their abilities. In *October Sky* the students carry out their projects according to their individual talents, and Homer has and uses the equivalent of the "ten talents" given to the servant in Matthew's Gospel. Another student who is also a talented science buff is ridiculed and intimidated by his fellow students (a 1950s version of the conflict between the jocks and the geeks). When Homer invites him to help with the experiments, this student is encouraged to develop and increase his talents, too.

The students win the competitions and receive their prizes. Homer, an admirer of the German scientist Wernher Von Braun who developed the liquid fuel rocket, actually gets to meet him. Because Homer has been "faithful" to his calling, he gets to "join in the master's happiness" when he becomes a space engineer and is hired by NASA to train astronauts for shuttle missions.

October Sky parallels today's Gospel again when Homer is faced with the decision to go to work at the mine to save his parents' home and must thus bury his talents. His talent would then have been taken, so to speak, and given to others. Even though work in the mine had its own dignity and value, this was not where Homer's talents lay.

KEY SCENES AND THEMES

- The mining town setting of *October Sky* is a case of discernment of talent and the opportunity to "seize the day."

- The townspeople watching as Sputnik circles the earth in the October sky, a new era of space exploration, the students' reactions; Homer inviting the "geeky" student to help make rockets, the work, the tests, the successes and failures.

- Homer's life at home, his father's coal mine and the threat of closure, the miner's strike; Homer's mother and brother; his chance for a sports scholarship, the "talents" in the family.

- Homer winning the local science fair, going to the nationals in Indianapolis; the collaboration to rebuild the stolen equipment; the final experiment with the townspeople's support; Homer asking his father to press the button; their reconciliation; each character's destiny using their talents; the mine's closing.

FOR REFLECTION AND CONVERSATION

1. Homer and his father have a complex relationship. There is anger, jealousy, pride, love, and finally acceptance and reconciliation. What kind of expectations does John have of his son? Does he recognize his talents? Why or why not? What are the social and cultural dimensions of this story that influence John's attitude?

2. Popular students and jocks, particularly in middle school or high school, can intimidate others through bullying. This is becoming an increasingly bigger problem in U.S. schools, and we see it in *October Sky*. Why does Homer reach out to the boy who is kind of a "geek" and a "nerd"? How are they both able to pursue their talents despite the fact that they will never be jocks?

3. Life is not always as simple as a two-hour movie can make it seem. The history of America as told in the movies is full of poor people who pulled themselves up by the bootstraps and made good. What is so special about a true story told through a film like *October*

Sky? How does such a film work on a patriotic level while inspiring our spirits at the same time?

Prayer

Help us, Lord, to recognize the talents in others and ourselves. Grant us the strength to use our gifts in response to the opportunities your Providence offers us. Amen.

Dead Man Walking

U.S., 1995 / 130 minutes

Actors: Susan Sarandon, Sean Penn, Scott Wilson,
Raymond J. Barry, R. Lee Ermey, Robert Prosky

Writer: Tim Robbins

Director: Tim Robbins

Dead Man Walking

Ministering on the Margins

SYNOPSIS

Sister Helen Prejean teaches children in the St. Thomas Housing Project in New Orleans. She receives a letter from Matthew Poncelet, who is on death row at Angola State Prison for rape and murder. She goes to see him and, despite the chaplain's wariness, she becomes Poncelet's spiritual director.

Helen listens to his story with compassion, but finds him angry, bigoted and insolent. She meets his family and offers them spiritual support. She then visits the families of the victims who assume she has come to support them. Hearing their bitterness, she is taken aback and realizes she must also appreciate their side of the situation.

Sister Helen campaigns against capital punishment and gets her bishop to join in protests and hearings. She persuades the Sisters of her community to allow Poncelet to be buried in the nuns' cemetery.

As the time for his execution approaches, Poncelet responds to her ministry and her love. He finally confesses his crimes and accepts personal responsibility for what happened. She assists him to the end, and he dies acknowledging what he did and expressing sorrow for it. The film ends with Helen and the father of one of the victims who disapproved of her death row ministry praying together in church.

COMMENTARY

Dead Man Walking is based on Sister Helen Prejean's best-selling book about the human face of the death penalty. The book recounts her work with death row inmates, her relationships with the victim's families, and her lobby against the death penalty. Sister Helen acted as technical adviser for this film that Tim Robbins wrote and directed.

Susan Sarandon shows her versatility yet again by playing Sister Helen Prejean in a more self-effacing style than in some of her previous roles, such as Marmee in *Little Women* (nice, strong, and motherly), Regina in *The Client* (forceful and shrewd as she fought for a victim), and Michaela Odone in *Lorenzo's Oil* (played with the fierce commitment of a mother fighting for her child).

Sarandon's portrayal of Sister Helen is probably the best on-screen portrayal of a contemporary nun in recent decades. Judging from the accuracy of the dialogue and representation of events, the team of Prejean, Sarandon, and Robbins worked incredibly well together. The sequences showing the nuns at home are just right. Sister Helen's dealings with the prison chaplain may seem stereotypical, but instead accurately reflect the situation.

For dramatic purposes, two actual convicts that Sister Helen ministered to on death row in the early 1980s were conflated by Robbins to create Sean Penn's character.

While Poncelet remains a most unsympathetic character to the end, the ethical, intellectual and emotional complexities of the death penalty are fairly dramatized. Audiences that favor capital punishment may not be persuaded to change their minds, but they will be forced to look again at their motives and the consequences of violence perpetrated and endorsed by the State. Audiences that are against capital punishment will have their stances reinforced and will have to extend their compassion to those who are driven by a sense of revenge and justice because they have been so tragically victimized.

DIALOGUE WITH THE GOSPEL

Focus: Sister Helen Prejean was caring for marginalized children when she was asked to be spiritual director to a prisoner on death row, truly the "least" of Jesus' brothers and sisters. By taking up this new ministry, she served the prisoner and Jesus himself.

This Gospel description of the Last Judgment, and the standard of mercy by which we will be judged, was chosen by the Church to complete the Cycle A Scripture readings for this year. The reading gathers together the themes of Matthew's Gospel by telling us that the standard by which we will be judged is the quality and extent of our mercy to the "least ones" in society.

It is not very hard to see that Helen Prejean fits into the category of those who will gain eternal life because they served the least in God's kingdom. Jesus says, "As often as you did it for one of my least brothers, you did it for me." Matthew Poncelet is guilty, rude, crass and unrepentant. Over time, he acknowledges his sin and guilt and takes responsibility for his actions, but he cannot undo his terrible deeds. He seems the least desirable and most contemptible of all Jesus' brothers. Yet everything Sister Helen did for Matthew, she did in the name of Jesus and for love.

This mandate to love the least among us is difficult enough under normal circumstances, but it seems like an almost impossible challenge to people like the parents of Poncelet's victims. In a veritable dilemma, Helen Prejean tries to minister to those who have been sinned against as well as the sinner. She never excuses herself when she fails to adequately respond to the victims and the victimizer, but keeps the image and words of Jesus before her always as the goal of love to be achieved.

- Sister Helen's memories: her vocational call, her family, the ceremony when she received her religious habit, the home movies; Sister Helen as a woman religious: her explanation of the vow of celibacy, her work in the inner city.

- Sister Helen visiting the parents of the victims, her desire to help; Mr. Delacroix accusing Helen of arrogance; the Percys' scorn.

- Poncelet's trust in Sister Helen, his confession and acceptance of responsibility; Poncelet seeing Helen as the face of love: her touch, her kiss, her singing; Poncelet's stretched-out body resembling a crucifix, his apology to the parents, his declaration against murder of any kind, including his own; the state-sanctioned killing of criminals.

1. One of the most difficult issues about the death penalty concerns the victims of criminal acts. Debbie Morris survived kidnapping and rape by Robert Lee Willie and his partner, Joseph Vaccaro. Willie was one of the two men who formed the character Poncelet in *Dead Man Walking*, and was executed for murder. In a compelling book entitled *Forgiving the Dead Man Walking* (1998), Morris wonders what her reaction will be when she gets to heaven after forgiving Robert Lee Willie and then meets him there, because he died repentant. How do we as Christians deal with this dilemma? How are both perpetrators and victims the "least of our brothers"?

2. The death penalty is a complex issue in the U.S. and some other countries in the world today. How does the film deal with the issue? Does the death penalty in today's society solve anything? How does *Dead Man Walking* show that capital punishment contributes to the culture of death? What does the *Catechism of the Catholic Church* (cf. nn. 2266–2267) teach about the death penalty?

3. Sister Helen's witness to religious life is one that can help us understand what it means to follow Jesus more closely in vowed life. She was always willing to admit her mistakes, to learn, and to grow. How did Sister Helen use the Gospel of love as her criterion and guide to serve the marginalized? If you are a single Catholic woman, would Susan Sarandon's portrayal of Sister Helen Prejean make you want to learn more about religious life?

Prayer

Jesus, you tell us that when we help those in need, even the most desperate people, we can recognize your face in them. Help us to see you in all people and to find within us the generosity to be the face of love to them. Amen.

Return to Me

U.S., 2000 / 116 minutes

Actors: David Duchovny, Minnie Driver, Bonnie Hunt,
Carroll O'Connor, Robert Loggia, James Belushi,
Joely Richardson

Writers: Bonnie Hunt and Don Lake

Director: Bonnie Hunt

Return to Me

A Graced Heart

Elizabeth Ruel is deeply in love with her husband Bob. She is a zoologist who works with gorillas. One evening, after a charity dinner, she is killed in a car crash. Because she is an organ donor, a young woman named Grace is the recipient of Elizabeth's heart.

SYNOPSIS

Grace belongs to a very Catholic, Irish-Italian family that runs a restaurant. Her grandfather and his partners sit around after hours playing cards and commenting on the world. Grace's friend Megan and Megan's husband, Joe, bring an air of family realism into Grace's life.

Bob Ruel comes into the restaurant on a double date he'd rather not be on. He is attracted to Grace and intentionally leaves his cell phone in the restaurant. When he returns for it, he asks Grace out.

Grace falls in love, but she is cautious, though family and friends urge her on. She is self-conscious about her surgery scars. By chance she discovers her own letter at Bob's house, mailed from the donor agency, and realizes that she received Elizabeth's heart and that Bob does not know. A few days later as she breaks the news to him, he is overcome by emotion and walks out. Grace, believing that their relationship is over, travels to Italy, but Bob follows her and declares his love.

COMMENTARY

The plot of this movie is just the kind that often leaves critics cringing, complaining about coincidences, sentimentality, and sweetness. But when *Return to Me* was released, reviewers felt that the seeming implausibility of the plot was handled with the right blend of humor and emotion, as in the case of such romances as *Sleepless in Seattle* and *Moonstruck*.

Return to Me is both entertaining and thoughtful. It is romantic but it takes romance to a deeper level, truly to the heart. Audiences sympathize with David Duchovny's character and his grief for his vivacious wife, played by Joely Richardson. Audiences also empathize with Minnie Driver's Grace, her illness and discovery of love. And they are certainly satisfied when Bob and Grace finally find each other.

The "old codgers," led by a benignly crusty Carroll O'Connor, provide a comic chorus. The down-to-earth scenes with Bonnie Hunt and James Belushi at home with their children give a feel for life's ironies and humor. Bonnie Hunt, as co-author of the script and director, gives *Return to Me* a certain warmth that makes it an above-average love story.

DIALOGUE WITH THE GOSPEL

Focus: In a world of disappointment and death, we need God's love as well as a new heart. Mary said yes to that love, showing the power of grace in the human heart.

The Feast of the Immaculate Conception is a celebration of Mary, full of grace. God presents Mary as his beloved from her earliest moment. There is nothing to impede the fullness of the gift of this Divine love, for Mary is conceived without original sin. Today's feast commemorates God's transforming love for all of us and Mary as the symbol of this amazing reality. God's invitation to say yes to the love present in our hearts enables us to love and to do great things.

The reading from Genesis reminds us that we live in an imperfect world, a world that needs redemption. The Gospel story of the Annunciation event presents for all time "Mary, full of grace," and reminds us of the ways in which God's love can change our hearts and, through us, the world.

Return to Me is a film about love, about hearts, and about a woman with the meaningful name of Grace. Bob grieves at the death of his wife Elizabeth, who has been generous and giving, even in death. Her loving heart is given to Grace, and the love of Grace's heart is doubled.

This love comes back to Bob when Grace says "yes" to the gift of the heart she has received and allows herself to risk falling in love. It is an imaginative reminder of Gabriel's encouraging words to Mary: "nothing is impossible for God."

KEY SCENES AND THEMES

- Elizabeth's death, the donation of her heart, the transporting of the heart and the dramatic gift of life given to Grace.

- Bob's encounter with Grace: the attraction, Grace's response; Grace and Bob's "coming alive in love" from the gift of the heart.

- Grace finding the letter, realizing the truth; Grace revealing the truth to Bob, his inability to face this reality; Bob's "change of heart," his journey to Italy to profess his love.

FOR REFLECTION AND CONVERSATION

1. Grace is God's life in us. How is the character of Grace and her heart transplant a symbol of God's grace to Bob and the other characters in the film? How are the characters "grace" to one another?

2. How is love communicated and symbolized in the relationships shown in the film, especially between friends, spouses, and family members? Talk about the

different cultures, races, and ages represented and how these work together to make *Return to Me* more meaningful.

3. From time immemorial, the heart has been the symbol of human and Divine love. What does the act of giving one heart so that another may live and love evoke in my thoughts and prayer?

Prayer

Mary, full of grace, show us how to say "yes" to God's invitation to love so that our hearts may be filled, like yours, with that love. Amen.

Terminator 2: Judgment Day
U.S., 1991 / 135 minutes
Actors: Arnold Schwarzenegger, Linda Hamilton, Robert Patrick, Edward Furlong, Joe Morton
Writer: James Cameron
Director: James Cameron

Terminator 2: Judgment Day

Single-Minded Mothers

SYNOPSIS

Sarah Connor, mother of the post-nuclear world leader of the future, John Connor, is held in a mental institution while her son is sent to live in foster homes. He is practically a juvenile delinquent and is totally unaware of his destined role in future events. (John's father returned to the future in the prequel to this film, *The Terminator.*)

In 2029 A.D., there is a war between robots and the human resistance to these machines. Enemies of the humans send a high-powered evil cyborg (a being that is part-human, part-robot) back in time to destroy John, the leader-to-be of the human resistance. At the same time, to save the boy, the future human resistance sends a "good" cyborg to protect John. The struggle between the "good" and "bad" cyborgs persuades John to believe that danger is imminent. John and the faithful cyborg go to rescue his mother, an intelligent and strong woman who has already managed to escape.

The hostile cyborg disguises himself by taking on the look and identities of others. He seems indestructible. There are shootouts, fights, amazing chases, escapes with special effects—all leading to a confrontation with a scientist who is developing lethal weapons to supposedly protect the world. When faced with the reality of what these weapons will do in the future, the scientist dies trying to eliminate them. Ultimately, the bad cyborg is terminated and Sarah and John destroy his computer chip to prevent it from being used for evil again.

COMMENTARY

Terminator 2 was the very successful sequel to *The Terminator,* a much smaller-budget science-fiction thriller that capitalized on the emerging popularity of Arnold Schwarzenegger in the 1980s. Many critics voted it one of the ten best films of 1984.

In the first film, Schwarzenegger played an evil cyborg sent from the future to destroy the child who was to save the world. In the sequel he plays a good cyborg assigned to save the child from another, deadly cyborg, played with malevolent intensity by Robert Patrick.

The focus is on the child: he is special and must be saved. John Connor's initials are J.C. This enables the audience to give the movie more of a Gospel interpretation, especially when we consider the role of John Connor's mother, her single state, the way she protects her son, and the role of the friendly cyborg (a kind of foster-father).

Interestingly, the movie takes an anti-violence stance while it enjoys the conventions of an action thriller. The cyborg has to learn not to kill people, the scientist destroys the weapons he develops, and the audience is instructed on the effects of violence and war on humanity.

DIALOGUE WITH THE GOSPEL

Focus: Jesus came in the fullness of time, a blessing to the world, born of a woman, Mary. Mary shares in all the experiences of her son, especially his infancy years.

The Feast of the Mother of God focuses on Mary's relationship to her son. The excerpt from the Letter to the

Galatians (cf. 4:4–7) is one of the few times Paul mentions Jesus and his mother. He stresses that Jesus came to save the subjects of the law, that they may receive their inheritance from God.

There are many hero-figures in the movies who save the world, but few whose mothers are featured in the stories as Sarah is in *Terminator 2*. It isn't easy to compare Sarah Connor with Mary. Sarah seems too rough to measure up to our images of the Mother of God. But Sarah's love, like Mary's, isn't only for her son. Her love has a social dimension. Sarah is a strong mother figure. Her life is threatened because her child is to be the Savior of the world. In the film, Sarah shares the same dangers as her son. Her heart is pierced, so to speak, because she shares the same anguish and pain as her son John.

The short excerpt from the Book of Numbers is a hope-filled blessing, fitting for a new year and a new beginning. In the *Terminator* mythology, the human race is under threat of nuclear devastation stemming from our knowledge of how to create weapons of mass destruction. The need for a savior means a need for blessing, peace, and re-birth. In the future, John Connor is to be the blessing for his people.

The Gospel highlights the Jewish ritual of circumcision and the fact that Jesus is named as Savior, which signifies his mission. It is the name given by the angel when Mary conceived him. Sarah Connor ponders the mysteries about her son, as Mary "treasured all these things and reflected on them in her heart."

KEY SCENES AND THEMES

- John Connor's rebelliousness, his initial unawareness of his role as the human race's future savior; John's separation from his mother, the threats on his life.

- Sarah's harrowing experience in the mental institution; Sarah as a strong-minded woman: protective of her son, concerned for the world's future; the creation of a new "family": the mother, the cyborg "foster-father," and the son; their flight into the desert.

• The two cyborgs, symbols of good and evil; Sarah, John, and the good cyborg's shared experience of joy and of suffering.

FOR REFLECTION AND CONVERSATION

1. *Terminator 2* is an anti-violence film with a flawed premise: it uses violence to "destroy" violence. Today is the World Day of Peace in addition to being the Solemnity of the Mother of God. How does the message of this feast celebrating the motherhood of Mary speak to the issue of violence and its resolution?

2. When John Connor witnesses another mother grasping two little boys who are playing with guns and threatening violence if their behavior doesn't change, he says to the Terminator: "We're not going to make it, are we?" The answer given is that it is within our nature to destroy ourselves. Do you think this is true? Why or why not? What is the real message of *Terminator 2*?

3. Some adolescent boys like *Terminator 2* because of the action. They want to identify with John Connor and hero-worship the "good" cyborg. Girls like the film because John is "cute." Adults worry that young people will be desensitized by violence in movies and miss the message that violence ultimately destroys. Do we talk with each other about the movies we watch and question what we see? Are we willing to watch movies

with young people and to share opinions and values
with respect? Why or why not?

Prayer

Mary, in becoming mother of Jesus, you promised to share in his life,
the pain as well as the joy. Be a mother to us in our time of need.
Amen.

FEAST OF SAINT JOSEPH
Samuel 7:4–5, 12–14, 16; Luke 2:41–51

My Life

U.S., 1993 / 116 minutes

Actors: Michael Keaton, Nicole Kidman, Queen Latifah,
Haing S. Ngor, Bradley Whitford

Writer: Bruce Joel Rubin

Director: Bruce Joel Rubin

 My Life

A Father's Love

SYNOPSIS

Bob Jones is dying of cancer. He grew up as Bobby Ivanovich in Detroit with the dream of having the circus come to his backyard. It never happened, and he was shamed in front of his school friends. As a young man, he left Detroit and moved to California with a new name, a wife, and a good job. Now he finds out he is terminally ill. His wife is pregnant and he wants something to bequeath to his child. He makes a video.

In the video, Bob talks to the unborn child and explains all the things that he himself would have wanted to know as a boy. His devoted wife, Gail, feels that he confides more to the video recorder than he does to her.

He goes to a Chinese healer who uses homeopathic techniques rather than traditional medicine to soothe stress. Bob is initially skeptical about the treatment but continues. He begins to examine and review aspects of his life.

The main opportunity for him to tie up the loose ends of his life comes when he returns to his parents' home for his brother's wedding. Bob's memories are bleak and he clashes with his parents, blaming them for not staying in touch with him more. When he gets home to California, he assists at the birth of his child. His parents come to visit and a circus arrives in his backyard before Bob dies.

COMMENTARY

Michael Keaton made his name in comedies like *Night Shift* and *Mr. Mom*, but he also has made a number of serious dramas, such as *Clean and Sober*, and has played a villain in *Pacific Heights* and *Desperate Measures*. Here Keaton has the opportunity to combine comedy and drama by portraying a dying man who has to come to terms with his life and wants to leave a legacy for his unborn child on video.

The movie was written and directed by Bruce Joel Rubin, who also wrote two other screenplays on death and afterlife: *Ghost* and the purgatorial fantasy, *Jacob's Ladder*.

Bob's talking to his son on video enables the screenplay to offer a fair amount of advice and "preaching." Although this is an obvious filmic device, some of the other dramatic sequences have a certain power, especially the awkward meeting with his parents when he blames them for his life.

Nicole Kidman is his wife and Haing S. Ngor *(The Killing Fields)* plays the doctor who uses personal and psychological techniques rather than traditional medicine.

Focus: In My Life, *a father wants to leave his son with some memories and fatherly advice. Joseph is the wise and just father who taught and guided his foster son, Jesus, before his own early death.*

DIALOGUE WITH THE GOSPEL

Joseph is one of the underrated characters of the Gospels. He appears in the infancy narratives of Matthew and Luke and is no longer mentioned after the finding of Jesus in the Temple.

Joseph follows the tradition of the just and wise men, the significant ancestors who are praised in the Jewish scriptures for today's feast. Nathan speaks to David of his descendants in the first reading, and Abraham is praised in the second reading as "the Father of us all" (cf. Rom 4:13, 16–18, 22). St. Joseph's namesake, the patriarch Joseph, was noted for his wisdom. Descriptions of the "wise man" abound in the psalms and other Wisdom books of the Bible.

Joseph is the caring father present at the birth of Jesus who becomes a fine role model for his young foster son.

Bob Jones wants to be a caring father as well, but like St. Joseph, he will disappear from his child's life. Because his illness is in remission, he is able to assist at his child's birth. For Bob, the most important aspect of fatherhood is putting his own life in order so that he can bequeath wisdom to his child. In this way his son can avoid the mistakes Bob made. The video is a visible legacy of wisdom and love for his son. Bob dies, leaving his son in the care of his wife.

KEY SCENES AND THEMES

- Bob as a child: at school, at home, his unfulfilled desire for a circus in his backyard, the haunting effect this has on him; Bob's love for Gail, his inability to communicate with her in comparison with what he confides on the video; Gail's sharing his illness and the deepening of their love.

- The process of making the video: the content, the practical wisdom and everyday advice, the deeper counsel; Bob's chance to speak his life aloud.

- Bob's visit home, his parents, their ordinariness and inability to change, Bob berating them; the parents' visit before he dies; Dr. Ho's wisdom in convincing Bob to look at his anxiety; Bob assisting at his son's birth; Bob's death.

1. Wisdom is one of the gifts of the Holy Spirit and is evident in the lives and teachings of many people in the Scriptures. Many people meditate on the Wisdom books of the Bible every day for guidance in their lives. How does Bob expect his son to use the video he is preparing for him? How will the video Bob leaves behind be wisdom for his son?

2. Dr. Ho tells Bob that if he becomes aware of the stress in his life, he can be free of it. How does Bob try to become more self-aware? How does this help him reconcile with his past? How are his memories like the video he is making for his son? What is the role of the circus in the story? Why is it so meaningful to Bob?

3. Though St. Joseph was the foster father of Jesus, we don't know how many years they spent together. The Scriptures do not give these details. Bob does not have any significant time with his son, but his memory, his words, his advice will continue through his image and the sound of his voice. What is the legacy each of us will leave behind when we die? If we were to make a video recounting our own lives for our loved ones, what would we say? If we could have a video of a parent or grandparent who has already died, what would we want to hear from them?

FOR REFLECTION AND CONVERSATION

Prayer

Joseph, patron of a happy death, may we be prepared for our passing from this life to the next by leaving what is best in us to those we love. Amen.

Mission to Mars

U.S., 2000 / 115 minutes

Actors: Gary Sinise, Tim Robbins, Don Cheadle,
Connie Nielson, Jerry O'Connell, Kim Delaney

Writers: Jim Thomas, John Thomas, Graham Yost

Director: Brian DePalma

Mission to Mars

Beyond this World

SYNOPSIS

The year is 2020, and an expedition to Mars investigates Cydonia, a mysterious mountain. The mountain inexplicably comes alive and destroys all the members of the team except Luke Graham. Mission Control has to decide whether to send a rescue team.

Woody Blake, in charge of the rescue mission, works with his wife Terri. He insists that Jim McConnell be co-pilot because it was McConnell, and his now deceased wife, who pioneered the project in the first place. When they reach Mars, meteorites wreck their vehicle. Blake tries to connect with a module. When it misfires he drifts away and dies.

The team discovers Luke in the greenhouse he has built. Together they try to interpret the data from the mountain that seems to want to communicate with them. They realize that the code sent to them is for DNA structure. When they respond appropriately, the mountain opens, offering air and a giant hologram of the solar system. This reveals that after a meteor explosion ages ago, all the Martians, with the exception of one, abandoned Mars for another part of the universe, while some went to Earth. The hologram vividly illustrates the whole process of evolution. When the group decides to go back to Earth, Jim, who still grieves for his wife, opts to accept the Martian's invitation to travel on to another world.

Mission to Mars encountered a very mixed reception. Many critics damned it for being a silly science fiction derivative, while the Cannes Film Festival invited director DePalma to be present for its principal screenings.

The film is reminiscent of many science fiction films, from *2001: A Space Odyssey* to *Contact* and *The Abyss,* as well as action adventures like *Total Recall.* It is a straightforward tale of a failed expedition and rescue mission. The movie also explores questions about the Earth and the existence of peaceful intelligent life in the universe.

In the 1990s, Brian DePalma switched from making Hitchcock-like thrillers to action adventures, such as the first *Mission: Impossible* film. In fact, rather than DePalma's usual approach, the heroics in *Mission to Mars* are more like Phillip Kaufman's *The Right Stuff,* and the meteor attacks are very similar to those in Mimi Leder's *Deep Impact* and Michael Bay's *Armageddon.*

Gary Sinise starred in *Apollo 13* and is able to sustain the heroic role of the astronaut with integrity and vision. Tim Robbins appears as a guest star who, halfway through the movie, drifts off into space and dies.

In view of the unsuccessful Mars probes in 1999–2000, the film takes a pro-American, patriotic stance that favors further exploration. As far as interpreting aliens and intelligence in the universe, the movie offers a vision of what might be.

COMMENTARY

Focus: Jesus' mission on Earth is accomplished. Now we wait for him to come again in glory. Mission to Mars, in the scientific spirit of our times, offers us an image of someone transcending our universe, going beyond it to a better place.

DIALOGUE WITH THE GOSPEL

The Ascension story from the Acts of the Apostles is more detailed than the one offered by the Gospel of John, which highlights Jesus' last words to his disciples. The Ascension celebrates the culmination of Jesus' mission on earth, when he returns to his Father in order to send his Spirit.

The science-fiction movie genre takes us into the realm of other worlds. Sometimes these films are fearsome and filled with disaster. At other times, they bring us into new worlds that offer hope. *Mission to Mars* is the latter kind of movie. It portrays the struggles of men and women from earth, and tries to transcend those struggles.

At the film's end, Jim McConnell has finished his life on Earth and come to terms with his grief over his wife's death. It is time for him to move on. A new and more beautiful world awaits him. Jesus, too, finished all that his Father had given him to do on Earth. However, Jesus returns to his Father not to receive something more, but to send his Spirit to come and remain with us forever.

KEY SCENES AND THEMES

- Jim McConnell refusing the mission because of his wife's death; Luke and the journey, Cydonia's attack, the overwhelming experience of destruction, the mountain's mystery.

- The new expedition: warm fellowship, a sense of mission; the meteor destruction and Woody's death; finding Luke, the attempt to solve the mystery; the realization that the code is made up of DNA patterns.

- The mountain opening, the universe hologram, the picture of evolution, the interpretation of intelligent life; the option to return to Earth or push on to a new world; Jim's decision to "ascend" to a new life.

1. *The Encarta 2000 Dictionary* defines science fiction as forms of media entertainment "based on futuristic science: a form of fiction, usually set in the future, that deals with imaginary scientific and technological developments and contact with other worlds." Brian Aldiss, a British science fiction writer, said that it is a "search for a definition of mankind and his status in the universe which will stand in our advanced, but confused state of [scientific] knowledge...." In what ways and how well do *Mission to Mars* and other science fiction films you may be familiar with fulfill these definitions?

2. How humans deal with grief generates many plots for literature, popular fiction, television, and movies. In *Mission to Mars*, Gary Sinise's character chooses to move on or back to some unknown place of promise. Consider other films that deal with grief (for example, *What Dreams May Come*). What do they have in common? How is hope in heaven expressed: directly or by metaphor?

3. We all have a mission on earth. The Feast of the Ascension commemorates the completion of Jesus' earthly work that the Father sent him to do. Which characters in the film "complete" their mission? What is that mission I have been given by the Father during my time on earth? How am I working to complete it?

Prayer

Jesus, you completed the earthly mission given to you by your Father. We celebrate what you have done for us and see you as Risen Lord, ascending to a new life at the right hand of your Father. Amen.

What's Eating Gilbert Grape

U.S., 1993 / 118 minutes

Actors: Johnny Depp, Leonardo DiCaprio, Darlene Cates,
Juliette Lewis, Mary Steenburgen, Kevin Tighe, Crispin Glover

Writer: Peter Hedges

Director: Lasse Hallstrom

What's Eating Gilbert Grape

Bearing Family Burdens

SYNOPSIS

Endora, Iowa is a small town located where open fields stretch into the distance and where most residents now go out of town to shop. Gilbert is responsible for his family and works at the small local grocery store.

His mother has retired to her couch since her husband's suicide and is enormously obese. His two sisters continually complain, and his mentally handicapped younger brother, Arnie, is not expected to live long. In general, Gilbert has been able to cope, but he is getting weary. There seems no end in sight to his burden. At one point Gilbert becomes angry with Arnie, hits him, and almost leaves town. Gilbert's situation is further complicated when he tries to get out of an affair with a bored housewife to whom he delivers groceries. Becky, a young woman about Gilbert's age, and her grandmother stay at a nearby trailer camp on their way West. She and Gilbert become friends and talk about life and its meaning.

Arnie is exuberant and sometimes uncontrollable. He especially likes to climb the town's water tower. When he is taken to jail after his latest escapade, the mother comes out of the house and goes to the police station to defend her son. After returning home and climbing the stairs to her room, she dies. Instead of removing their mother's body, the children burn down the whole house.

What's Eating Gilbert Grape is a slice of small-town American life that is both moving and entertaining. Written for the screen from a novel by Peter Hedges, the film is a sensitive look at ordinary people for whom life seems to be passing by.

Lasse Hallstrom is a Swedish director whose films include *My Life as a Dog, Once Around, Something to Talk About,* and *The Cider House Rules.* He was able to bring a kind of "outside-looking-in" perspective to this story about rural America.

During the 1990s, Johnny Depp specialized in vulnerable roles, from *Edward Scissorhands* to *Benny and Joon* and *Don Juan de Marco.* The tour-de-force performance in *What's Eating Gilbert Grape,* however, comes from the Oscar-nominated Leonardo DiCaprio.

The film invites us to look compassionately at people we might not notice if we passed them on the street, people who feel that they have nowhere to go but who have rich, strong personalities. This is particularly true of the large Bonnie Grape, played unself-consciously by Darlene Cates.

Focus: Gilbert Grape is one of the least, the little ones of this world that the Gospel mentions. His burdens are difficult to bear. While still quite young, he finds the love and the strength to bear his burden as the main support of his family.

The reading from Deuteronomy introduces us to the unusually lyrical passage from Matthew. In this first reading, God is seen as "setting his heart" on his chosen people. The point is not that they deserve God's love because they are a great and numerous people, but because they are the least of all people.

In the Gospel, Jesus bursts into prayer. He thanks his loving Father for letting those he loves receive the revelation of what God and Divine love are like. The people Jesus loves are not the "learned and the clever" but "mere children."

The Grape family more than qualifies for being considered among the least of all people and, like us all, the Grapes are candidates for receiving the good news of the love of God.

Jesus goes on to explain what he means by the revelation of God. It is an invitation to those who are tired and downhearted to rely on him. Those who are weary do not have to give up; they can shoulder their yokes, for Jesus himself will share the load. Jesus says that he, too, is like the least on earth (such as the "anawim" of Zephaniah and the Beatitudes). Jesus is gentle and humble of heart. If we allow him to carry our burden with us, it will be easy and light.

Gilbert Grape does not receive a revelation from God that helps him carry his burdens. God works in more indirect ways through people and events. Mrs. Grape is quite literally a heavy burden, but Gilbert knows his mother's love, shown as she proudly walks out of the house when Arnie is taken by the police. Becky's friendship, communication, and love also show Gilbert that burdens can be shared.

Gilbert's love for Arnie is conflicted. First he rescues Arnie from the water tower and then mistreats him. But he is sorry and realizes what grace there is in carrying the burden of his brother.

KEY SCENES AND THEMES

• Gilbert Grape's burdens at home: the busyness and the noise, his immobile mother needing to be served, the older daughter's unhappiness, the other daughter's snobbish and resentful attitude, Arnie's innocent and exasperating mirth.

- An overwhelmed Gilbert forgetting Arnie in the bathtub, Gilbert angrily slapping Arnie, Gilbert's bitterness and his attempt to leave town.

- Bonnie Grape leaving the house to get Arnie; Bonnie's death, the children burning the house and their mother's body as ritual, purification, new beginning.

FOR REFLECTION AND CONVERSATION

1. The Grape family personifies the "label" of dysfunctional; the father is gone and one of the children is raising the others and the mother as well. The burden is too much, and we can understand Gilbert's poor choices, lack of options, and his desire to flee. Why does he return? What kind of a person is Gilbert Grape? What's really eating at him? How and why is he different from his sisters in their relationship to their mother and Arnie? How does Gilbert grow? How does the placement of this story in a small town with dysfunctional citizens help to maintain the dramatic sense of the story?

2. Each member of the Gilbert family has a burden to bear. Arnie is mentally handicapped, but there is no limit to his love, especially for Gilbert. How does Arnie's unconditional love reflect the kinds of love shown by his mother, sisters, and Gilbert? Who carries whose burdens in this film? How and to what extent do the members of this family show their love for one another?

3. The scene where Gilbert returns home on Arnie's birthday to find his mother, Bonnie, sitting on her

bed and looking out the window—angry, sad, and remorseful at the same time—is an emotional high point of the film. How does this scene parallel the Gospel? How can we help to carry the burdens of others in imitation of Christ?

Prayer

Jesus, you invite all those who are weighed down by life to come to you because you have promised to bear our burdens with us. When we experience the heaviness of our lives and responsibilities, be with us so that we may feel the lightness of your presence. Amen.

Music of the Heart

U.S., 1998 / 126 minutes

Actors: Meryl Streep, Aidan Quinn, Angela Bassett,
Gloria Estefan, Cloris Leachman, Jay O. Sanders,
Isaac Stern, Kieran Culkin

Writer: Pamela Gray

Director: Wes Craven

Music of the Heart

Great Is Your Reward

It is 1998, and Roberta Guaspari is a divorced mother with two sons. After moving around the world with her Navy husband, she has been abandoned by him. Roberta purchases fifty violins and starts a music program for underprivileged kids in East Harlem. She brings with her a great deal of inner strength and a sense of vocation tinged with an irascible edge.

SYNOPSIS

Roberta receives support from the school principal but criticism from some of the staff and parents. But she perseveres and the students learn that her severity comes from her dedication. They decide that they want her to teach with discipline because they know she cares. They vie for places in her class. Roberta is a white teacher in a non-white school, and some of the parents think the music program is just another patronizing handout. They eventually see the benefits of the music program for their children.

Years pass and Roberta's reputation grows. Her work is covered in magazine articles. At the same time her sons feel that she has neglected them. When the music program is threatened because of budget cuts, the boys support her as do staff and students. To raise money and consciousness for music education, she holds a concert with past and present students in Carnegie Hall. Eventually, the music community of New York City, led by world-renowned violinist, Isaac Stern, comes to her aid. The program is saved.

Music of the Heart was originally entitled *Fifty Violins*. The film is so sentimental that it might well have been called "Heart Strings." *Music of the Heart* is based on a true story and promotes education in the arts.

Roberta Guaspari was the subject of a 1996 Oscar-nominated documentary, *Small Wonders*, by Allen and Lana Miller, that essentially tells the same story.

Meryl Streep had never played an instrument before this movie and had to learn the violin. She does so with the skill and panache that she consistently brings to all her roles. It could be said that she learned the violin the same way she learns accents.

Wes Craven directed *Music of the Heart* in what seems an extraordinary departure from twenty-five years of making horror films (*Nightmare on Elm Street*, *Wes Craven's New Nightmare*, and the *Scream* trilogy). The film seems to indicate that the creator of Freddie Kruger has a very soft heart; after all, Craven was a teacher before making movies. The plot is reminiscent of Steven Herek's 1995 fictional story, *Mr. Holland's Opus*.

There is plenty of music to enjoy in *Music of the Heart*, especially a Bach concerto in D Minor for the final performance.

DIALOGUE WITH THE GOSPEL

Focus: When Mary went to visit Elizabeth she carried life within her and brought joy to Elizabeth and the son in her womb. Mary sang and praised God. Roberta Guaspari's music of the heart brought joy to many students over the years. She did great things.

The Gospel tells the story of the Visitation and gives us the Magnificat. It is Mary's song-prayer and shows her generosity and holiness when she decides to visit her cousin Elizabeth who is with child. Roberta Guaspari is an instrument of life for her students. She gives herself completely to them with music because of what it can do for their characters and their lives.

Mary glorifies God for what she has received and foretells that future generations will speak of the wonders God has done through her. When Roberta's program is threatened and she feels let down by her principal and staff, they affirm her by recounting the wonders she has achieved for the children.

Roberta may not have pulled the mighty from their thrones, but she certainly challenged the authorities about budgeting priorities and the need for children's imaginations and souls to grow through the arts and music.

The concert in Carnegie Hall involves the generosity of family, parents, staff, and friends and is a testimony to Roberta and her students. The beauty and sacredness of the music, especially Bach's concerto, reflect the Divine.

KEY SCENES AND THEMES

- Roberta's marriage, her children, her husband who abandons her for a friend; Roberta bringing up the children; going to live with her mother; trying to start a new life; finding a job.

- Roberta's reaction to Harlem: the kids on the streets, the squalor, yet her decision to make her home there; Roberta's relationship with her sons and her students: her strictness, her teaching ability; her decision to introduce the students to violins: tests, practices, a sense of pride; Roberta feeding their ambitions, developing their skills, the joy in music for both the children and parents.

- Ten years later: Roberta's achievements, the program's cancellation, her decision to have the concert to raise money; the concert's impact, past and present students performing; Roberta's leadership.

FOR REFLECTION AND CONVERSATION

1. The Visitation was a moment when the Old Testament in the person of the older woman, Elizabeth, met the New Testament in the person of the younger woman, Mary. Reading, writing, and arithmetic have been the staples of educational content for centuries, while music and the arts always seem new and have to struggle for their place in the curriculum. Mary had the openness of spirit to recognize the value of the past embodied in Elizabeth, and Elizabeth recognized the beauty of the new in Mary. How can we today recognize the value of the past and the present to assure a rich educational, religious, and cultural future for coming generations?

2. Though the film is sentimental, it has an authentic feel because of how well Meryl Streep personifies Roberta's prickly personality. Though gifted, Roberta is not an easy person to like. What made Roberta the person she was? Why did the students respect and love her? What was Roberta's reward? What reward did the school, the children, and the city receive because of Roberta's persistence and dedication?

3. The alternative opening prayer for today's liturgy asks that we follow Mary's example in reflecting God's holiness and join Mary in her hymn of endless life

and praise. Why is music so central to spiritual and liturgical life, not to mention its role in our everyday lives?

Prayer

Mary, you glorified the Lord for the wonderful things he did for you. Help us to appreciate God's wonders in our lives and to give him thanks and praise as you did in the Magnificat. Amen.

Paradise Road

Australia, 1997 / 115 minutes

Actors: Glenn Close, Pauline Collins, Cate Blanchett, Frances McDormand, Jennifer Ehle, Elizabeth Spriggs, Johanna Ter Steege, Wendy Hughes, Pamela Rabe, Julianna Margulies, Clyde Kasatsu

Writer: Bruce Beresford

Director: Bruce Beresford

Paradise Road

Song of Salvation

SYNOPSIS

When Singapore falls to the Japanese in 1942 during World War II, British and Australian women and children are evacuated by ship. After the Japanese attack the ship, three survivors swim to the nearby shore of Sumatra. These, along with some Dutch women from the East Indies, are taken prisoner by the Japanese and marched to prison camps with only the clothes on their backs.

The women settle into the hardship of camp life and learn to deal with brutal treatment by the guards. Some decide to be "comfort women" to the Japanese in exchange for food and security. Others get sick and die. A Chinese woman who steals medicine for the sick is executed.

The group eventually discovers that several members know music; they compose original scores and form a human orchestra that enables them to survive the squalor, hunger, and humiliation of the camp. Friendships are formed and the singing touches even the Japanese soldiers.

Many of the women die during the war years and only a small group survives the ordeal, strengthened by the gift of music.

COMMENTARY

Paradise Road is a movie of women's stories. The final credits state that the screenplay is based on "reminiscences" of survivors of the Sumatra prisoner of war camps and that the women performed thirty works between 1943 and 1944. The music in the film was performed from original scores that survived. These true memories are filled with intense feeling. Written and directed by Bruce Beresford *(Tender Mercies, Driving Miss Daisy, Double Jeopardy)*, this film about the remote Belalau internment camp for women and children is compelling.

Paradise Road is about mourning and inspiration. It shows the range of the human spirit's ability to respond to despair with hope and to move from selfishness to self-sacrifice.

For the audience to be able to sit through such a serious and grimly graphic movie, the filmmakers had to combine themes of evil and suffering with self-sacrifice and the possibility for redemption without understating the horror of human cruelty and war. Beresford has done this most effectively by showing how the women were able to draw on deep inner resources to survive their ordeal together.

The first-rate ensemble cast revolves around Glenn Close, a good, capable woman who conducts the human orchestra the women create in the camp. Peter James' photography makes us wonder how such cruelty can be perpetrated in the midst of a natural paradise by contrasting the drab, brown hues of the prison camp with the luminous beauty of the mountains, lush jungle, and mistiness of the camp's setting.

DIALOGUE WITH THE GOSPEL

Focus: The Beatitudes of today's Gospel might be called the road to paradise. In the sufferings of the women in the prison camps of World War II we see weakness and heroism—the Beatitudes put into practice.

The women who survived the prison camp shown in *Paradise Road* are introduced by the first reading from the Book of Revelation, for they are like the saints, "the ones who have survived a great period of trial."

In *Paradise Road*, we see women from various walks of life—some selfish and pampered, others selfless and giving—who experience an ordeal that turns them into the humble of the earth, the poor in spirit. They mourn; they seek justice and peace for the world and an end to the war; they are gentle. Some are tested and find that to be pure of heart is too difficult. The women have to find mercy in their souls for their Japanese captors because they are persecuted in the cause of right.

The mystery of the Beatitudes is that many who are declared blessed do not survive to experience their recompense on earth. One aspect of the mystery is that through their sufferings and death they encourage others to persevere.

Rejoicing will be great in heaven when all will receive their reward. It is often difficult to remember this when we are faced with the pain of our earthly existence. The music made by the women in the camp helped them to be blessed in captivity and was a foretaste of the joy of paradise.

KEY SCENES AND THEMES

- The women in the camps: their punishments, torture, the executions; the jungle's tropical atmosphere, starvation, maltreatment, illness, confinement; the good women's strength of spirit, the selfish women's difficulty coping, ordinary women's heroism.

- The music in such a setting: the discipline that helped the women work together, the auditions and practices; music transcending their experiences.

- Adrienne's fear in being taken into the jungle, the guard singing to her; Margaret's sorrow and death, her praying the psalm as she dies; the middle-aged woman, "The Lord is my shepherd" and the poem, the reference to Paradise Road; the war's end, the Japanese, the women's liberation.

FOR REFLECTION AND CONVERSATION

1. Today we reflect on the saints who lived the beatitudes during their earthly lives. How did the women of *Paradise Road* live the Beatitudes? Identify which characters possessed and lived each Beatitude most significantly. Did any of the women exhibit qualities that would make her a saint? Or were these just ordinary women living in extraordinary times?

2. The experience in the prison camp forced the women to become a community. How did they share joys, prayer, suffering, work, song, and forgiveness? What would we have done in similar circumstances?

3. The Beatitudes form a blueprint for Christian living. They are not negative injunctions, but positive ideals that spur us on. How did the women in the camp combine the precepts of the Ten Commandments and the blessings of the Beatitudes? How did they show that living a moral life is a positive, life-giving endeavor?

Prayer

Lord, your Beatitudes show us the qualities and holiness of your saints. Help us to appreciate their example and to live in the blessed ways you ask of us. Amen.

Pay It Forward

U.S., 2000 / 124 minutes

Actors: Kevin Spacey, Helen Hunt, Haley Joel Osment,
Jay Mohr, James Caviezel, Jon Bon Jovi, Angie Dickinson

Writer: Leslie Dixon

Director: Mimi Leder

 *Pay It Forward*

Celebration of Blessings

SYNOPSIS

A journalist arrives at a crime scene in progress and his car gets smashed. A businessman gives him his Jaguar, no strings attached. Amazed and confused, the journalist pursues this act of generosity and discovers a trail of people who are "paying forward" rather than paying people back for gifts they received.

In Las Vegas, the disfigured teacher, Eugene Simonet, begins Social Studies class by challenging his adolescent students to find an idea to change the world. Trevor, whose mother Arlene is alcoholic and whose father has disappeared, comes up with a plan to help three people who, in turn, are to help three more people. Unwittingly, Trevor begins a movement to "pay it forward."

Trevor begins his project when he brings home a drug addict. This makes Arlene angry with Simonet, and Trevor maneuvers a meeting between them. They fall in love. Eugene tells Arlene about his violently abusive father who set him on fire. Unexpectedly, Trevor's father returns and Arlene feels she has to give him another chance. Simonet cannot forgive Arlene for this betrayal. Trevor's father soon abandons the family once again.

Meanwhile, the reporter traces the movement's roots from a prisoner who helped the Jaguar owner's asthmatic daughter in an emergency room, to a bag lady who is, in fact, Arlene's alcoholic mother. Hailed as a celebrity, Trevor is interviewed for television on his twelfth birthday. At school that day, Trevor tries to help his friend who is being bullied by some students. In the struggle, Trevor is stabbed and dies. Crowds gather for a candlelight remembrance vigil at his home.

Big cities are an image of the world. They offer both trash and treasure. Helen Hunt's Arlene sees herself as trailer trash, an alcoholic, promiscuous, the victim of a violent, drunken husband. Conversely, it is her son, Trevor (Haley Joel Osment of *The Sixth Sense* and *A.I.)* who discovers the treasure, the goodness in each person and their capacity for being selfless.

Most movies depend on a conflict between good and evil for their dramatic impact. It is very difficult to make a movie about goodness for its own sake. Plots about goodness often seem "too good to be true," or like sentimental wishful thinking. *Pay It Forward's* screenplay acknowledges this and often inserts sharp comments about do-gooders and the risks that come with being too optimistic. The Las Vegas work setting, street people, drug and alcohol addiction, physical abuse, dysfunctional families, schoolyard bullying and violence ensure that the audience knows that the film's world, where goodness is needed and is possible, is real.

Kevin Spacey's Eugene Simonet is a decent man scarred by child abuse who encourages students to engage with the world because, in fact, he is too fearful to do so. Helen Hunt embraces her role as a single mother, and Osment shows versatility and conviction as Trevor. Direction is by Mimi Leder, who brings her considerable experience to the movie from television's *Hill Street Blues* and *ER*, as well as the films *The Peacemaker* and *Deep Impact*.

Focus: Thanksgiving is an acknowledgment of God's blessing even in difficulties, and of gratitude for a better and fuller life. Pay It Forward shows us people blessing other people in thanksgiving for goodness received.

Thanksgiving is a time to celebrate the memory of people who struggled for their convictions by seeking a new world where they could live in freedom. They found this land and gathered to thank God for the blessings of a new home, food, and shelter. But Thanksgiving is not a finished event. It is celebrated every year by people who have experienced hardships and the struggle to survive, and yet who find goodness in their lives for which to be thankful.

This theme is described perfectly in the Hebrew experience of the first reading from 1 Kings. The final verse exhorts us to learn of this goodness in people's lives and God's loving action. The reading urges thanksgiving people to "pay it forward" and is a summary of what Trevor tries to do. This sharing attitude is what entered into the hearts of those who benefited from Trevor's scheme. It is what Trevor died for.

The reading from Colossians (cf. 3:12–17) amplifies the inner Thanksgiving attitude: a heartfelt celebration of God's blessing; or, when the love of God is not so immediately recognized and named, from the grace of the human heart. The characters in *Pay It Forward* are graced by each other in a love that transcends expectations because it is about generosity born of thanksgiving. Simonet grows beyond his scars, Trevor learns to believe when he thinks he has failed. Arlene, her mother, the prisoner, the businessman, the journalist— all become bearers of the gift of goodness.

The Gospel of the ten lepers reminds us that when Jesus healed people, not everyone was able to show gratitude. It is the Samaritan leper, who does not expect the gift of healing (like the characters in the movie), who returns to Jesus and becomes a symbol of Thanksgiving. Jesus tells him that his faith has saved him and sends him forth to "pay it forward."

- The businessman giving the car to the blundering journalist; his subsequent disbelief and confusion; his quest to discover the chain of goodness, his learning the stories.

- Simonet's class and his challenge; Trevor putting his plan into practice with the addict; the reactions: his mother, Eugene, his school friend; Trevor's successes and failure.

- Trevor's TV interview; the violence and sadness of his death; Trevor's pierced side and the Gospel overtones in his "martyrdom."

1. Eugene Simonet bears terrible scars, both internal and external. How does the film show his isolation in symbol (for example, when he irons the shirt) and in fact? How does the "pay it forward" theme interface with Eugene's reality and the way he grows as a person?

2. Though not a religious film per se, the relationships in *Pay It Forward* come to be "blessed" in Christian ways, such as forgiveness. Talk about the main characters in the film and how various values and virtues emerge as the story unfolds.

3. *Pay It Forward* shows us how good deeds can multiply and that the most unlikely people are capable of generosity when it is least expected. Is there any character in the film you can identify with? Who and why? What does *Pay It Forward* teach about gratitude and celebrating blessings?

Prayer

Lord, as we bless and thank you for your goodness to us, in thanksgiving may we always pass on your blessings to those more needy than ourselves. Amen.

Appendices

Contents By Movie Title

Contents By Movie Title

Movie Title	Sunday/Celebration	Gospel Text	Page #
Horse Whisperer, The	Week 2	Jn 1:29–34	151
Hurricane, The	Easter Sunday	Jn 20:1–9	102
Insider, The	Palm Sunday	Mt 26:14—27:66	80
It's a Wonderful Life	Christmas Dawn	Lk 2:15–20	25
Jesus' Son	Advent Sunday 3	Mt 11:2–11	9
Killing Fields, The	Week 27	Mt 21:33–43	279
Les Miserables	Trinity Sunday	Jn 3:16–18	141
Lion King, The	Christmas Midnight	Lk 2:1–14	19
Lorenzo's Oil	Week 20	Mt 15:21–28	243
Man for All Seasons, A	Easter Sunday 7	Jn 17:1–11	132
Marvin's Room	Week 6	Mt 5:17–37	171
Matewan	Week 25	Mt 20:1–16	268
Men with Guns	Week 11	Mt 9:36—10:8	195
Message in a Bottle	Easter Sunday 2	Jn 20:19–31	107
Miracle Maker, The	Good Friday	Jn 18:1—19:42	92
Miracle Worker, The	Lent Sunday 4	Jn 9:1–41	71
Mission to Mars	Ascension	Mt 28:16–20	332
Music of the Heart	Assumption of Mary	Lk 1:39–56	341
My Life	Feast of Saint Joseph	Lk 2:41–51	328
October Sky	Week 33	Mt 25:14–30	309
Oscar and Lucinda	Week 15	Mt 13:1–23	217
Paradise Road	All Saints Day	Mt 5:1–12	346
Pay It Forward	Thanksgiving Day	Lk 17:11–19	350
Phenomenon	Lent Sunday 2	Mt 17:1–9	62
Places in the Heart	Body and Blood of Christ	Jn 6:51–58	146
Pleasantville	Week 5	Mt 5:13–16	166
Prince of Tides, The	Easter Sunday 3	Lk 24:13–35	112
Return to Me	Immaculate Conception	Lk 1:26–38	319
Saving Private Ryan	Week 3	Mt 4:12–23	156

Contents By Movie Title

Contents By Sunday/Celebration

Contents By Sunday/Celebration

Contents By Sunday/Celebration

Contents By Gospel Text

Contents By Gospel Text

Gospel Text	Movie Title	Sunday/Celebration	Page #
Mt 3:13–17	*Tender Mercies*	Baptism of the Lord	47
Mt 4:1–11	*End of Days*	Lent Sunday 1	57
Mt 4:12–23	*Saving Private Ryan*	Week 3	156
Mt 5:1–12	*Paradise Road*	All Saints Day	346
Mt 5:1–12	*Snow Falling on Cedars*	Week 4	161
Mt 5:13–16	*Pleasantville*	Week 5	166
Mt 5:17–37	*Marvin's Room*	Week 6	171
Mt 5:38–48	*The Crossing Guard*	Week 7	175
Mt 6:1–18	*Cookie's Fortune*	Ash Wednesday	52
Mt 6:24–34	*Forrest Gump*	Week 8	179
Mt 7:21–27	*At Play in the Fields of the Lord*	Week 9	185
Mt 9:36—10:8	*Men with Guns*	Week 11	195
Mt 9:9–13	*The Doctor*	Week 10	190
Mt 10:26–33	*A Cry in the Dark*	Week 12	200
Mt 10:37–42	*Ben-Hur*	Week 13	207
Mt 11:2–11	*Jesus' Son*	Advent Sunday 3	9
Mt 11:25–30	*What's Eating Gilbert Grape*	Sacred Heart of Jesus	336
Mt 11:25–30	*Simon Birch*	Week 14	212
Mt 13:1–23	*Oscar and Lucinda*	Week 15	217
Mt 13:24–43	*Secrets and Lies*	Week 16	222
Mt 13:44–52	*Bagdad Cafe*	Week 17	226
Mt 14:13–21	*City of Joy*	Week 18	231
Mt 14:22–33	*Touch*	Week 19	236
Mt 15:21–28	*Lorenzo's Oil*	Week 20	243
Mt 16:13–20	*The Shoes of the Fisherman*	Week 21	249
Mt 16:21–27	*The Devil's Advocate*	Week 22	253
Mt 17:1–9	*Phenomenon*	Lent Sunday 2	62
Mt 18:15–20	*The Crucible*	Week 23	258
Mt 18:21–35	*Unforgiven*	Week 24	263

Contents By Gospel Text

Movie Ratings Chart*

Movie Title	MPAA (1)	BBFC (2)	OFLC (3)	USCC (4)
Apostle, The	PG-13	12	M	A-III
At Play in the Fields of the Lord	R	15	M	A-IV
Awakenings	PG-13	12	PG	A-II
Bagdad Cafe	PG	12	PG	A-III
Beach, The	R	15	M	A-IV
Ben-Hur	G	PG	PG	A-I
Big Night	R	15	M	A-III
Bob Roberts	R	15	M	A-III
Born on the Fourth of July	R	15	M	A-IV
Bridges of Madison County, The	PG-13	15	M	A-IV
Chorus Line, A	PG-13	12	PG	A-IV
City of Joy	PG-13	15	M	A-II
Civil Action, A	PG-13	15	M	A-II
Cookie's Fortune	PG-13	12	PG	A-III
Crossing Guard, The	R	15	M	A-III
Crucible, The	PG-13	12	M	A-III
Cry Freedom	PG	15	M	A-II
Cry in the Dark, A	PG-13	15	M	A-III
Dead Man Walking	R	15	MA	A-III
Devil's Advocate, The	R	18	M	O
Doctor, The	PG-13	12	PG	A-II
E.T.: The Extra-Terrestrial	PG	U	PG	A-I
End of Days	R	18	MA	O
Entertaining Angels	PG-13	12	PG	A-II
Erin Brockovich	R	15	M	A-III

* Information regarding the rating codes may be found on each organization's Web site.

(1) MPAA: Motion Picture Association of America, United States; www.mpaa.org

(2) BBFC: British Board of Film Classification, United Kingdom; www.bbfc.co.uk

(3) OFLC: The Office for Film and Literature Classification, Australia; www.oflc.gov.au

(4) USCC: United States Catholic Conference, www.nccbuscc.org

Movie Ratings Chart

Movie Title	MPAA (1)	BBFC (2)	OFLC (3)	USCC (4)
Family Man, The	PG-13	12	PG	A-III
Fisher King, The	R	15	M	A-III
Forrest Gump	PG-13	15	M	A-III
Girl, Interrupted	R	15	M	A-III
Horse Whisperer, The	PG-13	PG	PG	A-II
Hurricane, The	R	15	M	A-III
Insider, The	R	15	M	A-III
It's a Wonderful Life	NR	U	G	A-II
Jesus' Son	R	18	R	O
Killing Fields, The	R	15	M	A-II
Les Miserables	PG-13	12	PG	A-II
Lion King, The	G	PG	PG	A-I
Lorenzo's Oil	PG-13	12	PG	A-II
Man for All Seasons, A	G	U	G	A-I
Marvin's Room	PG-13	12	PG	A-II
Matewan	PG-13	15	M	A-III
Men with Guns	R	15	M	A-III
Message in a Bottle	PG-13	12	PG	A-III
Miracle Maker, The	NR	U	G	A-I
Miracle Worker, The	NR	PG	PG	A-II
Mission to Mars	PG	12	PG	A-II
Music of the Heart	PG	PG	PG	A-III
My Life	PG-13	15	M	A-II
October Sky	PG	PG	PG	A-II
Oscar and Lucinda	R	15	M	A-III
Paradise Road	R	15	M	A-III
Pay It Forward	PG-13	12	PG	A-III
Phenomenon	PG	PG	PG	A-III
Places in the Heart	PG	12	PG	A-II

Movie Ratings Chart

Movie Title	MPAA (1)	BBFC (2)	OFLC (3)	USCC (4)
Pleasantville	PG-13	12	PG	A-IV
Prince of Tides, The	R	15	M	A-IV
Return to Me	PG	PG	PG	A-II
Saving Private Ryan	R	15	MA	A-III
Secrets and Lies	R	15	M	A-III
Shadowlands	PG	12	PG	A-II
Shoes of the Fisherman, The	G	PG	PG	A-I
Simon Birch	PG	PG	PG	A-II
Sister Act	PG	PG	PG	A-III
Sixth Sense	PG-13	15	M	A-III
Snow Falling on Cedars	PG-13	15	M	A-III
Superman: The Movie	PG	PG	PG	A-II
Tender Mercies	PG	PG	PG	A-II
Terminator 2: Judgment Day	R	15	M	O
Touch	R	15	M	O
True Confessions	R	15	M	A-IV
Unforgiven	R	15	M	A-IV
What's Eating Gilbert Grape	PG-13	15	M	A-III
Where the Heart Is	PG	12	PG	A-IV

Recommended Reading on Movies and Religious Themes

Baugh, Lloyd, *Imaging the Divine: Jesus and Christ-figures in Film.* Kansas City, MO: Sheed and Ward, 1997.

A thesis-based study of the Jesus movies and some selected Christ-figure movies; defines what Christ-figure means; extensive and thorough, if somewhat controversial in interpretation.

Blake, Richard A., *After Image: The Indelible Catholic Imagination of Six American Film-makers.* Chicago: Loyola Press, 2000.

An exploration of imagination and its religious dimension in the movies of six Catholic-educated directors: Capra, Coppolla, DePalma, Ford, Hitchcock, Scorsese.

Eilers, Franz-Joseph, *Church and Social Communication, Basic Documents.* Manila: Logos Publications, Inc., 1993.

The texts of nine Vatican documents from 1936 to 1992, with the addresses for World Communications Day and quotations on communication from other official documents. Eilers provides introductions and some structure outlines of the documents.

Fraser, Peter, *Images of the Passion: The Sacramental Mode in Film.* Westport, CT: Praeger Publishers, 1998.

Selected movies are examined to illustrate how they implicitly dramatize aspects of the Gospel and the sufferings of Jesus.

Fraser, Peter and Neal, Vernon Edward, *ReViewing the Movies: A Christian Response to Contemporary Film.* Wheaton, IL: Crossway Books, 2000.

An application of the theory in Fraser's Images of the Passion to contemporary popular cinema in a wide-ranging survey.

Jewett, Robert, *Saint Paul at the Movies.* Louisville, KY: Westminster/John Knox Press, 1993.

A New Testament scholar writes an enlightening book about the Greco-Roman world of Paul. A movie enthusiast, Jewett has chosen ten popular movies to illustrate the virtues that Paul holds up to the Roman Empire.

Jewett, Robert, *Saint Paul Returns to the Movies*. Grand Rapids, MI: William B. Eerdmans, 1999.

A sequel which is as good as, perhaps better than, the original.

John Paul II, *Giovanni Paolo II e il Cinema, Tutti i discorsi*. Rome: Ente dello Spettacolo, 2000.

A collection of eight speeches by the Pope on cinema. Texts in Italian and in English with commentary articles on the Church and cinema.

Johnston, Robert K., *Reel Spirituality: Theology and Film in Dialogue*. Grand Rapids, MI: Baker Academic, 2000.

A theologian from Fuller Theological Seminary who loves cinema asks basic questions about the religious dimension of movies, opening up the spirituality implicit in so many mainstream movies. It has a wide range of film references.

Mahony, Roger M., *Film Makers, Film Viewers, Their Challenges and Opportunities*. Boston: Pauline Books & Media, 1992.

The text of Cardinal Mahony's pastoral letter to the diocese of Los Angeles, his synthesis of a contemporary Catholic approach to cinema.

Malone, Peter, *Movie Christs and Antichrists*. New York: Crossroads, 1990. (Originally, Sydney: Parish Ministry, 1988.)

A study of movies and meanings, focusing on the Jesus-movies (Jesus-figures) and the movies of characters who resemble Jesus (Christ-figures); also chapters on movies and antichrist symbols.

Malone, Peter, *On Screen*. Manila: Daughters of St. Paul, 2001.

An introduction to the study of movies and meanings.

Marsh, Clive and Ortiz, Gaye, eds. *Explorations in Theology and Film*. Oxford: Blackwell, 1997.

A collection of theological essays exploring specific contemporary popular movies like The Terminator, Groundhog Day, The Piano, Edward Scissorhands.

May, John R. *New Image of Religious Film*. Kansas City, MO: Sheed and Ward, 1997.

A collection of theological essays which examine theoretical aspects of religion, society, and cinema.

McNulty, Edward, *Films and Faith: Forty Discussion Guides.* Topeka, KS: Viaticum Press, 1999.

As the title indicates, discussion material for forty films. They are designed for the non-expert in cinema and provide detailed information about each film as well as some theological background. There are extensive questions for reflection.

McNulty, Edward, *Praying the Movies: Daily Meditations from Classic Films.* Louisville, KY: Geneva Press, 2001.

A collection of thirty-one devotions that connect movies and the spiritual life of moviegoers.

Romanowski, William D., *Pop Culture Wars, Religion and the Role of Entertainment in American Life.* Downers Grove, IL: InterVarsity Press, 1996.

A wide-ranging study of entertainment, including cinema, noting the hostile U.S. religious tradition, as well as the movements to find the religious values in media and entertainment.

Short, Robert, *The Gospel from Outer Space, The Religious Implications of E.T., Star Wars, Superman, Close Encounters of the Third Kind and 2001: A Space Odyssey.* San Francisco: Harper and Row, 1983.

The author of *The Gospel according to Peanuts* and *The Parables of Peanuts* offers the text of a multimedia presentation of Gospel parallels in popular science fiction and fantasy movies.

Stern, Richard C., Jefford, Clayton N., and Debona, Guerric, *Savior on the Silver Screen.* Mahwah, NJ: Paulist Press, 1999.

The authors have run courses on the principal Jesus movies from Cecil B. De Mille to *Jesus of Montreal.* This is the expanded course with a thorough rationale for studying these movies.

Stone, Bryan P., *Faith and Film, Theological Themes at the Cinema.* St. Louis: Chalice Press, 2000.

The framework for examining a range of generally well-known movies is the *Apostle's Creed,* enabling the author to highlight religious themes in movies in a context of faith and the exploration of faith.

Vaux, Sara Anson, *Finding Meaning at the Movies.* Nashville: Abingdon Press, 1999. The author wants to encourage study groups in schools, universities, and parishes by taking a range of popular movies and showing how they can be fruitfully discussed.

Index

ABOUT THE AUTHORS

PETER MALONE, MSC, is a Sacred Heart Father from Australia currently living in England. In 1998, he was elected president of the International Organization for the Cinema (OCIC), an appointment which received immediate Vatican approval.

Peter is known worldwide for his pastoral approach to integrating film, faith and life. He has served as juror at film festivals throughout the world, and is currently a consultant to the Bishops' Committee for Film in the Philippines.

Father Malone is the author of *Movie Christs and Anti-Christs, The Film, Films and Values,* and a co-author of *Cinema, Religion and Values,* and is a regular columnist in *The Universe* Catholic newspaper in the U.K.

ROSE PACATTE, FSP, is a Daughter of St. Paul and the Director of the Pauline Center for Media Studies in Boston. She has an MA in Education in Media Studies from the University of London, and gives workshops on media literacy education throughout the U.S. and abroad.

Rose was a member of the Catholic Jury at the Venice Film Festival in 2000 and has been a panelist at the City of Angels Film Festival and Boston's Faith & Film Festival. She is one of the directors of the annual National Film Retreat and is the author of *A Guide to In-House Film Festivals in Ten Easy Steps.*

BOOKS & MEDIA

The Daughters of St. Paul operate book and media centers at the following addresses. Visit, call or write the one nearest you today, or find us on the World Wide Web, www.pauline.org

CALIFORNIA
3908 Sepulveda Blvd, Culver City, CA 90230   310-397-8676
5945 Balboa Avenue, San Diego, CA 92111   858-565-9181
46 Geary Street, San Francisco, CA 94108   415-781-5180
FLORIDA
145 S.W. 107th Avenue, Miami, FL 33174   305-559-6715
HAWAII
1143 Bishop Street, Honolulu, HI 96813   808-521-2731
Neighbor Islands call: 800-259-8463
ILLINOIS
172 North Michigan Avenue, Chicago, IL 60601   312-346-4228
LOUISIANA
4403 Veterans Memorial Blvd, Metairie, LA 70006   504-887-7631
MASSACHUSETTS
885 Providence Hwy, Dedham, MA 02026   781-326-5385
MISSOURI
9804 Watson Road, St. Louis, MO 63126   314-965-3512
NEW JERSEY
561 U.S. Route 1, Wick Plaza, Edison, NJ 08817   732-572-1200
NEW YORK
150 East 52nd Street, New York, NY 10022   212-754-1110
78 Fort Place, Staten Island, NY 10301   718-447-5071
PENNSYLVANIA
9171-A Roosevelt Blvd, Philadelphia, PA 19114   215-676-9494
SOUTH CAROLINA
243 King Street, Charleston, SC 29401   843-577-0175
TENNESSEE
4811 Poplar Avenue, Memphis, TN 38117   901-761-2987
TEXAS
114 Main Plaza, San Antonio, TX 78205   210-224-8101
VIRGINIA
1025 King Street, Alexandria, VA 22314   703-549-3806
CANADA
3022 Dufferin Street, Toronto, Ontario, Canada M6B 3T5
  416-781-9131
1155 Yonge Street, Toronto, Ontario, Canada M4T 1W2
  416-934-3440

¡También somos su fuente para libros, videos y música en español!